1662—AND AFTER

Three Centuries of English Nonconformity

by

JOHN T. WILKINSON

LONDON : THE EPWORTH PRESS

FIRST PUBLISHED IN 1962

Book Steward
FRANK H. CUMBERS

SET IN MONOTYPE BASKERVILLE AND PRINTED IN
GREAT BRITAIN BY THE CAMELOT PRESS LTD
LONDON AND SOUTHAMPTON

1662—AND AFTER

Three Centuries of English Nonconformity

The Fernley-Hartley Lecture 1962

BOOKS BY THE SAME AUTHOR

Richard Baxter and Margaret Charlton: A Puritan Love-Story (Allen & Unwin)

Gildas Salvianus, or the Reformed Pastor, by Richard Baxter. Edited by J. T. Wilkinson

William Clowes, 1780-1851

Hugh Bourne, 1772-1852

Arthur Samuel Peake, 1865-1929. Essays in Commemoration. Edited by J. T. Wilkinson

Principles of Biblical Interpretation (A. S. Peake Memorial Lecture, 1960)

The Saints' Everlasting Rest, by Richard Baxter. Edited and Abridged by J. T. Wilkinson

DEDICATED TO

HETTIE M. WILKINSON
Sister: National Childrens' Home

J. LEONARD WILKINSON
M.D., Ch.B.(Manch.), F.R.C.S.(Eng.), L.R.C.P.

ALAN B. WILKINSON
M.A., Ph.D.(Cantab.)

IN GRATITUDE
FOR ALL THEY HAVE TAUGHT ME

PREFACE

THIS tercentenary year of the Act of Uniformity, 1662, provides a valuable opportunity for a survey of the three centuries of English Nonconformity which followed the passing of this crucial Act. To indicate the significance of this movement in the religious life of England is the purpose of this book.

I venture to hope that it may be regarded as timely. It is fifty years since the two substantial volumes of H. W. Clark entitled *The History of English Nonconformity* were published in 1911-13: a work which still remains a standard authority, but which is not now easily accessible. For a long time, C. Sylvester Horne's *Popular History of the Free Churches* was widely read, but that work appeared as early as 1903. Whilst there have been many studies of various aspects of English Nonconformity, only two brief volumes, since the Second World War, have covered the whole range. In 1944 Dr E. A. Payne produced a succinct account in *The Free Church Tradition in the Life of England*; in 1953 Dr Horton Davies contributed a useful volume to the Home University Library under the title: *The English Free Churches.* In each case, however, limitations of space precluded any detailed record.

Arising out of the arrangements made by the present Joint Committee for the due celebration of this tercentenary, a major work, *From Uniformity to Unity, 1662-1962,* is to be issued in the form of a series of essays by both Anglican and Free Church scholars, under the editorship of Dr Norman Sykes, Dean of Winchester, and Dr G. F. Nuttall.[1] A smaller book by Professor F. G. Healey, of Westminster College, Cambridge, has also been prepared for the more general reader at the request of the Joint Committee. It bears the title: *Rooted in Faith: Three Centuries of Nonconformity, 1662-1962.* Since the completion of my own manuscript I have had the pleasure of reading this smaller volume which is an explication of Free Church principles upon the historical background of these centuries, and I most warmly commend it.

In the present work, whilst I trust the more general reader may

[1] Owing to the lamented death of Dr Sykes, some changes have taken place.

find the record useful, I have also had in mind the more advanced student of Church history. In particular, it is important that the rising generation of both Anglican and Free Church ministries should be aware of the significance of this movement in English religious life, not least in view of the ecumenical issues which face us all at this time of closer approximation between the Churches.

I have deliberately confined this study to English Nonconformity. The development of Nonconformity in Wales, arising out of the passing of the Act of Uniformity forms really a distinct chapter, and could well form a separate volume. Similarly the developments in Scotland and Ireland also might well receive separate treatment.

In view of the enormous influence of the events of the seventeenth century—together with the particular interest associated with this tercentenary year—I have deliberately given a more detailed account of the earlier part of the story; in any case, material associated with the later period is more accessible to the modern reader.

The following pages will reveal that I owe a great deal to the many writers of studies of this period, to whom I would here acknowledge my debt. I have endeavoured to write objectively, and by confining myself largely to arrangement of material, I have for the most part refrained from critical comment. I desire that the record of these centuries should speak for itself.

I am deeply sensible of the honour bestowed upon me by the Fernley Hartley Trustees by their request that I should undertake this work and I acknowledge this with much gratitude.

I am also grateful for the help and encouragement of many friends, amongst whom I must name the following: the Rev. W. E. Farndale, D.D., whose friendship I have valued for many years; the Rev. Henry T. Wigley, B.A., B.D., a former Secretary of the Free Church Federal Council, and my friend since our college days together; the Rev. W. Gordon Robinson, M.A., B.D., Ph.D., Principal of the Northern Congregational College, Manchester; Professor F. G. Healey, M.A., of Cambridge, who in the early stages of my work kindly indicated, at my request, the pattern of his own book to which I have made reference above; to Dr Frank Cumbers, B.A., B.D., of the Epworth Press who has made this work his constant care; and to my younger son, the Rev. Alan B. Wilkinson, M.A., Ph.D., of St Catharine's College,

Cambridge, with whom I have discussed the subject of these pages. To the Librarian of Dr Williams's Library, the Librarian of the Library of the Society of Friends, and to my former colleague, the Rev. Bernard E. Jones, M.A., B.D., Librarian of Hartley Victoria College, Manchester, I am indebted for loan of material. Finally, and by no means least, to my wife for her constant encouragement and unfailing patience I am deeply grateful.

JOHN T. WILKINSON

KNIGHTON, RADNORSHIRE
January 1962

CONTENTS

ABBREVIATIONS

Bate	*The Declaration of Indulgence, 1672*, by F. Bate (1908)
Besse	*A Collection of the Sufferings of the People called Quakers*, by Joseph Besse (1753)
Bettenson	*Documents of the Christian Church*, ed. by H. Bettenson
Bosher	*The Making of the Restoration Settlement*, by R. S. Bosher
Braithwaite	*The Second Period of Quakerism*, by W. G. Braithwaite (edn 1961)
Broadmead Records	*The Record of a Church of Christ meeting in Broadmead, Bristol, A.D. 1640 to A.D. 1688*, by E. Terrill, ed. by N. Haycroft
Burnet	*History of His Own Times*, by Gilbert Burnet (edn 1897), 2 vols
Calamy, *Abridgement*	*An Abridgement of Mr Baxter's History of His Life and Times*, by E. Calamy
Calamy, *Account*	*An Account of the Ministers . . . who were ejected and silenced*, by E. Calamy
Calamy, *Continuation*	*A Continuation of the Account of the Ministers . . . who were ejected and silenced*, by E. Calamy
Cardwell	*A History of Conferences* (3rd edn), ed. by E. Cardwell
C.J.	*Journals of the House of Commons*
C.R.	*Calamy Revised*, by A. G. Matthews
C.S.P.D.	*Calendar of State Papers, Domestic*
Clarendon, *Hist.*	*The History of the Rebellion and Civil Wars in England* (edn 1843)
Cragg	*Puritanism in the Period of the Great Persecution, 1660-8*, by G. R. Cragg
Dale	*History of English Congregationalism*, by R. W. Dale
D.C.U.	*Documents on Christian Unity* (Four series), ed. G. K. A. Bell
D.N.B.	*Dictionary of National Biography*
Drysdale	*History of Presbyterianism in England*, by A. H. Drysdale (1899)
Ellwood	*The History of the Life of Thomas Ellwood*, ed. C. E. Crump (1900)

E.R.E.	*Encyclopaedia of Religion and Ethics*
Evelyn	*The Diary of John Evelyn*, ed. W. Bray
Gee and Hardy	*Documents illustrative of English Church History*, compiled by H. Gee and W. J. Hardy (1914)
Gould	*Documents relating to the settlement of the Church of England by the Act of Uniformity of* 1662, ed. G. Gould
Jordan	*Free Church Unity: A History of the Free Church Council Movement: 1896-1941*, by E. K. H. Jordan
Kennett	*A Register and Chronicle, Ecclesiastical and Civil*, by W. Kennett (1728)
L.J.	*Journals of the House of Lords*
Neal	*History of the Puritans* by D. Neal, 5 vols (1822)
Palmer	*The Nonconformist's Memorial*, by S. Palmer, 2 vols (1775)
Payne	*The Free Church Tradition in the Life of England*, by E. A. Payne
Pepys	*The Diary of Samuel Pepys* (edn 1924), 2 vols
Rel. Bax.	*Reliquiae Baxterianae, or Richard Baxter's Narrative of His Life and Times* (1696)
Robertson	*Select Statutes, Cases and Documents*, ed. C. G. Robertson
Stoughton	*History of Religion in England*, by J. Stoughton, 8 vols
Swainson	*The Parliamentary History of the Act of Uniformity*, by C. A. Swainson (1875)
T.B.H.S.	*Transactions of the Baptist Historical Society*
T.C.H.S.	*Transactions of the Congregational Historical Society*
T.U.H.S.	*Transactions of the Unitarian Historical Society*
Underwood	*A History of the English Baptists*, by A. C. Underwood
Whiting	*Studies in English Puritanism, 1660-8*, by C. E. Whiting
Whitley	*A History of British Baptists* by W. T. Whitley (1923)
W.R.	*Walker Revised*, by A. G. Matthews

CHAPTER ONE

THE CALL FOR REFORMATION

THE roots of English Nonconformity run far back into the beginnings of the English Reformation. Those men who sought to refashion the liturgy, discipline and government of the English Church 'according to the Word of God' were known as Puritans, a term which embraced English Baptists, Congregationalists and Presbyterians during the first century of their existence. From the middle of the seventeenth century until the close of the nineteenth the more negative terms 'Nonconformists' and 'Dissenters' were used to describe them.

The primary impulse towards further reformation on this biblical foundation arose in Geneva amongst those who were exiled during the Marian persecution. On their return they hoped to refashion the English Church after the Genevan pattern, but they were challenged by the rigidity of the terms of the Elizabethan settlement of religion. These eager reformers fell into two groups: the conforming Puritans who, remaining within the Church, hoped for such reformation; and the nonconforming groups who with still greater eagerness were prepared for 'reformation without tarrying for any', and therefore became Separatist. Though influential, the first group, finding their efforts unavailing, passed over into the nonconforming groups, either Presbyterian or Independent, though some left these shores for the Low Countries or the colonies of New England.

I

On 19th June 1567 a company of nonconforming Puritans, meeting at Plumbers' Hall, in London, were arrested for holding a meeting in defiance of the Act of Uniformity, 1559. They were not Separatist; they were only in temporary nonconformity, hoping that the enactments of Elizabeth would be repealed. In their defence before Archbishop Grindal they declared:

So long as we might have the worde freery preached, and the Sacraments administred with out the preferring of idolatrous geare about it, we never assembled togither in houses. But when it came to this, poynt, that all our preachers were displaced by your lawe, that would not subscribe to your apparaile and your lawe, so that wee could not heare none of them in any Church, by the space of seaven or eight wekes... and were we troubled & commaunded to your courtes from daye to daye, for not comming to our parish Churches, then we bethought us what were best to doe.... And if you can reprove ... anie thing that we hold by the word of God, we will yeelde to you, and do open penaunce at Paule's Crosse; if not, we will stand to it by the grace of God.[1]

Their position was strengthened by two documents which appeared in 1572, independently of this group, and which formed, in effect, an appeal for a Presbyterian system after the Genevan model.[2] The outcome was the establishment of the first Presbyterian Church at Wandsworth in 1572.

Meanwhile the other Puritan group, concerned for 'reformation without tarrying for any', had begun to set up Separatist meetings. Most of the pioneers were able and educated men, whose witness was to prove of far-reaching importance through their radical challenge to the prevailing policy of the enforcement of uniformity in doctrine and discipline. Robert Browne gathered a small company in Norwich in 1581, and maintained that essentially the Church consists of Christians.

The Church planted or gathered is a companie or number of Christians or beleeuers, which by a willing couenant made with their God and Christ are under the gouernment of God and Christ, and kepe his lawes in one holie communion: because Christ hath redeemed them vnto holiness & happines for euer, from which they were fallen by the sinne of Adam.[3]

Here we see that Nonconformist inheritance of spiritual religion which repudiates merely nominal membership of a Church; here is also 'the priesthood of believers'. Coming under notice of the authorities Browne and his followers fled to Middelburgh in 1582.

The mantle of Browne fell upon John Greenwood (d. 1593),

[1] *An Examinatian of certayne Londoners . . . before the Commisioners . . . 1567* in *A Parte of a Register* (? 1590), pp. 24-5.

[2] *An Admonition* and *A Second Admonition*. See also Scott Pearson, *Thomas Cartwright and Elizabethan Puritanism* (1925). Ch. 2.

[3] R. Browne, *A Booke which sheweth the life and manners of all True Christians* (1582). See *Elizabethan Texts* (1953), ed. Peel and Carlson, p. 252. For Browne, see F. J. Powicke, *Robert Browne, Pioneer of Modern Congregationalism* (1916).

who joined himself to a company of about a hundred Separatists meeting in London, and later he influenced Henry Barrow (1550?-93).[4] In 1596 Greenwood and Barrow were arrested, and, after several years of imprisonment, were hanged at Tyburn in 1593. A few months earlier an ardent Welshman, John Penry (1563-93),[5] joined the London company, but he also came to a swift end—in May 1593 he also was hanged. Part of the significance of these men is that they denied the validity of all set forms of prayer, and practised simple forms of worship and administration of the sacraments. In this group we find the origin of Congregationalism, afterwards to be described as Independency. In London in 1567 there was 'a Privie Churche', meeting under the leadership of Richard Fitz, and their adoption of a 'covenant' makes it congregational in character.[6]

An issue which had to be faced was the question of baptism. This was raised by John Smyth (*c.* 1554-1612),[7] a younger man, who, about 1606, joined the Separatist Church at Gainsborough. With him was Thomas Helwys (*c.* 1550-*c.* 1616). The accession of James I afforded no further hope of liberty, so this Gainsborough company migrated to Amsterdam, where, in 1609, Smyth became convinced that only believers' baptism was justified by the New Testament, and must therefore be the foundation of Church fellowship. He therefore baptized himself, then Helwys and others of his company. So the first English Baptist Church came into existence. The ideal of spiritual worship is reflected in the words of John Smyth:

We hould that the worship of the new testament properly so called is spirituall proceeding originally from the hart: & that reading out of a booke (though lawfull eclesiastical action) is not part of spirituall worship, but rather the invention of the man of synne it beeing substituted for a part of spirituall worship . . . in time of prophesjng it is vnlawfull to have the booke as a helpe before the eye.[8]

[4] See F. J. Powicke, *Henry Barrow and the Exiled Church of Amsterdam* (1900).

[5] See W. Pierce, *John Penry: His Life and Times* (1923); also *The Note-Book of John Penry* (Camden, Third Series, 1944), ed. Peel.

[6] R. W. Dale, *History of English Congregationalism* (1907), identifies this meeting with that at Plumbers' Hall, and also describes it as 'the first regularly constituted English Congregational Church'. It does not appear, however, to have formulated any Church polity, and the identification has been disproved by C. Burrage, *Early English Dissenters*, I.82-90.

[7] See W. H. Burgess, *John Smyth, Se-Baptist* (1911).

[8] J. Smyth, *The Differences of the Churches of the Separation* (1608).

About 1612 Helwys and about a dozen others returned to London despite the dangers involved in so doing, and in Spitalfields they founded the first Baptist Church on English soil. Soon Helwys was imprisoned, for whilst in Holland, he had written *The Mistery of Iniquity* (1612), in which he insisted upon the right of religious liberty for all. It was a bold declaration.

> Our Lord the King is but an earthly King, and he hath no aucthority as a King but in earthly causes, and if the King's people be obedient and true subjects, obeying all humane laws made by the King, our lord the King can require no more: for men's religion to God is betwixt God and themselves: the King shall not answere for it, neither may the King be jugd betwene God and Man. Let them be heretikes, Turcks, Jewes, or whatsoever, it apperteynes not to the earthly power to punish them in the least measure.[9]

This indicates a further emphasis expressed by these pioneers of the faith.

Sufficient has been said to show that for both Puritans and Separatists alike there was a recognition that the Church of England was in need of reformation. In course of time Puritans and Separatists were to join forces. The possibility of better times was frustrated under James I and eventually for many the only course was emigration so that they might worship according to the dictates of their own consciences. The passage of the Scrooby Separatists to Holland in 1607, and the subsequent settlement of some of them in New England, as 'The Pilgrim Fathers' of *The Mayflower* in 1620, is a familiar story. The importance of this enterprise, for America and beyond, would be difficult to exaggerate. Between 1620 and 1640 some twenty thousand of the finest English folk crossed the Atlantic in the hope of finding religious freedom.

There were those who remained in England, however, and it was to be their task to struggle for civil and religious liberty in the tumultuous days of the seventeenth century.

II

The extraordinary disregard of liberties by Charles I and the policy of Archbishop Laud for securing religious uniformity throughout the land were the two main factors which created the

[9] T. Helwys, *A Short Declaration of the Mistery of Iniquity* (1612), p. 69. Only four copies now survive, but in 1935 the work was reproduced by photo-litho in facsimile, by the Baptist Historical Society.

strong reaction of the Puritans towards the whole régime, and intensified their commitment to reformation both in Church and State.

The Puritans were for the most part Presbyterians whose aim, as we have seen, was to reform England after the Genevan pattern, and to establish Presbyterian classes in place of episcopal dioceses. They were not prepared, however, to acquiesce in the policy of toleration for which the Independents stood. The Presbyterians were insistent upon Presbyterian uniformity in an established Church, and under the initial decision of Parliament, sought to accomplish this through the famous Westminster Assembly which began in 1643, and which sought 'a due and necessary reformation of the government and liturgy of the Church'.[10] Parliament had come to the end of its patience with Charles I and already Laud had been impeached for treason.

The Independents came to power eventually on a wave of opposition to the autocratic demands of the Presbyterian party. As we have seen, in contrast to the Presbyterian system, they maintained the right of every congregation to govern itself. Much of their strength lay in the army, and it soon became evident that they stood for a considerable body of opinion. It was from Independency, not Presbyterianism, that eventually English Puritanism was to draw its power. In the light of these differences it is not surprising that a rift developed between the two groups.

The attempt to establish the Presbyterian system as the form of national religion ultimately failed, even though the Episcopalian system had virtually been disposed of. By 1653 the decline of Presbyterianism was complete. The reason is summed up in Miltons' oft-quoted line: 'New Presbyter is but Old Priest writ large.' 'Presbyterianism as a religious system in England fell for precisely the same reason as the Elizabethan Settlement dissolved, because men and women cannot be dragooned into a denomination, irrespective of their religious experience or predilections. Conformity by compulsion inevitably produces a defiant Dissent.'[11]

[10] Cf. the communication from the Scottish Assembly to Parliament in 1643. 'We now look for a perfect and thorough reformation: all may resort to the same public worship, and the names of Heresies or Sectaries, Puritans, Conformists, Separatists and Anabaptists may be suppressed. The prelatical hierarchy being put out of the way, the work will be easy' (quoted Payne, p. 42). It is important to note that the English Presbyterians must be distinguished from the Scottish Presbyterians, with whom they had no contact until 1643.

[11] H. Davies, *The English Free Churches* (1952), p. 81.

The new régime centred in Oliver Cromwell, who became 'the incarnation of Independency'. The system which he created did not survive, but his insistence upon toleration became part of our English heritage.[12] Under his religious settlement the Church was to be neither Episcopal, Presbyterian, nor Independent, though as 'apostles of toleration', the Independents were given some degree of favour. The system did not mean complete toleration,[13] but it gave a greater measure of toleration in ecclesiastical matters than had previously been known. The Independents stood for the entire separation of the spheres of Church and State.

With the death of Cromwell in 1658 the scene changed. Under the Restoration, Presbyterians, Independents and Baptists entered into a common experience of suffering, and into a new unity such as they had not known in the days of their triumphs.

III

Two other nonconforming groups must be given brief notice.

During the time of the Commonwealth, and at the time of the Presbyterian dominance, there came the rise of the Quaker movement. George Fox (1624-91), restless under ecclesiastical autocracy, critical of the bibliolatry of the Independents, and staggered by the formalism of much of contemporary religion, found spiritual peace in the authority of 'The Inner Light', the illumination of the Holy Spirit. Upon this foundation he withstood ridicule, persecution and imprisonment. The earliest Quaker congregation developed from a 'shattered' Baptist Society at Mansfield, in Nottinghamshire, in which Fox found fellowship and ultimately became the leader. The eccentricity which marked some of the early followers of Fox—in particular the messianism of John Nayler—is well-known. The extraordinary sufferings of the Quakers during the seventeenth century is the outstanding example, amongst Nonconforming groups, of the refusal to compromise.[14]

[12] A. S. P. Woodhouse, *Puritanism and Liberty* . . . (1938). 'The consciences of common men were a new phenomenon in politics and one that has never disappeared' (p. 53).

[13] Roman Catholics were excluded from livings, though on political as much as on theological grounds.

[14] For the history of the Quakers in the seventeenth century see W. G. Braithwaite, *The Beginnings of Quakerism* (1923), and *The Second Period of Quakerism* (revised edn, 1961).

It was also at this time that Unitarianism first appeared in England. John Biddle (1615-62), though not himself a Unitarian, has been described as 'the Father of English Unitarianism'. His doctrine was distinctly Socinian. Tried by Cromwell's Parliament he suffered imprisonment; that his life was saved by Cromwell's intervention is probable. On the grounds of liberty of conscience, both Independents and Baptists petitioned the Protector on his behalf, as against the Presbyterians who agitated for his being silenced. Biddle stood for the freedom of rational enquiry into matters of religion, and the movement which developed from his witness was to play its part in the progress of English Nonconformity.[15]

[15] See H. J. McLachlan, *Socinianism in Seventeenth-century England* (1951); E. M. Wilbur, *A History of Unitarianism* (1952), Vol. II.

CHAPTER TWO

THE RESTORATION OF EPISCOPACY

I

CROMWELL died on 3rd September 1658. His son, Richard, succeeded him, and at first it seemed as if he would be generally accepted. Loyal addresses came to him; the armies and the officers of the fleet assured him of their loyalty, and he received congratulations from foreign powers.[1] But there were other elements in the situation. There was discontent within the army; in the light of the deliverance from prelate and King which the army had achieved, there was a growing demand for an enlarged share in the government of the State; many regarded the work of deliverance as still incomplete; the liberties of the people must be finally secured. The Wallingford House party, under the leadership of Fleetwood, regarded Richard with suspicion: he had been outside the conflict and soon after his accession there was a demand that he should surrender the supreme command of the army to one of the generals, but this he refused to do. Suspecting that Richard had Presbyterian leanings, the Independents were doubtful as to whether he would preserve the settlement, and so they gave considerable support to the army. In addition, the Republicans, who deeply resented the vesting of supreme power in 'a single person', saw a second chance for their cause.

The first step taken by Richard Cromwell was the calling of a new Parliament, which met on 27th January 1658/9. A quarrel with the army broke out immediately, and the Wallingford House party demanded that Parliament should be dissolved.[2] Richard consented and the dissolution took place on 22nd April 1659. The early fall of Richard was now inevitable. The triumph of the Army was a triumph for the Republicans, and the Independents regarded the dissolution with satisfaction.

At the demand of the Republicans and the officers, the surviving

[1] Clarendon, *Hist.*, p. 864: 'Nothing was heard in England but the voice of joy, and large encomiums of their new Protector: so that the King's condition never appeared so hopeless, so desperate.'
[2] Ibid. p. 865.

members of the Long Parliament—The Rump—were called to resume their places at Westminster.[3] On 7th May forty-two of these met as a House of Parliament, and three weeks later voted for a free Commonwealth, without either a 'single person, or King, or House of Peers', and also claimed control of the army. The officers resented this and after fierce quarrel the army dismissed Parliament in October. A Committee of twenty-three was appointed to administer national affairs under the title of 'The Committee of Safety'. The officers were masters of the nation.

General Monck, who was commander of the Scots in Edinburgh determined that he would march south to restore Parliament. The threat of his coming induced the officers to recall The Rump on 26th December. Monck continued to move on towards London. He declared himself in favour of a free Parliament, and was ready to swear that he abjured the King and that he would be faithful to the Commonwealth. The members who had been excluded in 1648 now began to return to Parliament. This renovated assembly was predominantly Presbyterian, and within a short time, voted for the establishment of Presbyterianism. The Westminster Confession was adopted as the national confession of faith; the Solemn League and Covenant was printed and widely published, and was followed by a Bill for reorganizing the Church on a Presbyterian model.[4]

Although the second establishment of Presbyterianism was less effective than the earlier attempt, it resulted in the removal of some Independents.[5] On 13th March, the engagement to be undertaken by the next Parliament, namely to be faithful to the Commonwealth, 'without a single person, or King, or House of Peers', was repealed, and on 16th March this Parliament of the excluded members was dissolved. This definite assertion of Presbyterians was probably due to a suspicion that a return

[3] Although the Long Parliament had been violently dismissed, as an Act provided that it could not be abolished without its own consent, and therefore, though elected in 1640, eighteen years earlier, it was still the lawful Parliament of England.

[4] *C.J.*, 5th March 1659/60, VI.862.

[5] Under the influence of this brief Presbyterian reaction in 1659-60 Dr John Owen was removed from the Deanery of Christ Church, Oxford, in favour of Dr Reynolds, a distinguished Presbyterian. Owing to his association with Fleetwood and the Republican movement he had already lost his position as Vice-Chancellor of the University, Dr Conant, the Presbyterian Rector of Exeter College taking his place. Together with Thomas Goodwin, Owen had already been excluded from the pulpit of St Mary's.

of Charles was being planned, and so it would be wise to secure possession before any such return took place. The re-established Presbyterianism might have to be in modified form, but it would remain sufficiently strong to challenge the return of Episcopacy.[6] 'They resolved therefore that they should find their own ecclesiastical system impregnably established'.[7]

The way was now clear for the restoration of the old constitution and the return of Charles. For the forty days which intervened before the new Parliament met, government was in the hands of Monck and the Council of State, and this Council, predominantly Presbyterian, took up the projected treaty with the King.[8] The basis of the negotiations was to be the terms offered to his father at the Treaty of Newport in 1648: an act of indemnity; the confirmation of the sale of Church and Crown lands; the control of the militia and the permanent establishment of Presbyterianism. Monck intervened, however, and refused to consent to the proposals, declaring that the matter must be left to a free Parliament. This was a wise course. Nevertheless, Monck did not hesitate to make direct approaches to Charles. In answer to royal overtures for his assistance, Monck declared his faithfulness to the King, and then indicated the policy which he wished the latter should accept.[9] This represented a complete *volte face* on the part of Monck, who had previously declared himself in favour of the Commonwealth. To his cousin, Sir John Grenville, Monck indicated the terms. Charles was to promise a general amnesty with little exception; to confirm the possession of confiscated property, whether obtained by gift or purchase, and whether the lands were Crown lands, Church lands, or forfeited estate; to grant liberty of conscience to all his subjects. He also recommended that Charles should move to Breda. Grenville reached Brussels about 26th March, and the proposals were

[6] James Sharp, agent of the Scottish Church in London, reported in March: 'The great fear is that the King will come in, and that with him moderate Episcopacy, at the least, will take place here' (quoted Bosher, p. 103).

[7] C. H. Firth: *Cambridge Modern History* (1906), IV.553.

[8] On 16th March the inscription, '*Exit tyrannus Regum ultimus*', set up by the Commonwealth in the Exchange where the King's statue had once stood, was blotted out at noonday (*Camb. Mod. Hist.*, IV.554). At a Conference at Northumberland House where leaders of the moderate Presbyterian party assembled, 'the King's restoration was proposed in direct terms, as absolutely necessary to the peace of the kingdom and for the satisfaction of the people: and the question seemed only to be, upon what terms they should admit him; some proposing more moderate, others more severe conditions' (Clarendon, *Hist.*, p. 894).

[9] J. Price, *The Mystery and Method of his Majesty's Happy Restoration* (1680), pp. 116-18.

passed over by the King to Hyde and others. The basic principle that all concessions should be of grace rather than in terms of bargaining was accepted. But as to the degree of the concession there was doubt. It was therefore suggested that such should be referred to the decision of Parliament, Charles himself being satisfied that the forthcoming Parliament would not ask from him more that he was ready to consider. On these lines a declaration was formulated and was dated from Breda, 4th April 1660. The most important section of the document reads as follows:

And because the passion and uncharitableness of the times have produced several opinions in religion by which men are engaged in parties and animosities against each other; which, when they shall hereafter unite in a freedom of conversation, will be composed, or better understood; we do declare a liberty to tender consciences; and that no man shall be disquieted, or called in question, for differences of opinion in matters of religion which do not disturb the peace of the kingdom; and that we shall be ready to consent to such an act of parliament, as, upon mature deliberation, shall be offered to us, for the full granting that indulgence.[10]

The Declaration also stated that Charles had never relinquished the hope of recovering his rights; that his subjects by law might enjoy what was their own, as he also his; that under the Great Seal he would grant a free pardon to all who should accept his favour within forty days, save any who should be excepted by Act of Parliament; and that he desired that all note of discord and separation should be utterly abolished. In conclusion, it was promised to refer to Parliament all grants and purchases made by officers and soldiers who might be liable to action at law; also to pay arrears due to the army.

The new Parliament assembled on 25th April, and, on 1st May, to both Houses, Sir John Grenville delivered the Declaration together with a letter from Charles.[11] Both communications were read by the Speaker, Sir Harbottle Grimstone, and it was at once determined that the documents should be printed and published. The same afternoon a conference was held between the Lords and Commons, when it was agreed that according to the ancient and fundamental laws of this Kingdom, the Government is and ought

[10] For *The Declaration of Breda*, see *infra*, Appendix I.

[11] There were also letters to 'our trusty and well-beloved General Monck', and to the Lord Mayor and Aldermen and Council of the City of London. For all these documents, see Clarendon, *Hist.*, pp. 900-1; *C.J.* and *L.J.*, in loc.

to be 'by King, Lords and Commons'.[12] This conclusion formally re-established the monarchy in England. The majority of the members of Parliament were delighted beyond measure with the Declaration,[13] but some were cautious, and 'thought that the guilt of the nation did require less precipitation than was like to be used, and that the treaty ought first to be made with the King, and conditions of security agreed on before His Majesty should be received'. Further, the Presbyterian party 'seemed very solicitous that somewhat should be concluded in veneration of the Covenant: and at least that somewhat should be inserted in their answer to the discountenance of the bishops',[14] but the House dismissed such opinion.

There were some in the nation who were completely opposed to the recall of Charles. Milton sought to reverse this 'epidemic madness' which was driving the nation back to the servitude of kingship. To him a free commonwealth was 'the noblest, the manliest, the equalist, the justest government, the most agreeable to all due liberty and proportioned equality, both human, civil and Christian, most cherishing to virtue and true religion'. That most Englishmen preferred a monarchy troubled him little.[15]

> If we return to Kingship, and soon repent (as undoubtedly we shall when we begin to find the old encroachments coming on little by little upon our consciences, which must necessarily proceed from King and Bishop united inseparably in one interest), we may be forced perhaps to fight over again all that we have fought . . . losing by a strange after-game of folly all the battle we have won . . . treading back again with lost labour all our happy steps in the progress of reformation.

The situation throughout was a triumph for the King. 'The torrent of reviving loyalty was irresistible.' On 2nd May it was resolved to send a letter of thanks to the King, affirming the loyalty of Parliament and declaring the death of the late King to be 'the greatest reproach that ever was incurred by any of the English nation, an offence to all the Protestant Churches abroad, and a scandal to the profession of the truth of religion here at

[12] *C.J.*, VIII.8.

[13] 'So universal a joy was never seen within those walls. . . . The kind of reception was beyond what the best affected, nay, even the King could expect or hope' (Clarendon, *Hist.*, p. 904).

[14] Ibid. p. 904.

[15] J. Milton, *Ready and Easy Way to Establish a Free Commonwealth, and the Excellence thereof, compared with the Inconveniences and Dangers of readmitting Kingship in this Nation* (February 1660).

home'.[16] This letter also contained the following significant paragraph:

We have yet more cause to enlarge our praise, and our prayers to God for your Majesty, that you have continued unshaken in your faith; that neither the temptation of allurements, persuasions and promises from seducing papists on the one hand, nor the persecution and hard usage from some seduced and misguided professors of the Protestant religion on the other hand, could at all prevail on Your Majesty to make you forsake the Rock of Israel, the God of your fathers, and the true Protestant religion in which your Majesty hath been bred: but you have still been as a rock yourself, firm to your covenant with your and our God, even now expressing your zeal and affection for the Protestant religion, and your care and study for the propagation there of.[17]

On 8th May, Charles II was proclaimed in London. Sermons were preached in both Houses, and Richard Baxter preached in St Paul's, before the Lord Mayor and Corporation of London.[18] The proclamation was repeated speedily throughout the whole country. It emphasized the fact that Charles's title to the Crown dated from the moment of his father's death, and that it was not bestowed in virtue of any parliamentary recognition, but 'by inherent birthright and lawful undoubted succession . . . being lineally, justly and lawfully next heir of the blood royal of this realm'.[19]

Whilst Charles waited at Breda, both Houses sent deputations to assure him of the national loyalty.[20] The Presbyterians also sent a delegation which was cordially received by Charles at the Hague. They presented a letter from eighty London ministers who had met at Sion College on 7th May,[21] and four days later they travelled to Holland with the parliamentary commissioners. It is a proof of the confidence of the Presbyterians as to their standing, that they asked Charles, on his return to England, not to use the Book of Common Prayer, and to discourage the use of the

[16] The letter is printed in Clarendon, *Hist.*, pp. 904-5.

[17] Ibid. p. 905. Cf. *Rel. Bax.*, I.215, for further testimonies.

[18] R. Baxter, *Works* (1830), Vol. XVII. The text was Luke 10[20].

[19] For the text of the Proclamation, see Clarendon, *Hist.*, p. 906.

[20] Ibid. pp. 908-9.

[21] Register of Sion College, Vol. A, f. 204 (quoted by Bosher, p. 128). The delegation included Ed. Reynolds, Edmund Calamy, William Spurstowe, Thomas Case, and Thomas Manton from London, and Edward Bowles from Yorkshire (Clarendon, *Hist.*, p. 909).

surplice by his chaplains. He received them kindly, but, when they pressed these particular issues, he told them 'with some warmth' that 'whilst he gave them liberty, he would not have his own taken from him'; that the service in the Book of Common Prayer 'he thought the best in the world'; that the surplice 'had always been held a decent habit in the church, constantly practised in England till these late times'.[22]

One important element in the preparation for the restoration concerned the organization of episcopal authority. If Cromwell had lived ten to twelve years longer, episcopacy in England might have been lost beyond recovery. All the bishops in English sees would have died.[23] It was this situation that induced the ancient bishops to petition Charles to fill up vacant sees without delay, and in this they were supported by Sir Edward Hyde who prevailed with the King. Names were forwarded to Dr Barwick, to be put into the hands of the Bishops of London, Ely and Sarum in view of consecrations. There was difficulty in securing the right persons, but even greater was that of performing consecrations canonically because there were no deans and chapters to elect, and so none to receive the mandate. To prepare the ground for a resuscitation of episcopacy, testimonies as to the King's firm Protestantism had been procured early in 1660 from prominent Huguenot divines; other letters were obtained and the documents were published under the title: *Certain Letters evidencing the King's steadfastness in the Protestant Religion.* Baxter declared that through these 'mighty commendations of the King as to his temper and piety . . . the fears of many at that time were much quieted'.[24] Repeated efforts, largely in secret, were made to secure episcopal consecrations. It was suggested that the King should grant commissions to the bishops of each province to elect and consecrate, and on the basis of equality of balance between the universities. With the growing certainty of the Restoration,

[22] Ibid. Clarendon adds this comment: 'Though they were very much unsatisfied with him, whom they thought to have found most flexible, yet they ceased further troubling him, in hope and presumption that they should find their importunity in England made effectual.' But we may note the contrast in Baxter's comment: 'His Majesty gave such encouraging promises of peace, as raised some of them to high expectations' (*Rel. Bax.*, I.218). Also this comment from Pepys: 'At Court I find that all things grow high. The old clergy talk as being sure of their lands again, and laugh at the Presbytery . . . there being nothing now in any man's power to hinder them and the King from doing what they have a mind' (I.61; quoted Bosher, p. 131).

[23] By the end of 1650 all but nine of the twenty-seven sees were vacant.

[24] *Rel. Bax.*, X.215.

however, the question of episcopal succession seemed to grow less urgent, but there was some apprehensiveness as to a possible re-establishment of the old Presbyterianism.[25] Steadily, however, largely through the efforts of Dr George Morley and those associated with him, the way was being prepared for the re-establishment of the Anglican régime; in conversation with leading Presbyterians, lines of adjustment were suggested, but it is difficult to set aside the idea that this was no disinterested effort to bridge the gulf between the two groups.[26]

On 25th May King Charles landed at Dover. Neither bishop nor royal chaplain was there to greet him—and this omission, it would appear, was at Charles's own decision. It was a policy of discretion.[27] The King was received by the Mayor and Corporation, and a Bible was given to him by the Mayor's Chaplain, probably a Presbyterian minister. On 28th May the King entered London. Twelve Presbyterian ministers were officially present.[28] There were wide expressions of loyalty. The Independent ministers of London and Westminster expressed their gratitude for his Declaration at Breda.[29] There was allegiance on all sides, but the Episcopalians remained quiet, awaiting their opportunity.

The return of Charles II was the beginning of a long and tragic chapter in the fortunes of England, alike in matters of civil and of religious freedom. It is easy to say that the reason behind the coming of the King was that the nation as a whole was tired of the Puritan régime, and saw in the restoration of the monarchy the solution of the situation. But the reason is deeper than that. The desire for the King's return would not have arisen had it not been for a series of disastrous mistakes. Richard Cromwell's failure and his betrayal of the trust bequeathed to him by his father; the surge of republican interest and the party spirit of the Independents, not least in their jealousy of the Presbyterians; the ambition of the Presbyterian party to assert ecclesiastical supremacy, and their failure to secure firm guarantees for constitutional

[25] J. Gauden, *Slight Healing of Public Hurts* (1660): 'The little finger of rigid Presbytery hath been heavier than the loins of moderate Episcopacy' (quoted Bosher, p. 103).

[26] For a full account of these attempts, see Bosher, Ch. 3.

[27] *Life of John Barwick* (1724), pp. 270-2. Bosher, pp. 124-5.

[28] *Rel. Bax.*, I.218. 'As he past through the city toward Westminster, the London ministers in their places attended him with acclamation and by the hands of old Mr Arthur Jackson presented him with a richly-bound Bible, which he received, and told them it would be the rule of his actions.'

[29] *C.S.P.D.*, Charles II, I.4.

and ecclesiastical freedom, together with a blindness to the real purposes of the King, were all contributory factors to the situation. The dividing spirit which prevailed throughout the nation caused the sacrifice of those gains in civil and religious freedom which had been the result of the great rebellion during the previous decade.[30]

II

The months that followed the arrival of the King were crucial in the development of Church settlement. Although the Anglicans continued to work quietly in order to regain control, there was every reason to exercise a policy of caution. There were still grounds for a feeling of insecurity. The more radical elements in the nation still had influence, and Presbyterianism was still a force to be reckoned with. Although in the Convention Parliament the Presbyterians were outnumbered, if they and the Independents combined the position was reversed.[31] The situation was always uncertain, and far too delicately balanced to allow of any policy that might result in a Presbyterian crisis. Amongst the Presbyterians themselves there was uneasiness on the question of episcopacy.[32] Baxter has summarized the Anglican position:

When they came in, it was necessary that they should proceed safely, and feel whether the ground was solid under them before they proceeded to their structure; the land had been but lately engaged against them; the Covenant had been taken even by the Lords and gentlemen of their own party at their composition; there was the army that brought them in (who were Presbyterian as to most of the ruling part) to be disbanded; and how knew they what the Parliament would do? . . . How could they know these things beforehand? Therefore it was necessary that moderate things should be proposed and promised.[33]

There were some in the Government who declared that, since previous legislation without royal warrant was cancelled by the

[30] Dale, pp. 356-9.

[31] See *English Historical Review*, Vol. XXIII; L. F. Brown, 'The Religious Factors in the Convention Parliament', p. 63.

[32] A collection of speeches made in Parliament in 1641 was reprinted in 1660, with the title: *A Landskip: or a Brief Prospective of English Episcopacy*, 1641.

[33] *Rel. Bax.*, I.287.

restoration of the monarchy, it was therefore a natural consequence that the Church of England should assert its authority.[34] This was certainly the view of Hyde and his associates, though recognized as too severe a policy, at least for the time being.[35] Others who were not Anglican asserted that the Declaration of Breda, with its reference of all religious issues to the decision of Parliament, opened the road to readjustment, and it was this policy that both Charles and the Anglican group temporarily adopted, whilst at the same time working for the establishment of the old order. The procedure, which was marked by attempts to reassure the Presbyterians, was gradual, but nevertheless determined.

In June 1660, at the request of Parliament, the King issued a Proclamation maintaining all incumbents with their benefices for the time being. Soon afterwards, however, the King received an episcopal delegation seeking assurance as to their future to which Charles asserted that 'as his heart and mind was always most chiefly addicted and inclined to episcopal government, so he would labour to his utmost to see them restored and established; only, considering the present state of affairs, and the several interests and animosities of several parties . . . it were fit he should be advised by his Parliament herein'.[36] In the same month, the King appointed several Presbyterian ministers as royal chaplains,[37] and these were presented to the King by the Earl of Manchester, a strong supporter of the Presbyterian interest, at the latter's lodgings, Clarendon and other statesmen being present. On this occasion Baxter spoke at length.[38] He declared that Cromwell had done a great work for the nation, and 'had placed and encouraged many thousand faithful ministers in the Church'.

[34] Ibid. p. 229. 'The more Politick men of the Diocesan way understood that upon the King's return, all the laws that had been made in nineteen years, viz. since his father's departing from the Parliament, were void, and so that all their ancient power, and honour and revenues would fall to them without any more ado; and that they had nothing to do but to keep the ministers and people in quietness and hopes, till time should fully do the work.'

[35] *L.J.*, XI.46. 'We taking notice that several riots have been committed and forcible entries made upon the possessions of divers of our subjects . . . and that without any order of Parliament or legal evictions . . . do by the Proclamation . . . declare that no person or persons ecclesiastical or temporal, shall presume forcibly to enter upon or disturb the said possessions . . . till our Parliament shall take orders therein, or an eviction be had by due course of law.'

[36] Add. MSS., Brit. Mus., 19,526, f. 40 (quoted by Bosher, p. 150).

[37] *Rel. Bax.*, I.229. Among these were Baxter, Reynolds, Calamy, Bates, Spurstow, and Manton.

[38] Ibid. p. 230.

He hoped that the King 'would never suffer himself to be tempted to undo the good which Cromwell or any other had done, because they were usurpers that did it, or discountenance a faithful ministry because his enemies had set them up; that he would rather out-go them in doing good'. Baxter spoke of the advantage that union would be both to the King, to the people and the bishops, and that it could be easily procured 'by making only things necessary to be terms of union; and by the true exercise of church discipline against sin; and not casting out the faithful ministers that must exercise it, nor obtruding unworthy men upon the people'. The King gave

not only a free audience but as gracious an answer as we could expect; professing his gladness to hear our inclination to agreement; and his resolutions to his part to bring us together; and that it must not be by bringing one party over to the other, but by abating somewhat on both sides and meeting in the midway . . . that he was resolved to see it brought to pass, and that he would draw us together himself.[39]

Either at this meeting or shortly after, the King requested his Presbyterian chaplains 'to draw up and offer him such proposals as we thought meet, in order to agreeing about church government; for that was the main difference; if that were agreed there would be little danger of differing in the rest'.[40] The King promised that when their scheme was prepared he would invite a few of both sides to consider it. The ministers agreed forthwith to meet daily at Sion College and others joined them, but there were divided opinions.

In these debates we found the great inconvenience of many actors, though there cannot be too many consenters to what is well-done; for that which seemed the most convenient expression to one, seemed inconvenient to another, and that we that all agreed in matter, had much ado to agree in words.[41]

Two or three weeks later a paper of proposals was offered to

[39] *Rel. Bax.*, I.231. 'Old Mr Ash burst into tears with joy, and could not forbear expressing what gladness the presence of His Majesty had put into his heart.'

[40] Ibid. pp. 231-2.

[41] Ibid. p. 232. As Bosher (p. 153) points out the disagreement was deeper than Baxter's account suggests. He quotes a letter of James Sharp (Wodrow, *History of the Church of Scotland*, I.46): 'Some friends of the Presbyterians way are very solicitous about the business, fearing that what they do now may conclude all their party, and lest they fall into an error *in limine* which cannot be retracted; that is, if they give in their paper of concessions, those will be laid on, and made use of by the other party as granted.'

the King.[42] These proposals were moderate and conciliatory. They asked that that godliness should not be discouraged; that each congregation should have 'a learned, orthodox and godly pastor residing amongst them'; that none should be admitted to the Lord's Supper 'till they competently understand the principles of Christian religion' and possess 'a creditable profession of faith and obedience', and that only unto such confirmation (if continued in the Church) may be administered'; and that 'effectual course be taken for the sanctification of the Lord's Day'. In matters of Church government, though dissenting from 'that ecclesiastical hierarchy as disclaimed in the Covenant', yet they would agree to 'the true, ancient and primitive presidency as it was balanced and managed by a due commixion of presbyters therewith', and then they declared themselves willing to accept the scheme of modified episcopacy drawn up by Archbishop Ussher in 1641.[43]

They affirmed the lawfulness of liturgy, provided it was not 'too rigorously imposed; nor the minister so confined thereto but that he may also make use of those gifts for prayer and exhortation which Christ hath given him'. In the Book of Common Prayer, the use of which had been long discontinued, they regarded some things as needing amendment, and they suggested that suitable divines of both persuasions should be commissioned at least to revise the book, and to draw up alternative services in scripture-phrase, to be used at the minister's choice. In regard to ceremonies they expressed their willingness that a proper authority should determine the forms of worship, 'ordered by the light of nature and Christian prudence', according to the general rules of Scripture, remembering that Divine worship is 'certainly most pure and most agreeable to the simplicity of the Gospel . . . when it hath least of human admixtures of things in themselves confessedly unnecessary, adjoined and appropriated thereunto', and which have so often 'occasioned . . . great separations . . . lest they should by perpetual permanency and constant use be judged by the people as necessary as the substantials of worship themselves'. The proposals declared particular ceremonies to which they objected. They requested that kneeling at the Lord's Supper and the keeping of holy days, as being of human institution,

[42] *Rel. Bax.*, I.232-7. See Gould, pp. 12-21, and Cardwell, pp. 277-86.
[43] See Appendix V.

should not be enforced; that the wearing of the surplice, the use of the Cross in baptism, and bowing at the Name of Jesus 'rather than . . . other Names whereby that Divine Person, or either of the other Divine Persons is nominated' be abolished. Also they desired that certain innovations not sanctioned by the Prayer Book and the laws of the land be forbidden, such as the erecting of altars and bowing towards them. Such ceremonies they declared 'have been imposed and urged upon such consideration as draw too near to the significancy and moral efficacy of the sacraments themselves'.

Some days after the Presbyterians had submitted their proposals to the King (10th July), they received a written reply from the surviving bishops,[44] which shows that not only were they in no mood to make concessions, but declined any conference upon the issues involved. Baxter described it as 'a paper of bitter opposition by way of confutation of our former proposals',[45] a description which, at first sight hardly seems justified, for the language of the document is moderate. The paper was a traditional defence of the Anglican position. The bishops, defending the constitution as before the war, and treating the 'Reduction' as inconsistent with Ussher's other discourses, resisted the proposals for a 'moderate episcopacy'. Two assertions, which at first sight seemed to be concessions, were in fact not so, as subsequent events clearly revealed. Defending the liturgy the bishops remarked:

Nor are ministers denied the use of their gifts in praying before and after the sermon, although such praying be but the continuance of a custom of no great antiquity . . . and ought therefore to be used . . . with the greatest inoffensiveness and moderation possible. . . . Nevertheless we are not against revising of the Liturgy by such discreet persons as His Majesty shall think fit to employ therein.

Further, as to the use of the surplice, the Cross in baptism, and bowing at the Name of Jesus:

Although we find not here any sufficient reason why they should be utterly abolished, nevertheless how far forth in regard to tender consciences a liberty may be thought fit to be indulged to any, His Majesty according to his great wisdom and goodness, is best able to judge.

They concluded with the judgement that to concede to the proposals of the Presbyterians would

[44] *Rel. Bax.*, I.242-6; Gould, pp. 27-39. [45] Ibid. p. 241.

prove the seminary of new differences, both by giving dissatisfaction to those that are well pleased with what is already established; who are much the greater part of His Majesty's subjects; and by encouraging unquiet spirits when these things shall be granted, to make further demands.[46]

It is plain that the answers of the bishops refused any essential alteration in the old system, but rather asserted its comprehensiveness.

The Presbyterians, 'not insensible of the unworthiness of this dealing', desired Baxter to write an answer, but on second thoughts, considered that it 'would increase the discord'. 'So what I had written', says Baxter, 'was never seen by any man, lest it should hinder the peace'.[47] This document, which bore the title, *A Defence of our Proposals to His Majesty for Agreement in Matters of Religion*, is available to us.[48] It reveals something of the wounded feeling natural to one writing under such circumstances, and had it been issued might well have provoked resentment, for it is undoubtedly challenging. It remained, however, a private matter. It reveals, however, the impressions made upon the minds of the ministers by the answer of the bishops, for their document left scarcely a vestige of hope, even at this early stage of the proceedings. Those things concerning the Church which had largely contributed to the convulsions of the civil war were all to be retained. Nothing was to be learnt from the experience of the previous twenty years. They were convinced that the bishops were even then resolved on their ultimate policy. The document concluded:

Your desires concerning us are like to be accomplished. You are like to be gratified with our silence and ejection, and the excommunication and consequent sufferings of Dissenters . . . and though we are stopped by you in our following of peace, and are never like this publicly to seek it more . . . yet are we resolved by the help of God . . . to live peaceably with all men.

Some of Baxter's friends were now inclined to give up further attempts at accommodation, but though he had 'low expectations' of success, he determined to persevere. His words are memorable.

[46] *Rel. Bax.*, I.242-7.
[47] Ibid. p. 242.
[48] Ibid. pp. 248-58; Gould, pp. 39-63. From internal evidence F. J. Powicke was undoubtedly right in assuming that this was written by Baxter (*Life*, I.193).

We abhor all thoughts of sedition and rebellion. . . . I looked to the end of all these actions, and the chief things that moved me next the pleasing of God and Conscience, is that when we are silenced and persecuted, and the history of these things shall be delivered to posterity, it will be a just blot upon us if we suffer as refusing to sue for peace, and it will be our just vindication when it shall appear, that we humbly petitioned for it and earnestly pursued after Peace, and came as near them for the obtaining it, as Scripture and Reason will allow us to do, and were ready to do anything for Peace, except to sin and damn our souls. And for my own part, I could suffer much more comfortably when I had used these means, and been repulsed than if I had used none.[49]

At this point it is worth while to look at the situation in perspective. An opportunity had arisen in the history of the Church in England for the healing of a wound of long-standing. For the two great parties into which the Church had been so long divided, a moment had arrived for facing their differences in a spirit of wisdom and charity. Admittedly the differences were deep. With profound confidence the Presbyterian group set their cause before the tribunal of Scripture, and on this basis asserted their doctrine of the equality of all ministers of Christ; they maintained that in the New Testament the terms 'bishop' and 'presbyter' are used interchangeably, and that there is no trace of clerical hierarchy. The story of the Church in the succeeding centuries had convinced them of the change from the episcopacy of the primitive Church to an elaborate system of prelatical power, marked by the pride of ambition, not seldom marked by corruption. Their reflection upon the Laudian régime convinced them further that the Church was in danger of Romanizing tendencies. They were prepared to defend the actions of the Long Parliament as necessary politically and ecclesiastically, and despite the sectarianism of the Commonwealth, they asserted that a more spiritual religion had spread through the nation. Though still contending against the prelatical episcopacy of the earlier days, they now asserted their willingness to accept a moderate form of episcopacy, nor did they condemn liturgy as such, not even the Book of Common Prayer if certain alterations could be secured. As to their loyalty to the Crown there was no question whatsoever. As to their ministries, they had been educated at the universities;

[49] *Rel. Bax.*, I.249.

many of them had been episcopally ordained, and had proclaimed the gospel effectively in their parishes into which they had been placed by the law of the land. So they urged that if they were to be silenced, it was without justification.

On the other hand, the Episcopalians declared that they valued the historic succession of the Church on the ground that the Church of England had not been founded in the reign of either Elizabeth or Henry VIII; but that then it had only been reformed and that it was part of the Catholic Church. For their doctrine they claimed the support of the early Christian Councils and the Fathers; that their orders were of great antiquity and that the early distinction between bishops and presbyters was proof of its sanction by apostolic authority. That there had been abuse of episcopal authority, in medieval times, was not the issue in the immediate controversy: episcopacy had been part of the English constitution until the time of the Civil Wars. The ecclesiastical changes which followed under the Long Parliament were illegal and unconstitutional. They asserted that with the Restoration the old constitution of King, Lords and Commons, together with episcopal government of the Church and the use of the Book of Common Prayer had returned. They declared that the Presbyterians in the day of their power had been ruthless; they had proscribed the Prayer Book; they had persecuted the episcopalian clergy; and now they were treating of things which involved no question of principle as a matter of conscience. Moreover, for some Episcopalians, the problem of a sacramental theology was at stake.

Each of the parties looked on the matters in dispute from its own point of view, and it is important to remember that both parties were advocates for a national establishment of religion. As in most controversies, both were marked by faults of reasoning and at times faults of temper. Yet the blame was not equally shared. It is not too much to assert that, even if we allow fully that the Puritans were often marked by prejudice, there is more evidence of a spirit of consideration and charity on the Puritan side than on the other.

Turning now again to the happenings of the time it must be noted that, behind these preliminary negotiations, there was a considerable measure of activity on the part of the Episcopalians. Throughout the latter half of 1660 there were frequent applications for restoration to benefices;[50] petitions from the counties were numerous and 'there can be little doubt that they gave welcome encouragement to a government officially professing one religious policy, and in fact, nervously engaged upon another'.[51]

There is abundant evidence that the settlement of the old system was intended, and would not wait either for the decision of Parliament, or an accommodation with the Presbyterians. Appointments to cathedral chapters, the restoration of Anglican rites in the universities, and the ejection of nonconforming Fellows; the growing use of the Prayer Book in the parishes—all anticipated Parliamentary action. By the end of August the work was moving rapidly to completion.[52] Many of the Puritan incumbents, seeing what seemed inevitable, quietly relinquished their possessions. Baxter records that 'before this time (10th July) by the King's return many hundred worthy ministers were displaced and cast out of their charges because they were in sequestrations'.[53] By the end of the year some 695 incumbents were silenced.[54] All these things naturally resulted in a growing tension between Presbyterians and Anglicans, the attack being largely upon the Puritan side, though with speedy reply in the Anglican defence.[55]

As the summer of 1660 moved on, the debate began to shift to Parliament, and on 6th June the House decided to resolve itself into a Grand Committee to consider matters of religion on each successive Monday.[56] In the opening of discussion of a bill for 'the maintenance of the Protestant religion'—a Puritan measure —an Anglican moved the inclusion of the Thirty-nine Articles; this proposal was interpreted on all sides as involving the re-establishment of episcopacy. This gave the whole ecclesiastical policy a new publicity. It was clear that in Parliament the die had been cast.

On 4th September 1660 the draft of a Declaration of In-

[50] *C.S.P.D.*, 1660-1, pp. 218-86. Stoughton (III.47-8) notes that in the month of August alone there were no less than 143 documents presented.

[51] Cf. Bosher, p. 156. E.g. *The Humble Petition of the Nobility and Clergy of the Six Counties of North Wales*, presented 28th June.

[52] Cf. Bosher, pp. 157-61. During September nominations to bishoprics were made, and on 28th October Sheldon was consecrated in the Abbey, the first consecration in the Church of England for sixteen years.

[53] *Rel. Bax.*, I.241.

[54] *C.R.*, Introduction, pp. xii-xiii.

[55] This is reflected in the sudden increase of controversial tracts from the beginning of July onwards (see *Thomason Tracts*, British Museum). Bosher, pp. 165-6.

[56] *C.J.*, VIII.82.

dulgence[57] from the King was shown to Baxter and his friends. They suggested omissions and modifications, some of which were accepted. On 22nd October representatives of both parties met the King at Worcester House, the home of Clarendon, to listen to the revised document; several statesmen were present and six bishops; the Presbyterians numbered six, including Baxter. Clarendon read the revised Declaration and as he read the bishops and divines offered their objections.[58] After discussion on the subject of the power of episcopacy and reordination, towards the close of the meeting, Clarendon drew from his pocket another paper observing that the King had been asked by Independents and Anabaptists to grant toleration. He proposed therefore to insert in the Declaration which had been read, a clause stating that persons not members of the endowed Church should 'be permitted to meet for religious worship, so be it, they do it not to the disturbance of the peace'. All present were silent—until Baxter, suspecting that 'the liberty of the Papists' was the aim, declared that he and his friends must distinguish 'the tolerable parties from the intolerable', and that for such as Papists and Socinians 'we cannot make toleration our request'. The King replied that 'there were laws enough against the Papists'; to which Baxter said that the real question was 'whether those laws should be executed on them or not'.[59] What was the importance of this intrusion? Certainly it widened the gulf between Presbyterians and Independents. It has been suggested that, as the King's real aim in all these negotiations was the establishment of universal toleration, this outspoken word of Baxter caused the King's resentment against the whole Puritan party.[60] Dr Bosher is right in

[57] *Rel. Bax.*, I.252-65; Gould, pp. 63-78; Cardwell, pp. 286-98. Also a lengthy document entitled *A Petition to the King, upon our sight of the First Draft of his Declaration* was drawn up by Baxter on behalf of the ministers; it was delivered to Clarendon, but they 'were never called to present it to the King'. This document is printed in *Rel. Bax.*, I.265-74; Gould, pp. 79-98. Instead they offered *Alterations of the Declaration*, printed in *Rel. Bax.*, I.275-6; Gould, pp. 98-101.

[58] *Rel. Bax.*, I.276. 'The business of the day was not to dispute . . . each party was to speak to what they disliked, and the King to determine how it should be, as liked himself.'

[59] Ibid. p. 277.

[60] Cf. F. J. Powicke, *Life*, p. 185: 'Probably this speech . . . did more to cool the King's zeal for a fair settlement . . . than anything else.' Cf. also Dale, p. 397: 'What happened at the close of the meeting was of critical importance in its effect on the policy of the King.' But cf. *Rel. Bax.*, I.286, where Baxter records his later conversation with the King: 'I told him I feared my plain speeches, October 23 . . . might have been displeasing to him. But he told me that he was not offended at the plainness or freedom or earnestness of them, but only when he thought I was not in the right; and that for my free speech he took me to be the honester man.'

asserting that such a theory is 'no more than a hypothesis', and that 'there is no ground for supposing that the King was not in accord with the Chancellor's religious policy'.[61] The whole occasion, so well staged, was part of the strategy skilfully employed by Clarendon and his associates at this period—'a master-stroke of policy well-calculated to relieve the dangerous state of tension'.[62]

At the close of the meeting a small committee of two Presbyterians and two Episcopalians was appointed to revise the Declaration.[63] Baxter was not a member of this committee. He left the Conference 'dejected . . . and resolved to meddle no more in the business, but patiently suffer with other Dissenters' being 'fully satisfied . . . that the Declaration . . . would not attain that concord which was our end'.[64] Three days later, on 25th October, the Declaration was issued. Baxter heard men crying it in the streets, bought a copy and stepped within a house to read it. To his surprise he found that some of the Presbyterian proposals had been accepted, and that 'now the terms were such as any sober, honest ministers might submit to'. At once he resolved to do his best to persuade his friends to conform—'cheerfully to promote the concord of the Church and brotherly love which this concord doth bespeak'.[65]

The Declaration itself is a remarkable document. It did not contain the clause which Clarendon had proposed, permitting persons who did not conform to meet for religious worship. Its aim was to make the Church sufficiently comprehensive to include those Presbyterians who accepted a moderate episcopacy yet were troubled by want of discipline in the Church and by the undue authority of the bishops and by the ceremonies. The following concessions were offered to the Presbyterians. Suffragan bishops were to be appointed where the situation required it; bishops were not to ordain nor exercise ecclesiastical jurisdiction without the advice and assistance of presbyters; no person was to be confirmed without the consent of the minister of the place to which that person belongs, and no person was to be admitted to the Lord's Supper without credible profession of faith. As to the Prayer Book a royal commission of divines 'of both persuasions' should revise the liturgy, and make any alterations deemed necessary, and also

[61] p. 188. [62] Ibid. p. 190. [63] *Rel. Bax.*, I.278.
[64] Ibid. [65] Ibid. p. 279.

'some additional forms', the minister to use one or other at his discretion. Meanwhile all ministers were to be requested to use as much of the unrevised Book as their consciences would allow. It also declared that none should be compelled to kneel at the Lord's Supper; or bow at the Name of Jesus, or use the Cross in baptism, or wear the surplice in parish churches. It is clear that this Declaration closely resembled the proposals made by the Presbyterians after the meetings in Sion College. Never before had such concessions been offered to dissenting Puritans, and it is understandable that they were received by the moderate men with gratitude. But, as Dr Bosher points out, if the question is asked as to whether the decision were intended to be interim or final in character, the document yields no answer. 'The Declaration defines its own intent with masterful ambiguity—to give some determination to matters in difference until a synod be called to give such further assistance as is necessary'.[66] In reading the Declaration it is difficult to avoid the feeling that in purpose and spirit it is marked by sincerity: it is when it is related to its context that the duplicity becomes apparent. It was with this situation in mind that afterwards Baxter's shrewd and final estimate of the Declaration was set forth:

It was necessary that moderate things should be proposed and promised; and no way was so fit as by a Declaration, which being no law is a temporary thing, giving place to laws. And it was needful that the calling of a synod were delayed till the Presbyterians were partly cast out, and a way to keep out the rest secured. And if when all these things were done, the former promises were . . . like an Almanack out of date.[67]

Shortly before the meeting at Worcester House unofficial offers of preferment had been made to some of the leaders of the Presbyterian party. After the Declaration Baxter was offered the see of Hereford, Calamy that of Lichfield and Coventry, and Reynolds that of Norwich.[68] Acceptance of such preferment would have lessened the influence of these leaders of the Puritan party and all declined the offers, except Reynolds, who accepted 'on the terms

[66] Bosher, p. 189.

[67] *Rel. Bax.*, I.287-8; cf. p. 281: 'I feared that this Declaration was but for a present use, and that shortly it would be revoked or nullified.'

[68] Ibid. pp. 281ff. In addition Manton was offered the deanery of Rochester, Bates that of Lichfield, and Bowles that of York. All declined.

of the King's Declaration'. This reaction reveals the uneasiness of the Presbyterians as to the permanence of the settlement proffered by the King. Nevertheless they determined to carry the whole issue a stage farther by urging that the Declaration should become law in terms of a Royal Proclamation. When the House returned on 6th November the matter was raised. A motion to return thanks to the King was accepted without dissent,[69] but when the proposal was put forward to make the Declaration a matter of law the difficulty arose. For the Church party it was an awkward dilemma, in that, if the Declaration were so thankfully accepted, why should Parliament not approve it in legal terms. To resist seemed to question the King's sincerity towards the Presbyterians: to agree involved an ecclesiastical settlement in terms of comprehension such as they had never envisaged. The discussion was fierce, and eventually the Bill was lost by 157 to 183 votes.[70] It was a crucial decision. It was the destruction of the Presbyterian hopes: yet the failure had now made it clear that the Declaration was but an expedient in the Anglican policy. In addition to the growing strength of the Episcopalians, there was a further cause for the defeat of the Bill. Clarendon declares that earlier the King desired to have the whole matter under his control, and was averse to any Act of Parliament on questions of religion.[71] He cared a great deal about the royal prerogative. It may be assumed that the King did not want the Declaration to become law. That Morrice, one of the Secretaries of State should advise that the Bill should not pass is significant. Charles wished to keep the Presbyterians quiet as long as possible, to secure a few of their leaders into the Church and to use others —to whom he held out hopes of toleration—as tools for securing liberty to the Papists. In this policy Clarendon had supported him throughout; he desired to restore the Church on its old basis, and with the purpose of winning over the Presbyterians to episcopacy, he was willing to make a few concessions. But any wish to base the Church on the principles of the Declaration was inconsistent with his own declared purpose. His frequent expressions of favour

[69] On 16th November a deputation of London ministers came to Whitehall with a loyal address of thanks to the King. *Rel. Bax.*, I.284-5; Gould, pp. 101-4.

[70] Some of the Independents voted with the majority and in so doing illustrated the gulf that existed between themselves and the Presbyterians, something which cost the latter dearly. Bosher, p. 198.

[71] Clarendon, *Hist.*, p. 1034: 'The King desired no more than that they should do nothing, being sure that in a little time he should himself do the work best.'

towards some of the Puritan party were but part of his diplomacy in an endeavour to reach his objective.[72]

Parliament was dissolved on 29th December 1660. It had had great opportunities for the settlement of religion in England but it failed to use them. The crucial moment had been lost.

III

Although there were attempts at negotiation during these months following the King's return, there was an insistent and steady infiltration of the old system within the parishes. In September 1660 there was a significant reminder that the ancient laws were regarded as still in force,[73] and these 'constituted an arsenal of weapons with which the magistrate and others could, if they were so disposed, grievously disturb their Puritan neighbour'.[74] Both Canon Law and Statute Law could be invoked. The magistrates, being appointed by the Crown, were often men of wide powers against the Puritans. There was widespread prosecution of ministers who refused to read the Prayer Book; others for refusal to observe holy-days; others for criticism of Anglican usage and ceremonies. Thus many were harassed and suffered minor penalties and cases were widely scattered through the counties.[75] The King's Declaration seems to have afforded only a very limited protection. Baxter speaks of the situation:

For the fulfilling of it there was nothing at all done which the Declaration mentioneth, save only this year's suspension of the law against us. And some men were so violent at a distance in the country that they indicted ministers at the Assizes and Sessions notwithstanding the Declaration, taking it for no suspension of the law; which put us on many ungrateful addresses to the King and the Lord Chancellor for their deliverance. For the brethren complained to us from all parts, and thought it our duty, who had procured the Declaration, to procure

[72] E.g. in a letter to Dr Barwick (*Life*, p. 525): 'It would be no ill-expedient to assure them of present good preferments in the church.'

[73] A publication entitled *Acts of Parliament now in force establishing the Religion of the Church of England* contained the texts of Acts in the reign of Elizabeth and Proclamations of James I and Charles I. The Preface contains the following: 'It hath been thought expedient to reprint certain Acts of Parliament . . . remaining still in full force and power, to the intent that everyone may be informed both of the duties and penalties by the law enjoined.' See Bosher, p. 200.

[74] Stoughton, III.135-7.

[75] From the pages of *C.R.*, Bosher (p. 201) lists the following counties: Shropshire, Sussex, Staffordshire, Nottinghamshire, Cheshire, Middlesex, Devon, and Northumberland.

the execution of it. And when we petitioned for them they were commonly delivered from that suffering.[76]

It would seem, therefore, that the Government did nothing to modify the activity of the magistrates; indeed it would appear that the procedure was quietly encouraged.[77] Such would explain the sudden outburst of persecution which we have just noted.[78]

One further factor was operative at this time against the Nonconformists, namely, the deep-seated fear of uprising against the monarchy. It was natural that in the Royalist mind this should become associated with the sectaries, the Presbyterians in time having become listed with 'the Fanatic party'. More and more religious discontent became interpreted in terms of political conspiracy. There had been suspicion of danger in December 1660.[79] On 2nd January 1661 an order in council was issued, forbidding large meetings, 'in secret places and unusual times', of Anabaptists, Quakers and other sectaries and restricting their assembly to their own parishes. On 10th January a Royal Proclamation appeared 'prohibiting all unlawful and seditious meetings and conventicles under pretence of religious worship'.[80]

[76] *Rel. Bax.*, I.II.286. Bosher (pp. 202-3) gives the example of Peniston Whalley, J.P. for Nottinghamshire, who instructed his jury to apply the statute of Elizabeth to offenders in the matter of the Prayer Book and to those who had worshipped in any other form. The evidence is in a tract of Whalley: *The Civil Rights and Conveniences of Episcopacy delivered in a Charge to the Grand Jury, at the General Quarter Sessions held at Nottingham, April 22, 1661* (1661). Bosher asserts that Whalley, 'in his plan for legal sophistry and abusive irony anticipated the great Jeffreys'.

[77] Kennett, *A Register and Chronicle, Ecclesiastical and Civil* (1728), p. 308: 'In September and October 1660 the justices of Peace by instructions sent to them had met in their several divisions to give out orders for restoring the use and public reading of the Liturgy of the Church of England according to the laws in being.'

[78] It may be observed that in Wales, as early as May 1660, the storm of persecution broke out, and before the end of June scarcely a prison was without Nonconformists. The Quakers were particularly involved; several Nonconformists were imprisoned at Carmarthen, and the jail at Montgomery was so full of Independents, Baptists and Quakers, that some had to be packed into garrets. Records speak of sufferers who during May and June (1660) were dragged out of beds into prison, driven into parish ponds like cattle, and led in chains to the Quarter Sessions. T. Rees, *History of Protestant Nonconformity in Wales* (2nd edn, 1883), pp. 97ff; Besse, *Abstract of the Sufferings of the People called Quakers* (1733), *passim.*

[79] Letter of Sir Ed. Nicholas, dated 7th December 1660 (quoted Bosher, pp. 204-5): 'The Fanatic party . . . have been designing their revenge in the nation's disturbance. . . . The King, God willing, will have a full occasion of cutting off by present justice and a continued severity that obstinate unreconcilable sect of men.'

[80] Gould, pp. 104-6. Cf. Kennett, pp. 352, 357-8, where the entry in the Council Book is printed under date 2nd January and the Proclamation under 10th January.

On 6th January there was a mad outbreak in London of Fifth-Monarchy men[81]—Venner's insurrection—and this was regarded as representing one in which nonconformists were involved, and therefore a much wider rebellion than a mere fanatical outburst of Fifth-Monarchists.[82] After the insurrection, Independents, Anabaptists and Quakers protested that they were in no way connected with the uprising,[83] but this did not suffice to remove suspicion, with the result that these groups began to suffer insult and persecution. In addition, because the Quakers refused to take the oath of allegiance the weight of suffering fell more heavily upon this group of nonconformists.[84]

On 9th March 1661 writs were issued for the electing of a new Parliament. The City of London took the lead and ten days later in the Guildhall there was an uprising through the challenge of dissenting opinion, and the hall echoed with the cries of 'No Bishop'—it was protest against the resurgence of episcopacy. Four presbyterians were voted into the office of burgess. This was a surprise for the Royalists, and it revealed the fact that the nonconformists were presenting a united front against the religious policy of the Government. Following this moment of victory, many citizens of London wrote to their friends in the country to urge constituents to follow the London example. These letters never reached their destination; they were intercepted.[85] The object of this interception was to discover how far there was anything treasonable, and to prevent any influence in the county

[81] The Fifth-Monarchy men were a millennial sect in the middle of the seventeenth century who aimed at bringing in the 'Fifth Monarchy' (Daniel 2^{44}) which should succeed the four empires of Assyria, Persia, Greece and Rome, and during which Christ should reign for a thousand years (Revelation 20^{4}). Believing that the Commonwealth was a preparation for this new monarchy they supported Cromwell, but finding their theocratic hopes unrealized they turned against him. After Venner's insurrection its leaders were beheaded and the sect as such died out.

[82] A comparison of the texts of the Proclamation with that of the Order in Council shows that its general text had been prepared prior to the Venner rising, and the reference to the Fifth-Monarchy men inserted following the insurrection.

[83] See Hanbury, *Memorials of the Independents*, III.592-5: *The Humble Apology of some commonly called Anabaptists* (1660)—A declaration drawn up by George Fox and Richard Hubberthorne and presented to the King, 25th January 1661. See Fox's *Journal* (ed. 1765), p. 316.

[84] In a few weeks some 4,230 imprisonments took place. See *A Briefe Relation of some of the Cruel and Inhumane Usages . . . of above 4230 . . . Quakers* (1661), reprinted in *The Friend* (1846). For instances, see Besse, *Abstract of Sufferings* (1753), Vols. I and II. Cf. W. G. Braithwaite. *The Second Period of Quakerism* (2nd edn, 1961), pp. 9-13.

[85] These letters (preserved in the P.R.O.) are summarized in *C.S.P.D.* (1660-1), Nos. 83-147. Some extracts may be found in Stoughton, pp. 150-3.

constituencies. The occasion was viewed in terms of a possible conspiracy against the Government.[86] The election proved to be in favour of the Royalists: the Presbyterians were so reduced in number as to prove ineffective.[87] The situation, together with apprehensiveness through recent events, marked a change in the official attitude. Presbyterians and sectaries were now looked upon as one company.

At this point we must note two important decisions concerning ecclesiastical affairs.

The first of these was taken by the King on 25th March 1661—so soon after the episode in the Guildhall that the two things cannot be unrelated. On that day the Royal Warrant was issued[88] calling representatives of the Anglicans and Presbyterians to meet 'in the Master's Lodging' for the purpose of revising the Book of Common Prayer, 'for the growing satisfaction of tender consciences and the restoring and continuance of peace and unity in the churches under our protection and government'. Despite the events that had occurred since the King's Declaration this seemed to suggest that the religious issue was still without settlement. The Commissioners were summoned to meet on 15th April.

The second decision was that of summoning Convocation. This matter had been raised at the Council on 10th April, five days before the Commissioners were to meet, and it was then ordered that writs should be drawn up for this purpose. If it had been intended to implement the Declaration of Breda, and also that at Worcester House, such a decision was really unjustified. The implication was now that the old constitution had become asserted, and that the ancient ecclesiastical order was virtually established. Clarendon's words are significant:

At the same time that he [the King] issued out his writs for the convening the Parliament, he had likewise sent summonses to the bishops, for the meeting of the clergy in Convocation, *which is the legal synod in England:* against the coming together whereof the Liturgy would be finished,

[86] Zachary Crofton, a prominent champion on the side of the anti-episcopalian party, was sent to the Tower a few days after the election, but obviously a general repression was inadvisable at such a time.

[87] 'The few divines and politicians who in 1660 represented the presbyterian cause were leaders without an army.' G. M. Trevelyan, *England under the Stuarts,* p. 279 (quoted Bosher, p. 211).

[88] *Rel. Bax.,* I.303-5; Gould, pp. 107-11; Cardwell, pp. 298-302.

which His Majesty intended to send thither to be examined, debated and confirmed.[89]

IV

Any attempt to understand the Savoy Conference must take into account the background of events upon which it was set. The situation was favourable for the Episcopalians and for the Presbyterians decidedly otherwise. This meant that the two sides were prevented from meeting on terms of equality.[90] The decision of Parliament in refusing to make the King's Declaration legal, the summoning of Convocation, the coronation of the King on 23rd April in Westminster Abbey by rites and ceremonies entirely episcopal indicated where the emphasis fell for any decision by the Conference. When the new Parliament assembled, 'constituted of men fitted and devoted to the Diocesan interest' on 8th May, followed by the order of Parliament on 22nd May, 'the National Vow and Covenant was burnt in the streets by the hands of the common hangman'.[91] It was in this atmosphere that the Commissioners met at Savoy. There was little hope of a free conference.

The first meeting was on 15th April 1661. Baxter has left a long account of the proceedings.[92] Formally opened by Archbishop

[89] Clarendon, *Hist.*, p. 1047. (Italics ours.) Note the error as to date. The writ for Parliament was issued 9th March and the summons for Convocation 11th April. Further the assumption of the operation of the old order is implied in 'the legal synod in England'. Again, the phrase, 'the Liturgy would be finished', could not mean that this was to be done in the Conference, for that would be against the policy of the bishops. It implied that the King intended that the Liturgy should be finished by the bishops themselves without regard to the transactions at Savoy. In point of fact the Liturgy was finished by Cosin and others before Convocation met. This means further that the issue of the Conference was determined at its commencement. Stoughton, III.158-9.

[90] Stoughton, III.160. 'A meeting at the Savoy between the divines of the two schools, in the spring of 1660, would have been different from such a meeting in the spring of 1661. Something at least like equal terms might at the former date have been secured, but it is plain that afterwards the men of Geneva stood no chance with those of Canterbury. Episcopacy and the Liturgy were in possession.'

[91] *Rel. Bax.*, II.333-4.

[92] Ibid. II.305-429. As Bosher indicates (p. 226) we are almost entirely dependent upon this account for material relating to the Conference, but on the episcopalian side he quotes at length a letter from Dr Ferne, written four days after the Conference ended. It is in *substantial* agreement with the main course of Baxter's account, though Dr Bosher suggests two points of discrepancy: (1) regarding Baxter's assertion that the bishops had paid little or no attention to the 'exceptions' handed in by the divines; (2) that Baxter gives the impression that the Reformed Liturgy was handed to the bishops much earlier than, according to Ferne's letter, was actually the case. Space forbids the development of a discussion on these points, but we are inclined to think that Dr Bosher has hardly established his contention that the attitude of the bishops was not a *non possumus*.

Frewen, who declared his ignorance of the business to be considered, the leadership of the Conference was put into the hands of Sheldon, Bishop of London, who insisted that, because the Presbyterian divines were 'seekers of the Conference' they should first hand in their exceptions to the Prayer Book. The divines disagreed as to this procedure on the grounds that the King's commission required all 'to meet together, advise, and consult', and 'that by conference we might perceive as we went on what each would yield to'. However, Baxter agreed to the Bishop's proposal, and persuaded his brethren to do likewise—not upon the grounds that Sheldon had asserted, but because a written statement would show a common mind. Discussion might show division amongst the Presbyterians themselves. The conference then adjourned until 4th May, during which interval Baxter drew up an entirely new Liturgy[93] as alternative and the rest of his brethren prepared 'Exceptions' to the old Liturgy. The more general 'Exceptions' relate to the use of the Scriptures, the Apocrypha not being admissible; the use of free prayer; the question of ceremonies. The chief feature of *The Reformed Liturgy* is that the prayers are generally more lengthy; there is a closeness to scripture phrase; the version of the psalms is alternative;[94] a recurrent optional 'at the discretion of the minister'—in the rubrics. The work was done by Baxter within a fortnight with only Bible and concordance at hand.

The reply of the bishops being long delayed,[95] Baxter became apprehensive as to the outcome of the Conference, and so he persuaded his brethren to offer a petition in the spirit of personal rather than official approach.[96]

We humbly crave that we may not in this be more rigorously dealt with than the pastors and people of the ancient churches were. If we may not have liberty of the primitive times, when . . . no liturgical forms were imposed . . . yet at least let us have the liberty of the following ages when . . . there were diversities of liturgies and particular

[93] See *An Accompt of all the Proceedings of the Commissioners of both Persuasions* (1661), which contains the four main documents. See also *Rel. Bax.*, I.II.316-33, Gould pp. 111-19, together with other papers given in at the Conference.

[94] The metrical versions were those of Barton (1644) and the Scottish version (1656) —'both to be printed . . . and publicly used at least until a better than either of them shall be made'.

[95] The answer of the bishops was not given in until June.

[96] Although published anonymously in *An Accompt of the Proceedings* . . . Baxter seems to have been responsible for the separate publication of the Petition and the Text of the Liturgy under the title: *A Petition for Peace with the Reformation of the Liturgy* (1661).

pastors had the power of making and altering them for their particular churches.[97]

The document closes with this appeal:

We are petitioners for those that are faithful to God and the King, that fear offending, that agree with you in all things necessary to salvation. We have now faithfully, and not unnecessarily or unreasonably spread before you the case of thousands of the upright of the land. We have proposed honest and safe remedies for the present distraction. . . . We humbly beg your favourable interpretation of our plain and earnest language, which the urgency of the cause demands, and your consent to these necessary requests.[98]

That such a petition should have been offered in this way and under such circumstances is a testimony to the sincerity of the divines and to their sense of the urgency of the cause of unity. They had been commissioned under the King's warrant *in common with the Bishops*, yet they undertook the attitude of petitioners to those who were really colleagues in the common task. The very presentation of such a document goes far towards supporting the feeling that the episcopal attitude was that of a *non possumus*.

When the reply to the 'Exceptions'[99] was handed in by the bishops it was seen that the attitude was one of intransigence. The following passage indicates the tenor of the answer thus given:

For the preservation of the church's peace we know no better way . . . than our set liturgy. . . . We conceive there is no such way to the preservation of peace as for all to return to the strict use and practice of the form. . . . We judge that if the liberty should be allowed . . . the generality of the soberest and most loyal children of the Church of England would be justly offended.

This reply was received by the ministers with profound regret, and they at once resolved upon 'a plain answer', the preparation of which was 'imposed' on Baxter, who immediately retired to the house of Dr Spurstow, in Hackney, and in the space of eight days completed the document.[100] In it the answers of the bishops are dealt with *seriatim* and we need not stay to give illustration of its direction. Its inordinate length—'the largeness of which I saw displeased them'—together with the pressing of every argument to the last possible extent could do little or nothing to mollify

[97] *A Petition for Peace* . . ., p. 9.
[98] Ibid. p. 21.
[99] *An Accompt* . . .; Gould, pp. 146-76.
[100] Ibid. pp. 201-345.

the attitude of the bishops. It illustrates what was Baxter's fundamental weakness, yet something which could be at times his greatest strength—his powers of logical analysis.

By this time, less than a fortnight remained to the end of the period allowed for the Conference. When they met, the situation resolved itself into a series of lengthy and largely irrelevant disputations in which tempers were frayed upon both sides. It was agreed that three members upon each of the two sides should undertake the discussion. Baxter found that the bishops were prepared to listen rather than to argue, and it was he who declared that the ministers were defendants against impositions which commanded either obedience or else silencing and possible imprisonment. 'Our wandering discourses', says Baxter, were succeeded by 'our as unprofitable disputes'.[101]

Baxter's final word in the Conference was to Bishop Morley, regarding the account of the proceedings which was to be given to the King. It was arranged that all that should be transmitted was this: 'That we are all agreed on the ends of the church's welfare, unity and peace, but after all our debates were disagreed of the means.' Baxter adds laconically: 'This was the end of that assembly and commission.'[102]

Throughout these proceedings of the Savoy Conference one thing stands out in bold relief. It is the zeal and fearlessness of Baxter in advocacy of the cause of unity. It must be admitted that discretion was sometimes wanting on his part, but he was passionate for one thing alone, namely, the victory of truth as he perceived it. Dominating his own party to an amazing degree—it would appear largely at the behest of the brethren themselves—he fought without guile or subtlety; yet the result was a hardening of the Episcopalians rather than their conciliation. 'Baxter's combativeness and voluble self-assertion was highly exasperating to the Anglicans', says Dr Bosher, 'and militated against any friendly *rapprochement* between the two parties'.[103] This is a true statement, but Baxter's motive must be properly understood. He was without personal ambition. His self-defence is moving:

The reason why I spake so much was because it was the desire of my brethren, and I was loth to expose them to the hatred of the bishops, but was willing to take it upon myself. . . . And I thought it a cause I

[101] *Rel. Bax.*, I.II.376. [102] Ibid. 237. [103] Bosher, pp. 229-30.

could comfortably suffer for and should as willingly be a martyr for charity as for faith.[104]

The Conference broke up in July, and by this time the Government had declared its policy quite plainly. When the Conference was over the London ministers waited on the Chancellor to present an account of their position, and also to consult about a petition to the King. They considered that, the bishops having the ear of the King and the Government, it was wise to forestall any misapprehensions. It was agreed that such a course be taken and that Baxter should be responsible for drawing up the document.[105] The following passage indicates the basic principles upon which the ministers had acted throughout the debates.

We humbly beseech Your Majesty to believe that we own no principle of faction or disobedience. . . . It is granted by all that nothing should be commanded by man which is contrary to the Word of God: that if it be, and we know it, we are bound not to perform it . . . and that to go against conscience, even when it is mistaken, is sin and danger to him that erreth. And on the other side, we are agreed that in things no way against the law of God, the commandments of our governors must be obeyed; and if they command what God forbids we must patiently submit to suffering, and every soul be subject to the higher power for conscience sake and not resist. . . . These are our principles.

We must pursue the matter a little farther, for the consequences of the failure of the Savoy Conference were unhappy. Baxter writes:

Our calamities began to be much greater than before: we were called all by the name of 'Presbyterians'—the odious name—though we never put up one petition for presbytery, but pleaded for primitive episcopacy. . . . We could not go abroad, but we met with daily reproaches and false stories of us . . . either we were feigned to be plotting or to be disaffecting the people.[106]

Baxter himself fell under the charge of sedition and became the centre of widespread calumny. 'No sermons that I preached scarce escaped the censure of being seditious, though I preached only for repentance and faith and morality and common virtue.'[107]

[104] *Rel. Bax.*, I.II.364.
[105] For this document, entitled *The Due Account and Humble Petition of the Ministers of the Gospel lately commissioned for the review and alteration of the Liturgy*, see *Rel. Bax.*, I.II.366-8; Gould, pp. 379-86.
[106] *Rel. Bax.*, I.II.373. [107] Ibid. p. 374.

This antipathy against Baxter spread even to Kidderminster; at Cleobury Mortimer, where he had an engagement to preach, but was unable to attend, a company of soldiers prevented the occasion altogether, the churchwardens having forbidden anyone who did not hold the bishop's licence.[108] Baxter, together with Calamy, was burlesqued on the play-house stage.[109] The most serious issue for Baxter was the decree of Morley, Bishop of Worcester, that Baxter should be silenced. 'I was the first man silenced in England.'

On 8th May, four days after the ministers had put in their 'Exceptions' at the Savoy, Convocation met for the first time since 1640.[110] It had been summoned without regard to the 'concurrent commission' of the Conference 'which indeed was an antecedent commission to us and has been a great *remora*'.[111] An early act of Convocation was the framing of orders of service for two royal occasions; the anniversary of the King's birth and that of his father's death. In June the King issued the letters patent authorizing Convocation to make canons and constitutions. Additions to the Prayer Book were made at this very time when the commissioners at the Savoy were discussing its existing contents; nevertheless Convocation refrained from doing more than this until the Conference had ended.[112] It was, however, an anomalous situation that Convocation, 'constituted of men fitted and devoted to the diocesan interest', should be making plans for the future when the whole question was *sub judice* at Savoy.

It should be noted that the Independents took no part in the meeting at Worcester House nor at the Savoy Conference; and indeed were not consulted by the Presbyterians. Obviously, in the light of their principles expressed before the Restoration, they could not participate in a scheme for comprehension. All they could hope for was toleration. 'Their prosperity under the

[108] *Rel. Bax.*

[109] *Diary of Henry Newcome* (Chetham Society, 1849), pp. 7-8.

[110] Even if it be allowed that the Church of England might be an episcopal Church *de jure* it was not at that time *de elege* or *de facto*. No new Act of Uniformity had been passed and the Presbyterians still regarded themselves as part of the English clergy. On 2nd May the London ministers chose Baxter and Calamy as representatives for Convocation, but Sheldon 'having power of choosing two out of four . . . did give us the great use of being both left out, and so we were excused, and the City of London had no Clerk in the Convocation'. *Rel. Bax.*, I.II.333.

[111] Comment of Dr Ferne, the first Prolocutor of Convocation (quoted Bosher, p. 230).

[112] The Acts of the Lower House of Convocation were destroyed in the Fire of London; those of the Upper House escaped, and may be seen in Cardwell's *Synodalia*, II.631. See Swainson, pp. 13-15.

Protectorate necessarily entailed their adversity at the Restoration. . . . They had embraced principles conducive to the freedom and spirituality of the church, and they were destined to take an important part in the development of English Christianity through the diffusion of those principles. Their disconnection with the establishment harmonized with that destiny.'[113] The Baptists for similar reasons were outside the Commission.

V

We must now turn to a brief survey of the issues in the new Parliament, the most royalist and Anglican so far, which had been summoned on 8th May 1661. It was opened with great ceremony by the King. In words full of sinister intent Clarendon raised the ecclesiastical issue.

> I must recommend to your utmost vigilance, utmost severity and to no part of your leniency and indulgence . . . the seditious preachers. . . . If you do not provide for the thorough quenching these firebrands, Kings, Lords and Commons shall be the meanest subjects, and the whole kingdom kindled into one general flame.[114]

On 17th May, Parliament resolved that the Covenant should be publicly burnt;[115] on 26th May that all members were required to receive the Sacrament at St Margaret's, Westminster, according to the Anglican rite, refusal to comply bringing disqualification.[116]

Several bills were now introduced for the purpose of restoring episcopacy and crushing dissent. On 30th May a bill was brought in to secure seats for the bishops in the Upper House. The ancient constitution could be pleaded in favour of this, but it now involved the principle of State-establishment of religion, and also the recognition of episcopacy as the form it should take.

Next came a bill requiring that all members of corporations should not only take the Oath of Supremacy, but should swear that it was unlawful under any pretence to bear arms against the King, and that the Solemn League and Covenant was illegal; also any who had not within one year received the Sacrament

[113] Stoughton, III.191.
[114] *Parliamentary History of England*, ed. W. Cobbett (1808), IV.184-5 (quoted by Bosher, p. 219).
[115] Stoughton, III.193; *C.J.*, VIII.254, 256.
[116] *C.J.*, VIII.247.

according to the Anglican rites should be ineligible for municipal office.[117]

On 25th June, the House appointed a Committee to report 'how far the coercive powers of the ecclesiastical courts are taken away, and to prepare a Bill for settling the same'.[118] Later, in July, this Bill was duly passed, thus giving legal status by Parliamentary authority to episcopal jurisdiction. This Bill involved the further re-establishment of Anglican rule.

The same Committee was entrusted with further instructions which were to be of far-reaching importance. This was 'to view the several laws for confirming the Liturgy of the Church of England . . . and to bring in a compendious Bill to supply any defect in the former laws and to provide for an effectual conformity to the Liturgy of the Church for the time to come'—a decision which was in entire disregard of the Savoy Conference at that time in being.[119] It was recommended that the preparation of the Bill should be entrusted to Serjeant Keeling.[120] The Bill came to the Commons on 29th June; a second reading was on 3rd July. Simultaneously with the second reading, an order was given 'for calling in all seditious schismatical books and pamphlets', and the names of those members who had not taken the Sacrament as commanded were reported. 'The House with one hand thus exercised Church discipline whilst with the other hand it was making Church Law.' A third reading on the 9th July was given to the 'Bill for the Uniformity of Public Prayer and Administration of the Sacraments', and a copy of the Prayer Book (1604) was annexed.[121] The Bill came to the Upper House on 10th July but received no reading for five months, probably because to make an enactment when the Royal Commission was still at work would have been difficult to justify; also the bishops did not take their seats in the House until 20th November, and their presence was important. The terms of the Bill demanded that every incumbent should read Morning and Evening Prayer, as

[117] Bettenson, pp. 391-9; Robertson, pp. 10-12. The Bill was first read on 19th June, but did not receive royal assent until 20th December.

[118] *C.J.*, VIII.279.

[119] Ibid.

[120] Keeling had taken part in the trial of the regicides in 1660; later, in 1662, he conducted the prosecution of Sir Henry Vane; in 1663 he became a judge and subsequently Chief Justice.

[121] Stoughton, III.201; *C.J.*, VIII. It would seem that this Prayer Book was attached because the examination of the Prayer Book had not been completed by Convocation.

appointed, on some Sunday before Michaelmas Day, 1661; that he should declare his assent and consent to the use of all things prescribed in the Book. Any person refusing was to be deprived of his preferment; every person hereafter presented or collated was to read the Prayers, and declare his assent and consent to the use of the Book within two months of taking possession. All lecturers were to do the same, on penalty of imprisonment for refusal.[122]

On 30th July Parliament adjourned. For the consolidation of the Anglican position a great deal had been achieved.

In the months that followed there was not only widespread episcopal activity, but as the news of the doings of Parliament spread through the provinces, annoyance of Nonconformists increased,[123] and a host of broadsides and pamphlets came forth against them.

Parliament reassembled on 20th November, with royal ceremony. The King came, in honour of the re-establishment, and his words are significant:

> I know that the visit I make you this day is not necessary . . . yet if there were no more in it, it would not be strange that I come to see what you and I have so long desired to see, the Lords Spiritual and Temporal and the Commons of England met together.[124]

In such a situation the Anglicans were now satisfied to leave further developments in the hands of Parliament.

The temper of the new session is illustrated in an episode which has been largely overlooked.[125] It had reference to the Act for Settling Ministers which had been passed by the Parliament in 1660. It took the form of a Bill 'for confirming the Act', and the Commons prepared amendments which changed the whole intent of the previous enactment, and of which the following are the most significant. For a period of six months from 1st February 1662 there should be the exercise of patronage where this had been overridden; all ministers in sequestered livings should pay one-fifth of the profits of the entire incumbency, and this could be recovered by the sequestered minister; all ministers who had shown any favour towards the execution of Charles I, either

[122] Swainson, pp. 12-13.
[123] E.g. Philip Henry, *Life*, pp. 91-2; Oliver Heywood, *Diaries*.
[124] *Parliamentary History of England*, IV.222, 224; Stoughton III.206.
[125] Bosher, pp. 239-43, gives a succinct account of this, to which I owe some of the above details.

before or after, should be deprived; any surrendered benefices during the Commonwealth by reason of 'fraud, poverty or force or fear' was rendered void; any minister causing sequestration should be deprived; plurality of livings should be restored to all sequestered ministers who had held them; there should be no confirmation of any minister not episcopally ordained by 25th March 1662, or who had failed to administer the sacrament according to the Anglican rite for a whole year.

The Bill was sent to the Upper House.[126] In February 1662 the Lords confirmed the Act of 1660 *without alterations*.[127] A serious situation was thus avoided, but the episode reveals the depth of growing antagonism. Clarendon was responsible for the rejection of the Bill, as an unwise procedure in view of forthcoming proposals regarding uniformity by which refusal to conform to the new requirements would mean legal disqualification. Thus the Commons rejected the proposed Bill.[128]

On 21st November, the day following the reassembling of Parliament, Convocation resumed deliberations of the Book of Common Prayer.[129] The work was carried forward speedily, for much had been prepared already. Within a month the work was finished. Forms of prayer were inserted.[130] About six hundred alterations were made in the body of the Book, some following the suggestions of the Puritans at the Savoy, but none of importance. On the other hand some were added which were more distasteful.[131] On 19th December the Upper House committed to Bishop Cosin of Durham, and Bishop Henchman of Salisbury, the preparation of a form of subscription, and the same afternoon this was

[126] *L.J.*, viii.341. [127] *L.J.*, xi.376. [128] *C.J.*, VIII.367.

[129] The first Reformed Liturgy in England was in 1549, under Edward VI; the second, which showed further advance on the side of the Reformation, was in 1552; the third was under Elizabeth, in 1559; with slight alteration the fourth was in 1604. It was the Book prepared in the reign of Elizabeth which Convocation was called to revise. See Proctor and Frere, *A New History of the Book of Common Prayer* (1906), pp. 196 ff.

[130] It is worth noticing that the Prayer of General Thanksgiving was drawn up by Bishop Reynolds, and that 'For all sorts and conditions of men' by Dr Gunning.

[131] The word 'priest' was substituted for 'minister'; in the absolution 'Bishops, Priests and Deacons' instead of 'Bishops, Pastors and Ministers'; the words 'rebellion and schism' were added to the petition against sedition. Lessons from the Apocrypha were included in the Calendar. The Laudian influence, however, has often been exaggerated. It is sometimes suggested that the manual acts in the Communion Service were due to the influence of the High Church party but it should be remembered that in the 'Exceptions' to the Prayer Book given in by the Puritans they declared that 'the manner of consecrating the elements was not sufficiently explicit', and 'the ministerial breaking of the bread is not so much as mentioned' (Gould, p. 12). Baxter's *Reformed Liturgy* specified the manual acts.

completed. The next day, 20th December, the two Houses of Convocation adopted and subscribed the Book.[132] This must have been on the basis of canon law and not upon statute law, the Act of Uniformity not having yet been passed.

In the 'Preface' to the revised Book the Bishops declared their own satisfaction with the completed work:

> Our general aim . . . in this undertaking was not to gratify this or that party in any their unreasonable demands: but to do that which to our best understandings we conceived might most tend to the preservation of peace and unity in the Church: the procuring of reverence, and exciting of Piety and Devotion in the publick worship of God: and the cutting of occasion from them that seek occasion of cavil or quarrel against the liturgy of the Church.

Baxter declared that 'the Convocation had made the Common Prayer Book more grievous than before'.[133]

It was not until 24th February that the completely transcribed Book was ready for presentation to the King; the following day Clarendon presented it to the Upper House with a letter from the King recommending that it should be enforced 'by the intended Act of Uniformity'.[134]

It is not unimportant to observe that in the month of December, which saw the completion of the labours of Convocation on the Prayer Book, two significant episcopal occasions took place. In Westminster Abbey, Sharp, Archbishop of St Andrews, Fairfoul, Archbishop of Glasgow, Leighton, Bishop of Dunblane, and Hamilton, Bishop of Galloway, were consecrated. Also on 20th December, Monk, Bishop of Hereford, was buried with full episcopal ceremonial.[135]

[132] Swainson (p. 17) suggests that it is difficult to think that the whole volume was written out between 13th December, when it was ordered, and 20th December, when it was subscribed. 'My belief is that the Book may have been subscribed, as we say in faith: the subscription form is blank.'

[133] *Rel. Bax.*, II.384. Dr Bosher (p. 249) thinks that 'apart from an increased use of the Apocrypha in the lectionary it is not easy to find basis for the charge'. The point behind Baxter's comment, however, is that, by the refusal of Convocation to allow any serious concessions to the Puritan view, and the insertion of things which were anti-Puritan, and the fact that the new Book was to make uniformity with no alternative possible rendered the possibilities of a settlement of religion far more difficult—as events certainly proved to be the case.

[134] *L.J.*, XI.392-3.

[135] Evelyn, *Diary*, in loc. 'It was a decent solemnity. There was a silver mitre with episcopal robes, borne by the Herald before the hearse, which was followed . . . by all the Bishops with divers noblemen.'

CHAPTER THREE

THE ACT OF UNIFORMITY, 1662

I

AS we have already seen, the Bill for the Uniformity of Public Prayers and Administration of the Sacraments was read a third time in the Commons on 9th July 1661, nearly six months before the Book of Common Prayer (the use of which it was intended to enforce) had been revised by Convocation. It was read in the Lords for the first time on 14th January 1662. A fortnight later the Commons pressed the Upper House for 'a convenient expedition' of the work.[1] On 25th February Clarendon presented the revised Book to the Lords, together with a letter from the King recommending that it should be enforced 'by the intended Act of Uniformity'.[2] Early in March the King declared to the Commons that he would get the Act carried, 'with all convenient speed'.[3] On 17th March the Book was approved, and 'the alterations and provisos' sent forward by the Committee were considered and the preamble was agreed upon. On the same day, Clarendon told the House of a proviso recommended by the King.[4] This was to exempt from the penalties of the imposed Act such ministers in possession of their benefices on 29th May 1660, and 'of whose more peaceable and pious disposition His Majesty shall be sufficiently informed and satisfied'. No such minister should be deprived for not using the surplice or the sign of the cross in baptism, provided he allowed another minister to perform the office when requested. This was included in the Bill passed by the Lords on 9th April.[5] A further proviso by the Lords was to the effect that if the deprived incumbent be regarded by the bishop as 'of peaceful disposition' he might claim one-fifth of his former living as the King might seem fit. This was also approved on 9th April.[6]

It is on the basis of these provisos that it is often stated that the Lords were more lenient towards the defeated Presbyterian

[1] *L.J.*, XI.364-72; *C.J.*, VIII.352. For detailed account of the whole parliamentary procedure, see Swainson; also Gould, pp. 408-55.
[2] *L.J.*, XI.406, 408, 409, 423. [3] *C.J.*, VIII.277; *L.J.*, XI.392-3.
[4] Swainson, p. 46. [5] *L.J.*, XI.425. [6] Swainson, p. 46; Gould, p. 422.

party than was the case with the Commons.[7] Such sympathy, however, is not so real as it might seem. Some of the changes introduced into the Bill by the Upper House increased the severity of it. The change of the date upon which the Act should be enforced from Michaelmas to Midsummer Day, and then owing to delay in passing the Bill, finally to St Bartholomew's Day, 24th August, meant that either of the two dates deprived outgoing incumbents of their Michaelmas tithes. The required declaration of assent and consent was changed to 'all and everything contained and prescribed'. Subscription to all the Thirty-nine Articles was required, not merely to those 'which only contain the confession of the true Christian faith and the doctrine of the Sacraments', as in the former Act of Elizabeth. The original Bill gave some discretion to magistrates as to the enforcing of the law, but as it left the Lords the Bill removed all discretionary powers.

On 10th April the Bill was received back by the Commons.[8] There the two provisos in the direction of leniency were rejected, and before the end of the month the Bill became marked by greater stringency.[9] After a conference between the Lords and the Commons on 30th April, and after the report of a speech by Serjeant Charlton asserting the views of the Commission, on 8th May the Lords accepted all amendments.[10] On 19th May, amid great ceremony, the Royal assent was given to the Bill as *An Act for the Uniformity of Public Prayer and Administration of Sacraments, and other Rites and Ceremonies; and for Establishing the Form of Making, Ordaining and Consecrating Bishops, Priests and Deacons in the Church of England.*[11]

The Speech to the Throne contained the following:

We cannot forget the late disputing age, wherein most persons took a liberty, and some men made it their delight; The hedge being trod down, the foxes and the wolves did enter; the swine and other unclean bests defiled the temple. . . . At length it was discerned, the smectymean plot did not only bend itself to reform ceremonies, but sought to

[7] Swainson, p. 47.

[8] Ibid. pp. 29ff gives the text of the Bill as it left the Lords, and includes the material later rejected by the Commons.

[9] *C.J.*, VIII.413, 414; Gould, pp. 437-8. Note the comment of Burnet, I.335: 'A severity neither preached by Queen Elizabeth in the enacting of her Liturgy, nor Cromwell in ejecting the Royalists, in both which a fifth part of the benefice was reserved for their subsistence.'

[10] *L.J.*, VI.446-50; Gould, pp. 441-52.

[11] 13 and 14 Car. II, c. 4.

erect a popular authority of elders, and to root out episcopal jurisdiction. . . .

Your Majesty, having already restored the governor and government of the Church, the patrimony and privelege of all churchmen; we hold it now our duty, for the reformation of all abuses in the public worship of God, humbly to present unto Your Majesty, a Bill for the Uniformity of Public Prayer and Administration of Sacraments.

We hope the God of order and unity will conform the hearts of all the people in the nation to serve him in this order and uniformity.[12]

The moment of Anglican triumph had been attained.

II

We must now examine briefly the terms of the Act of Uniformity.[13]

The preamble refers to the Act of Uniformity in the first year of Elizabeth's reign and describes it as 'very comfortable to all good people desirous to live in Christian conversation, and most profitable to the estate of this realm'. This passage then occurs:

Yet this notwithstanding a great number of people in divers parts of this realm, following their own sensuality, and living without knowledge and due fear of God, do wilfully and schismatically abstain and refuse to come to their parish churches, and other publick places where common prayer, administration of the sacraments, and preaching of the Word of God is used upon the Sundays and other days ordained and appointed to be kept and observed as Holy-Days.

This is an extraordinary description of Nonconformists—and it was not repealed later even by the Toleration Act of 1689.

After an account of the revision of the Prayer Book the Act declares:

In regard that nothing conduceth more to the settling of the peace of this nation . . . nor to the honour of our religion, and the propagation thereof than an universal agreement in the publick worship of Almighty God: and to the intent that every person within this realm may certainly know the rule to which he is to conform in Publick Worship and Administration of the Sacraments. . . . Be it enacted . . . that all and singular ministers in any Cathedral, or Parish Church and Chapel, or other places of publick worship within this realm of England, Dominion of Wales and Town of Berwick-upon-Tweed, shall be bound to say and use the Morning Prayer, Evening Prayer, Celebration and

[12] *L.J.*, XI.470-2. [13] See *infra*, Appendix II.

Administration of both Sacraments, and all other the publick and common prayer, in such Order and Form as is mentioned in the said book annexed and joined to the present Act.[14]

Intended therefore to regulate all public worship in England, the Act excluded every kind of public worship not provided for in the Prayer Book.

Further, by the Act, 'every Parson Vicar or other Minister whatsoever' holding any benefice or promotion was required on or before the Feast of St Bartholomew (24th August 1662) to read Morning and Evening Prayer in his church,[15] and in the presence of his congregation to make the following declaration:

I, *A.B.*, do here declare my unfeigned assent and consent to all and everything contained and prescribed in and by the Book entitled The Book of Common Prayer and Administration of the Sacraments, and other Rites and Ceremonies of the Church, according to the use of the Church of England, together with the Psalter and Psalms of David, pointed as they are to be sung or said in Churches; and the Form and Manner of Making, Ordaining and Consecrating of Bishops, Priests and Deacons.[16]

Any incumbent who failed to read the Prayers and make the Declaration, on or before 24th August, 'shall be deprived of all his spiritual promotions'. Where 'some lawful impediment' prevents this compliance a month's grace is to be allowed at the discretion of the bishop.[17] Every clergyman hereafter appointed to a benefice must make the same Declaration within two months after the possession of the living.[18] Further, every holder of any ecclesiastical dignity, every curate, every Master, Fellow, Chaplain and Tutor of any College, every University Reader or Professor, 'every schoolmaster keeping any publick or private school, and every person instructing or teaching any youth in any house of private family' is required to subscribe the following declaration:

I, *A.B.*, do declare that it is not lawful, upon any pretence whatsoever, to take arms against the King; and that I do abhor that traitorous position of taking arms by his authority against his person, or against those that are commissioned by him; and that I will conform to the liturgy of the Church of England as it is now by law established: and I do declare that I do hold there lies no obligation upon me or on any

[14] Ibid. § II. [15] Ibid. § III. [16] Ibid. § IV. [17] Ibid. § V. [18] Ibid. § VI.

other person, from the Oath commonly called The Solemn League and Covenant, to endeavour any change or alteration of government either in Church or State: and that the same was in itself an unlawful Oath, and imposed upon the subject of this realm against the known laws and liberties of this Kingdom.[19]

Any refusal was to be punished by deprivation of ecclesiastical benefice or collegiate or university office.[20] Schoolmasters or other teachers failing to obtain from the bishop a licence to teach and to make the declaration are to be imprisoned for three months for the first offence; for the second a similar imprisonment and a fine of five pounds.[21]

As most persons who had taken the Covenant were likely to be dead within twenty years, the clause dealing with this should be omitted after 1682.[22]

All clergymen who have not received episcopal ordination, unless this has been secured by St Bartholomew's Day, 'shall be utterly disabled', and deprived of their livings:[23] from that date no person is to be admitted to any ecclesiastical promotion or benefice, 'nor shall presume to consecrate and administer the Holy Sacrament . . . before such time as he shall be ordained priest, according to the Form and Manner in and by the said Book prescribed, unless he have formerly been made Priest by episcopal ordination; upon pain to forfeit for every offence the sum of one hundred pounds'.[24]

Further, a 'lecturer', i.e. a clergyman approved to preach without pastoral charge, is required to read the Prayer before preaching and to declare 'assent and consent' to everything contained in the Prayer Book, and to do this every month as long as he shall hold the lectureship. Failure to comply is to be punished by three months' imprisonment in the common jail.[25]

As we have seen the tithes of the clergy were usually due at Michaelmas and therefore as the date for submission was 24th August those clergy who refused to conform would lose a year's income.

[19] See infra, Appendix II, §§ VIII and IX. [20] Ibid. § X. [21] Ibid. § XI.
[22] Ibid. § XII. [23] Ibid. § XIII. [24] Ibid. § XIV.
[25] Ibid. §§ XIX, XX, XXI. From the time of Elizabeth to the Civil War Puritan ministers who had difficulty regarding conforming could hold 'lectureships' instead of parish incumbencies, and by these Puritanism had kept much of its strength. Laud had gone far towards suppression: by the Act of Uniformity they were eliminated.

III

From this brief summary the difficulties presented for Nonconformists become clear at once.[26]

One of the greatest was the question of ordination. Of those who had been placed in livings under the Commonwealth some had Presbyterian ordination; a few were Independents; some were without any formal ordination at all. There had been very occasional instances of incumbents in the Church of England who had not been episcopally ordained; most of these had been originally ministers of foreign Churches. If it were argued that by the Act of Uniformity a slur was cast on these foreign Churches, the Anglican answer was that there was a difference between such Churches that had no bishop through no fault of their own, and those, which, denying episcopacy set up a new scheme of ordination altogether.[27] Even allowing for a small number of exceptions, the Church of England unquestionably was based upon the ancient episcopal succession and so demanded that her clergy be thus ordained.[28] Those holding presbyterian ordination refused to be 're-ordained'.[29] The essence of the Anglican view was that 'they had not been ordained at all, but had been merely set apart for a Presbyterian ministry by people who had no right to ordain'.[30] Calamy stated the nonconformist position quite clearly:

Being . . . convinced that the requiring them to be episcopally ordained, who had been in a regular way ordained by presbyters before, tended

[26] See Palmer, I.37-50; Drysdale, pp. 383-5; *Rel. Bax.*, II.396-429.

[27] It is sometimes stated (Stoughton, II.243-4 note) that by 'An Act for the Ministers of the Church to be of sound religion' (13 Eliz. c.12, 1571) a particular form of ordination was not then requisite for ministration in the Establishment. The sentence quoted is this: 'That every person under the degree of a bishop which doth or shall pretend to be a priest or minister of God's Holy Word and Sacraments by reason of any other form of institution, consecration or ordering than that set forth by Parliament . . . before the Feast of the Nativity of Christ next following . . . shall declare his assent and subscribe to the Articles of religion.' For discussion of this point see A. J. Mason, *Episcopacy and the Church of England* (1914), pp. 489-511; N. Sykes, *Old Priest and New Presbyter* (1956), pp. 85-117.

[28] See 'Preface' to the Ordinal in the Book of Common Prayer.

[29] It was argued that the Church of England did not allow reordination and as proof of this, it was declared that if a Roman priest joined the Church he was not reordained. The point here, however, was that there was no reordination in his case, because he was a priest already. The Presbyterian was not a priest, and would therefore have to receive episcopal ordination (Clarendon, *Hist.*, p. 1077). The suggestion that not reordination but conditional ordination was required was put forward. 'The Form may be: "*If thou hast not been already ordained, then I do ordain.*" If the former ordination were good this is void: if the other was invalid or defective, he hath reason to be glad that it be thus supplied' (Ibid. p. 1078).

[30] Whiting, p. 15.

. . . to multiply their past orders, and invalidate their consequent ministrations, and at the same time to reflect on Foreign Churches who have no episcopal orders, as destitute of valid gospel ministrations, they durst not submit to it.[31]

A further problem for the Nonconformist was that of 'assent and consent'.[32] It would appear that some distinguished between the two terms. Baxter declared that the more latitudinarian conformists interpreted the phrase as referring not to the Book of Common Prayer, but to the use of it.[33] This is hardly defensible. The numerous 'Exceptions' given in by the ministers at the Savoy Conference show clearly that the differences between Nonconformists and Anglicans on this issue were very considerable, and for the former involved questions of conscience.[34] As to ceremonies, for example, Baxter states the position:

For my own part as I would receive the Lord's Supper kneeling rather than not at all, so I have no censure for those that wear the surplice, though I never wore it. But that man may adjoyn such a human Sacrament as the cross in Baptism to God's Sacrament, I am not satisfied in: and cannot assent and consent to it.[35]

Another difficulty was that the Nonconformists were required to take the oath of canonical obedience, and swear subjection to their ordinary according to the canons of the Church. They could not comply because they regarded several things in these canons as highly exceptionable. Further they found that the episcopal government was managed by lay chancellors' Courts, and they

[31] E. Calamy, *Abridgement*, p. 199. Cf. *Rel. Bax.*, II.427: 'At best to be reordained seemeth but a taking of God's name in vain, and a solemn prayer to God for what we have already, and a pretending *de novo* to *receive* that authority which they had before.'

[32] Clarendon, *Hist.*, p. 1078: 'They could be content to read the book in the manner they were obliged to do, which showed their consent; but declaring their unfeigned assent to everything contained and prescribed therein would imply . . . it was so perfect that nothing therein could be amended.'

[33] *Rel. Bax.*, II.427. The phrase 'all things' seems to be conclusive. Baxter points out that in preparatory discussion for the Conventicle Act (1663) the Commons refused a proviso of the Lords 'that those who declared assent and consent . . . should be obliged to understand it only as to the use of what was required of them, and not as to the things in themselves considered'. Baxter comments: 'Now the Parliament hath expounded their own words, and there is no more pretence left for the Latitudinarian equivocation.' In 1865 the *Act to amend the Law as to the Subscription and Declaration to be made and Oath to be taken by the Clergy* (28 & 29 Vic., c.122) the requirement was expounded in more general terms. 'I assent . . . to the Book of Common Prayer . . . and in Public Prayer and Administration of the Sacraments I will use the Form in the said book prescribed and none other, except as shall be ordered by lawful authority.'

[34] Cf. Whiting, p. 16.

[35] *Rel. Bax.*, II.428.

believed that the discipline of the Church should be exercised through the pastor, with appeal to a synod in case of abuse.[36]

Nonconformists were also required to abjure the Solemn League and Covenant.[37] Many had not taken the Covenant, and some had always resisted the imposing of it; yet their consciences would now allow such a renunciation as was demanded by the Act. They knew that the King himself had lawfully taken it three times and they regarded this renunciation as involving the guilt of perjury not only on the King but upon thousands of his subjects.[38]

Further there was the requirement of subscription to what was a political declaration.[39] The Nonconformists were ready to give any reasonable assurance of peaceful loyalty, but they demurred at subscription to this demand for fear of contributing to any betrayal of the liberties of their land. They realized that the law and the monarchy can be contrary to each other. The events which followed in 1688 proved that they were right in this refusal.[40]

Such were the grounds of nonconformity, and the refusal had to be made.

If but *one* thing had been made necessary to their continuing in their place, which upon due enquiry they thought sinful, they had been bound to have refused. But there were many things which they knew they would not yield to without sin, and because their consciences would not suffer them to do it, henceforward the church-doors were shut upon them with contempt and others filled their vacant pulpits.[41]

Beneath all the aforementioned grounds for this dissent, the basic difference between Anglican and Nonconformist was in respect of Church government. The bishops stood for a hierarchical pattern as primitive and divinely appointed: the Nonconformists did not believe it to be either.

[36] E.g. they would be condemned if they declared that the Book contained 'anything repugnant to the Scripture' (Canon 4); if they affirmed any of the Thirty-nine Articles 'to be erroneous' (Canon 5); if they asserted that the government of the Church of England by Archbishops, Bishops and Deans were 'repugnant to the Word of God' (Canon 7); if they questioned the requirement that 'all children without exception' should be offered to them for baptism (Canon 68).

[37] §§ IX, XII.

[38] Whiting, p. 17: 'Probably the authorities would have been wiser if they had let the Covenant sink into oblivion . . . but to the government it was still a dangerous standard of rebellion."

[39] § IX.

[40] Palmer, p. 50: 'The ejected ministers by their refusal helped . . . to pave the way for that glorious revolution.'

[41] Ibid. p. 51.

The bishops were for a reformed Catholicism; the Nonconformists were Puritan and Protestant. It was not merely a question of wrangling and possible compromise over details. The theological strife of the previous hundred and thirty years had produced two opposing parties with a different outlook and habit of mind; two parties which could not possibly settle down side by side in the same communion, holding opposing systems of worship and doctrine. . . . The division must have come sooner or later. That is sad enough, but what is still more sad was that the division should have brought with it such bitterness and uncharitableness.[42]

IV

The interval between the passing of the Act of Uniformity and its enforcement on 24th August 1662 was marked by uneasiness and fear of Puritan resistance. The bishops on the whole were resolved to force the Act to the limit, though in certain instances there were attempts to soften the severity.[43] The attitude of some Anglican laymen was equally antagonistic.[44] It was to be a policy of 'no compromise'.

In this situation of tension the King and Clarendon decided—without the bishops—upon a more conciliatory move. This took place a few days before the law came into operation and raised expectations[45] of an indulgence 'to be hoped for in some cases'. The ministers of London drew up a petition but 'could not get it delivered, and came away more dissatisfied than they went'. To any idea of indulgence Sheldon was entirely opposed and determined to hold to the law without mitigation.

The publication of the revised Prayer Book did not take place until 6th August.[46] This meant that in many cases in the provinces copies did not reach incumbents before the Act came into force.[47] Some allowance was made however in the Act for such delay.[48]

Baxter had decided openly upon nonconformity as early as a

[42] Whiting, p. 17.

[43] Ibid. p. 18.

[44] Bosher, pp. 255-7.

[45] Newcome, *Diary*, pp. 113, 115-16. Cf. *Rel. Bax.*, II.429.

[46] Gould, pp. 458-9. In folio form it was provided at a cost of six shillings for all churches and chapels.

[47] M. Henry, *An Account of the Life of Mr Philip Henry* (1765), p. 119: 'The printing and publishing of the New Book of Common Prayer was so deferred that few of the ministers except those in London could possibly get a sight of it, much less duly consider of it before the time prefixed.'

[48] § V. A certificate, dated 17th August 1662, 'allowing a lawful impediment', and given by the Bishop of Peterborough, is printed in Gould, pp. 458-9.

week after the Act had received royal assent. He preached his last sermon on 25th May 1662 and gave his reasons for his early silencing. 'I would let all ministers in England understand in time whether I intended to conform or not; for had I stayed until the last day, some would have conformed the sooner upon a supposition that I intended it.'[49]

[49] *Rel. Bax.*, II.364.

CHAPTER FOUR

THE AFTERMATH

I

SUNDAY 17th August 1662—one week before the Feast of St Bartholomew—was a day of farewells to crowded congregations, in the churches of those who could not conform. Many of these farewell discourses were afterwards printed, and they afford an insight into the prevailing temper of those about to be cast out.[1] Not all made direct reference to the situation, but in every case the theme implies it, and the sermons are exhortations to their flocks to stand firm in the spiritual things of which they had been taught. We take the following examples.

Preaching at St Dunstan's, London, Dr Bates concludes his discourse:

I know you expect I should say something as to my nonconformity. I shall only say this much. It is neither fancy, faction nor humour that makes me not conform, but merely for offending God: and if after the best means used for my illumination, as prayer to God, discourse and study, I am not able to be satisfied concerning the lawfulness of what is required; if it be my unhappiness to be in error, surely men will have no reason to be angry with me in this world, and I hope God will pardon me in the next.

Here is Dr Thomas Jacomb, of St Martin's, Ludgate:

Be good in bad times; be patterns of good works to those that shall behold you. . . . Walk as becometh the Gospel. . . . Let me require this of you, to pass a charitable interpretation upon our laying down the exercise of our ministry. . . . I censure none that differ from me, as though they displease God; but yet as to myself, should I do thus and thus, I should certainly violate the peace of my own conscience and offend God, which I must not do, no, not to secure my ministry, though that is, or ought to be, dearer to me than my very life; and how dear it is, God only knoweth.

[1] *A Collection of Farewel-Sermons* (1662); *A Compleat Collection of Farewel Sermons* (1663). The latter contains forty-two sermons.

Thomas Watson, Rector of St Stephen's, Walbrook, declared:

I have exercised my ministry now among you for about sixteen years, and I rejoice and bless God that I cannot say the more I love you the less I am loved. . . . Why should there be any interruption made? Where is the crime? . . . I desire to be guided by the silver thread of God's Word and of God's Providence. . . . There is an expression in the late Act, that we shall now be shortly, as if we were naturally dead:[2] and if I must die, let me leave some legacy with you before I go from you.

Thomas Lye, Rector of All Hallows, expresses an even more personal note.

Beloved, I prefer my wife and children before a blast of air of peoples' talk. I am very sensible what it is to be reduced to a morsel of bread.[3] Let the God of Heaven do what he will with me. If I could have subscribed with a good conscience I would: I would do anything to keep myself in the work of God, but to sin against my God, I dare not do it.

Beyond London similar occasions of farewell occurred. Thus Matthew Newcomen, Lecturer in Dedham, Essex 'for almost twenty-six years' spoke to his congregation:

The day is at hand wherein I and many others of my brethren shall be . . . evilly dead, dead in law, dead as to the work of the ministry. . . . It is not the laying by of the man but of multitudes, fifty in one place, threescore in another, and fourscore in another, and this not by a single bishop but by an Act of Parliament, which makes this wound wider and more incapable of cure; and shall we not be sensible of this?

Robert Atkins, of St John's, Exeter, declared:

I beg that you will not interpret our nonconformity to be an act of unpeaceableness and disloyalty. We will do anything for His Majesty but sin. We will hazard anything for him but our souls. We hope we could die for him, only we dare not be damned for him. We make no question however we may be accounted of him; we shall be found loyal and obedient subjects at our appearance before God's tribunal.

[2] This figure of speech, describing the effect of the ejection, is found very frequently in these farewell discourses.

[3] On 24th August 1651 Lye had preached his farewell sermon under sentence of banishment because he refused to take the Engagement (*C.S.P.D.*) 'because I would not swear against my King'.

Some of the preachers perceived the Hand of God in the impending calamity. 'God hath a special design in hand . . . which is always a design of faithfulness; just so far shall the enemy go.'[4] Again:

The Ark of God will not be lost . . . because God hath done already great things for this nation. . . . I argue from the abundance of praying people that are in this nation . . . and God never did forsake a praying people. . . . I am to exhort you that you would all of you contribute your utmost endeavours to keep the Ark of God from being taken.[5]

It was suggested that the very occasion of despair could provide deeper spiritual opportunity. 'Our sequestering from our preaching work for you will give us advantage to lay out more time to fetch sighs from our hearts in praying work for you.'[6] Further, the spirit of hopefulness for the future is by no means absent from these discourses.

When it is nearest day then it is darkest. There may be an hour of darkness that may be upon the Gospel, as to its liberty, purity and glory: and yet there may be a sun-shining day ready to tread upon the heels of it.[7]

The words of Joseph Caryl, Rector of St Magnus, London, when preaching from the text, 'And they shall walk with me in white; for they are worthy' (Revelation 3^4), are revealing:

I would only say this to you. . . . If I should have no more opportunity among you, that as you have been stirred up to get into the white of grace, that you and I may meet in the white of glory where we shall never part.

Throughout these farewell discourses the call of conscience rings clear; they reveal the kind of men about to be cast out of the Church. As to learning and eloquence the ejected ministers varied considerably, but underneath their differences 'lay a common faith of no ordinary character, a faith of that rare kind that makes the confessor'.[8] The spirit of these men is gathered up

[4] Elias Pledger, of St Antholin's, London.
[5] Edmund Calamy, of St Mary's, Aldermanbury, London.
[6] John Crodacott, Chaplain of St Saviour's, Southwark.
[7] Thomas Brooke, Rector of St Margaret's, New Fish Street, London.
[8] Stoughton, III.277.

in Baxter's poem, 'The Resolution'[9]—'written when I was silenced and cast out'—some lines of which are familiar:

He wants not friends that hath Thy love,
And may converse and walk with Thee;
And with Thy saints here and above;
With whom for ever I must be.
In the communion of saints,
Is wisdom, safety, and delight
And when my heart declines and faints,
It's raised by their heat and light. . . .
Must I be driven from my books,
From house, and goods, and dearest friends?
One of Thy sweet and gracious looks
For more than this will make amends. . . .
As for my house, it was my tent,
While there I waited on Thy flock;
That work is done; that time is spent:
There neither was my home nor stock. . . .
As for my friends they are not lost:
The several vessels of Thy fleet,
Though parted now by tempests tost,
Shall safely in the heav'n meet.
Still we are centred all in Thee;
Members tho' distant of one Head:
In the same family we be
By the same faith and spirit led.
Before Thy throne we daily meet,
As joint petitioners to Thee:
In spirit we each other greet
And shall again each other see.
The heavenly hosts world without end
Shall be my company above:
And Thou, my best and surest Friend:
Who shall divide me from Thy love? . . .
Christ seeth all that I would see:
The way and end to Him are known:
He hath prepared the place for me,
He'll love and use me as His own.

[9] *Poetical Fragments* (1699).

II

Despite the fear of reaction, against which the authorities had taken precautions,[10] St Bartholomew's Day passed without serious incident, and with little sign of popular discontent.[11] Amongst those who came out the far greater part were Presbyterians, though the number of Independents was considerable.[12] There was also a small group of Baptists among the ejected.[13]

To determine the exact number of the ejected is probably impossible, but according to Mr A. G. Matthews, the number deprived in 1662 is approximately 936; with the addition of those already displaced following the Restoration the total is estimated at 1,760.[14] When they discovered that the law against them would be pursued they began to take steps for mutual assistance. Lists of ejected ministers were made in the counties,[15] and money was collected for meeting necessitous cases.

Though now ejected, the majority resolved to exercise their ministry as opportunity should afford. Until better days might come they gave themselves to such private ministrations as were possible.

The Puritan pastor was concerned in all the passing events of the several families under his spiritual charge. . . . In sickness and sorrows, in festivities and congratulations, the minister had his appropriate duties. . . . The baptizing of infants, the catechizing of children, the welcome of the young folk to their first communion, the departure of some to

[10] Evelyn, *Diary*, 20th August 1662: 'There were strong guards in the City this day, apprehending some tumults, many of the Presbyterian Ministers not conforming.'

[11] Pepys, I.291: 'Things are quiet. . . . For aught I can see the Presbyterian clergy are gone out very peaceably, and the people not so much concerned therein as expected.'

[12] Lyon Turner (*T.C.H.S.*, VI.25) has proved that there were 389 ejected Congregational ministers, to which number another 100 might be added as probable, thus giving the Presbyterians a majority of five to one. F. J. Powicke, *Essays Congregational and Catholic*, ed. Peel (1931), p. 296. See also *T.C.H.S.*, XIV.156ff.

[13] W. T. Whitley (*T.B.H.S.*, I.24ff; cf. also his *History of British Baptists* [1923], p. 160) has examined the careers of eighty Baptists of whom it has been asserted that they held posts in the Established Church and has shown that not more than twenty-six were ejected in 1662, the majority being from the Welsh dioceses. He points out that a Baptist with a thorough grasp of his principles could never be a Nonconformist in the sense of one who declined to conform to the conditions on which he held his post.

[14] *C.R.*, Intro., pp. xii-xiii; xxxviii-ix. To the above number must be added 149 names from universities and schools, thus making a total of 1,909. See *infra*, Appendix IV.

[15] E.g. *An Exact Catalogue of the Names of Several Ministers lately ejected out of their Livings in Several Counties* (1662).

places of business, the espousals and the marriage of daughters, recoveries from sickness, removals to new habitations, intrusions of death in their families—these and other incidents of social life were appropriate occasions for the spiritual assistance of the pastor.[16]

The numerous diaries of the ejected ministers show the frequency of 'private days' with their friends, some of whom made gifts for the maintenance of their ministers. Forbidden to preach publicly, they conducted religious services in their own houses or in those of their friends, and in these exercises introduced 'repetitions' of their own or other discourses. As time went on they began to exercise this private ministry beyond their own localities. So the principles of an organized nonconformity gradually developed. As we shall see later, it was not long, however, before such opportunities became more and more restricted under penal laws. Frequently the ministers attended the parish churches for divine service, and on occasion, received the sacrament of communion.[17]

The loss of their livelihood was more or less serious, except in a small number of cases. It should be remembered again, that they went out before their September tithes were due, and in many cases they could not gain any support from their successors. By the legal position they were largely prevented from entering into the learned professions, such as law, medicine or teaching, though the legal restrictions were not enforced with equal rigidity in all regions. About a hundred kept schools, including, in nine cases, academies for the training of ministers, though at times they suffered interference. In some cases they acted as tutors to the sons of families who readily recognized the academic qualifications which the ministers possessed.[18] Some took to farming, and others became tradesmen. Nearly sixty are recorded as practising

[16] R. Halley, *Lancashire: Its Puritanism and Nonconformity* (2nd ed, 1872), p. 392.

[17] R. Baxter, *The Nonconformist's Plea for Peace* (1679), pp. 235-6. 'The greatest part of them forebore all public preaching and only taught some few in private at such hours as hindered not the public assemblies, and many of them lived as private men.... Those that live where they find small need of their preaching, or else have no call or opportunity and cannot remove their dwellings do hold no assemblies, but as other men content themselves to be auditors. Those that live where are godly and peacable ministers in public, who yet need help, do lead the people constantly to the parish church, and teach them themselves at other hours and help them from house to house. This is ordinary in the countries, and even in London with many ministers . . . that were ejected out of city parish churches.'

[18] *C.R.*, Intro., p. lvi. (Kennett's *Register* [pp. 888ff] lists occupations but with a tendency to lessen the hardships of the ministers.)

medicine.[19] Nearly fifty others held chaplaincies or domestic posts in the households of the nobility.[20]

Some of the deprived ministers were in the fortunate position of receiving charitable relief from benefactions amongst the nobility and gentry, though these sympathizers would be few in number because most of the upper classes upheld the Anglican settlement.[21] In the years immediately following the ejectment, London merchants assisted the ministers in this way.[22] The wills of the period show many legacies left for the same purpose[23] and the diaries of the ministers indicates many small amounts similarly bestowed.[24] Some of the ministers had private means, and it is noteworthy that some of these financially assisted their more needy brethren.

It should be noted further that between thirty and forty of the ejected ministers left these shores, some for Scotland, Ireland, and America, though in some cases the absence was only temporary.[25] Though there may have been some suggestion of a more general emigration nothing developed in this direction.

In view of the above it would seem that the distresses of the ejected were not as intense as might be thought. On the part of some historians there has certainly been a tendency to exaggerate. Nevertheless there were cases of great severity. In his *Account* Calamy notes about thirty of these, and in addition, scattered throughout his record there are many more cases where the distresses, though less severe, were none the less real. There are contemporary testimonies which cannot be refuted.

The best known record which must be recorded at length, is from the pen of Baxter, who wrote when the further penal acts had intensified the sufferings of the ejected.

Hundreds of able Ministers, with their Wives and Children, had neither House nor Bread: For their former Maintenance served them

[19] *C.R.* (Two ministers, Edward Hulse [*C.R.*, p. 283] and Richard Morton [*C.R.*, p. 357], rose to high rank in the profession.)

[20] Ibid. (See also Whiting, p. 20.)

[21] Ibid. The following are listed: Philip, Lord Wharton; the Earl of Bedford; Lord Fairfax in Yorkshire; The Harleys, in Herefordshire; Mary, Countess of Warwick; the Barringtons, in Essex; the Dunches in Hampshire and Berkshire; the Barnardisons in Suffolk; the Boscawens in Cornwall. Also it is reported that the King gave £1,000 to Dr John Owen for distribution.

[22] Ibid.

[23] Ibid.

[24] E.g. Newcombe's *Diary, passim.*

[25] Calamy (*C.R.*, Intro., p. xiv) lists fifteen as going to America, ten to Holland (probably encouraged by the Dutch), and six to Ireland.

but for the time, and few of them laid up anything for the future: For many of them had not past 30 or 40*l.* *per Annum* apiece, and most but about 60 or 80*l.* *per Annum*, and very few above 100*l.* and few had any considerable Estates of their own. . . . And if they had a poor Cottage to live in, and no Money to pay their Rent, nor to buy Fire, Food or Cloathing, they had much less enough to take another House, and pay for the removal of their Goods afar off, and the Charges of new Settlement; and there to dwell among Strangers, far from those whose Charity relieved them, was but to turn their Families to famish. . . . And indeed in many Countries, it was hard to find many places which were not within five Miles of some Corporation, or of some place where we had Preached before. . . . And if such a place were found, was it like that there would be Houses enough found untenanted, to receive so many Ministers? Or if there were, perhaps the Landlords would be so much for Prelacy, as to refuse such Tenants, or so timorous as to be afraid, lest by receiving such, they should bring themselves under Suspicion of favouring Non-conformists, and so be ruined; or so covetous, as knowing their advantage, to ask more for their Houses, than poor Ministers that had hardly any thing left to subsist on, could be able to give. Besides that, almost all Country Houses are annexed to the Farms or Lands belonging to them. And Ministers are ill Farmers, especially when they have no Money to Stock their Land.

Yea, they allowed them not to be kept as common Beggars, on the Alms of the Parish; but when by the Law, every Beggar is to be brought to the place of his Birth, or last abode, and there to be kept on Alms; No Minister must come, within five Miles of the Parish where he ever exercised his Ministry; nor any that were born in Cities and Corporations, must come within five Miles of them for relief.

In this strait, those Ministers that had any Maintenance of their own, did find out some Dwellings in obscure Villages, or in some few Market-Towns which were no Corporations: And those that had nothing, did leave their Wives and Children, and hid themselves abroad, and sometimes came secretly to them by night. But (God bringing Good out of Men's Evil) many resolved to preach the more freely in Cities and Corporations till they went to Prison: Partly, because they were then in the way of their Calling, in which they could suffer with the greater peace; and partly, because they might do some good before they suffered; and partly because, when they lay in prison for preaching the Gospel, both they, and their Wives and Children, were like to find more pity and relief, than if they should forsake their People, and their Work. Seeing therefore the Question came to this, Whether Beggary and Famine to themselves and Families, with the deserting of their Callings, and the People's Souls, was to be chosen, or the faithful performance of their Work, and a Prison after, and the People's Compassion? They thought the latter the more eligible. . . .

Alas! it is not now and then a Shilling, or a Crown given (very rarely) which will pay House-Rent and maintain a Family. Those Ministers that were unmarryed, did easlier bear their Poverty; but it pierceth a Man's Heart to have Children crying, and Sickness come upon them for want of wholsom Food, or by drinking Water, and to have nothing to relieve them. . . . I heard but lately, of a good Man, that was fain to spin as Women do, to get something towards his Family's relief. . . . Another (Mr. *Chadwick* in *Somerset*)[26] for a long time had but little but brown Rye Bread and Water for himself, his Wife and many Children, and when his Wife was ready to lye in, was to be turned out of Door, for not paying his House-Rent. But yet God did mercifully provide some Supplies, that few of them either perished, or were exposed to sordid unseemly Beggary.[27]

Another witness is Francis Tallents, of Shrewsbury, who gives the names of thirteen Shropshire ministers, 'very poor and had wives and many children'. . . .

Others were very poor but had no charge. Others had a little. . . . And some few might have to the value of 40*l.* a Year: Scarce any above. So the richest of them were brought low; and the rest into great Want and Straits: But he that feeds the Ravens has provided for them and theirs, amidst the Fewness and Poverty of their Friends, one way or another, in a wonderful manner.[28]

An interesting testimony comes from the pen of a Conformist, Edward Pearse, who produced four treatises in defence of reasonableness towards Nonconformists.

After the Act of Uniformity took place it is impossible to relate the number of sufferings, and great trials, with Hardships upon their Persons, Estates and families by uncomfortable Separations, Dispersion, Unsettlement and Removes, Disgrace, Reproaches, Imprisonments, chargeable journeys, Expenses in Law, tedious Sickness and uncurable disease ending in death; great disquietments and frights to their wives and families, and their doleful effects upon them. . . . Though they were as frugal as possible, they could hardly live; some lived of a little more than brown bread and water; many had but sight of ten pounds a year to maintain a family, so that a piece of flesh has not come to one of their tables in six weeks time. Their allowance would scarce afford them bread and cheese. One went to plough six days and

[26] *C.R.*, p. 107. [27] *Rel. Bax.*, II.385, III.3-4. [28] Calamy, *Account*, p. 573.

preached on the Lord's Day; another was forced to cut tobacco for a livelihood.[29]

Yet these suffering folk continued under a deep sense of the sufficiency of divine providence.

In all conditions various appearances of Divine Providence, great support, various deliverances and strong resolutions with a clear satisfaction of conscience as to the cause of their sufferings are impartially to be observed.[30]

This is reinforced by Calamy in his *Abridgement:*

Did God disown these Worthies when the Great Ones cast them off? Let any Persons observe and judge. They and their Families were supply'd by an invisible Hand. A noted Man among them (who himself had a good Estate) reckon'd up as many who were Ejected within a few Miles round him, as with their Wives and Children made up above a Hundred, who were all turn'd out to the wide World, and Liv'd upon Providence: Concerning whom he observ'd, that though they were oft in straits, yet they were not forsaken. Nay the same Person (when he had been Young, and then was Old) observ'd, that tho' many of the Ejected Ministers were brought very Low, had many Children, were greatly Harrass'd by Persecution and their Friends generally Poor, and unable to Support them, yet in all his Acquaintance he never knew, nor could remember to have heard of any Nonconformist Minister that was in Prison for Debt. Providence was instead of Livings to those who left their Livings for the sake of their Consciences.[31]

The sufferings of the ejected were greatly increased under the penal Acts which followed the Act of Uniformity: to the account of these we shall come in due course.

III

That the Church of England suffered no small loss by the going forth of these ministers is not to be gainsaid, though it would be easy to exaggerate the situation. There still remained in the Church men of distinguished piety and scholarship.[32] Nevertheless the

[29] *The Conformists Fourth Plea for the Nonconformists* (1683) pp. 40-1.
[30] Ibid.
[31] Op. cit. p. 193.
[32] Whiting (p. 24) lists some of these: Wilkins, Sanderson, Thorndike, Cosin, Barrow, Pearson, Jeremy Taylor, Whichcote, Cudworth, More, Sancroft, Patrick, Stillingfleet, Sparrow, Bull, Leighton, South—and other names might be added to the list.

ejected were godly men, a large proportion of whom had received university education,[33] and in some cases had attained to considerable degree of scholarship. Calamy has summarized this quality which marked these men.

They were men that would have been highly esteemed and honoured in the Primitive Church. . . . They were men of great Faith and Trust in God, and by their Integrity silenc'd many that apprehended Religion a Fancy. They rejoic'd in the Usefulness of their Brethren, while they themselves were Discountenanc'd. They Pray'd heartily for their Civil Governours, and all in Authority, while treated as Seditious Persons, and unworthy of any Favour. They were own'd of God in all their Troubles, carry'd through a great many Difficulties, gain'd upon many of their Enemies by their Patience and Quietness, and at last were taken under the Protection of the Government. . . . Cautions were entered against them, in all ways of Lively-hood they were capable of; and yet they Liv'd comfortably, and maintain'd their Families credibly; many of them bred up their Sons to the Ministry . . . And they died at last in peace, and were laid in their graves with Honour.[34]

We may recall a more modern recollection of their greatness found in a sonnet by William Wordsworth:

Nor shall the eternal roll of praise reject
These Unconforming; whom one rigorous day
Drives from their Cures, a voluntary prey
To poverty, and grief, and disrespect.
And some to want—as if by tempests wrecked
On a wild coast; how destitute! did They
Feel not that Conscience never can betray,
That peace of mind is Virtue's sure effect.
Their altars they forego, their homes they quit,
Fields which they love, and paths they daily trod,
And cast the future upon Providence;
As men the dictate of whose inward sense
Outweighs the world; whom self-deceiving wit
Lures not from what they deem the cause of God.[35]

[33] In *C.R.*, Intro., p. lxi, Mr A. G. Matthews shows that 1,285 had received university education (733 at Cambridge, including 68 Fellows; 513 at Oxford, including 36 Fellows; 20 at Scottish Universities; 12 at Harvard; 2 at Trinity College, Dublin). The greater part had graduated: about 150 had lists of publications.
[34] *Abridgement* (1713), pp. 192-3.
[35] 'Clerical Integrity.'

To find successors to fill the places of the ejected ministers certainly proved a difficult problem to solve. The supply of ordinands was considerably less than the demands of the parishes, and there is no doubt that some persons who were incompetent crept into the Church.[36]

IV

In any attempt to estimate the significance of the Act of Uniformity, it is important to recognize that primarily it belongs to the history of Presbyterianism rather than to the history of the other nonconforming groups. The Independents, the Baptists and the Quakers had taken no part in the earlier ecclesiastical negotiations of Charles II's reign, and in the scheme for comprehension discussed between the Episcopalians and the Presbyterians no place was contemplated for these smaller groups; indeed such inclusion was not possible if the idea aimed at was that of uniformity of worship, for by their principles, they were completely against the idea of a national Church. The Act of 1660 had already dismissed many; in fact all these separatist groups had met the challenge from the very time of the King's return, and a definite denunciation of their gathering for worship was made in the Proclamation of 1661. Even whilst the negotiations for a comprehensive Church were proceeding between the Episcopalians and the Presbyterians, they had suffered and the Act of Uniformity did not imply any change in their legal status: it merely ratified the illegality of their position. Although the Act does not make special reference to these separatist groups yet in declaring its purpose 'that every person within this realm may certainly know the rule to which he is to conform in public worship' it allowed no exception. It is therefore hardly true to look upon the year 1662 as if it were of supreme importance to those nonconforming groups of the separatist type, for such were already outside the Established Church, and had been so since the days of their origins in the reign of Elizabeth. This does not mean that the Act of Uniformity had no importance for the separatist groups. The importance for these lay in the fact that it marked an increase of the forces of this separatist nonconformity

[36] E.g. Oliver Heywood records that, in the course of a year and a half following his ejection, there were six successors in his incumbency (*Life*, p. 149). Cf. *Life of Adam Martindale* (1845), p. 169; and also Halley, *Lancashire; its Puritanism and Nonconformity* (2nd edn, 1872) pp. 392-3.

by the addition of those who had hitherto been 'internal' Nonconformists. For it was in 1662 that Presbyterianism, which began as a movement within the Church of England in the days of Elizabeth, now came to its final collapse. 'With the Act of Uniformity Nonconformity within the Church reached its term.'[37]

This, then, was the narrower and more immediate significance of the Act: it was essentially a Presbyterian defeat. Yet as we have just observed it was not this defeat and the failure of the plan for comprehension which inaugurated the Nonconformist struggle for existence. This struggle had already begun—and would also continue. 'The driving of the Presbyterians into union with an "outside" nonconformity which, even without the Act, would have had to fight for its life, was the only result which the Act of Uniformity really brought about.'[38]

By this fact of severance, the Presbyterians now expelled and the Independents already outside had by force of circumstance to share a common fate. The ejected Presbyterian ministers and their congregations finding the maintenance of a Presbyterian scheme impossible, tended to approximate to the Independent type,[39] each congregation being more or less isolated from the rest. So there came about the gradual approach between Presbyterianism and Independency on the congregational model, which resulted in the union, temporarily successful, following the Toleration Act of 1689.

St Bartholomew's Day, therefore, must not be regarded as 'the birthday of Nonconformity'—as is sometimes suggested—in the modern understanding of the term. The *name* did appear at that time; but only the *name* was new. There had been for a long time separatists from the Church of England. Arising out of the enforcement of the Act of Uniformity these 'new separatists'—who gradually after 1662 formed Congregational, Baptist, and so-called Presbyterian Churches—styled themselves 'Nonconformists', or 'Nonconforming Churchmen'; the Church people called them 'Dissenters'.

[37] Clark, II.32.

[38] Ibid. p. 31.

[39] This approximation was more to the Independent model than to the Baptist, because the special Baptist doctrine proved to be a difficulty. An outward sign of a new bond between them was a united sacramental service held at St Bartholomew's, Thames Street, when the Act of Uniformity became law (*C.S.P.D.* [1661-2], p. 396).

What the Act of Uniformity did was to accept the facts, and the date of its coming into operation merely marks the day when a new schism took effect and some old ones were recognized as permanent. Henceforth the idea of reuniting all the sects into the national Church becomes increasingly recognized as hopeless, and Dissent is accepted as a permanent factor in the national life.[40]

[40] Whiting, p. 26.

CHAPTER FIVE

FURTHER PENAL MEASURES

I

WITHIN four months of the enforcement of the Act of Uniformity, the King, in typically Stuart manner, returned to his previously tried expedient. On 26th December 1662 he published a Declaration in which he spoke again of 'liberty for tender consciences',[1] and affirmed that he intended to ask Parliament in the next session to grant him legally a dispensing power such as he believed was inherent in the Crown. He perceived that any concession to Roman Catholics must be joined to similar concessions to Nonconformists.

Naturally Parliament challenged this request; equally the bishops were against it,[2] and to some Nonconformists it seemed 'to their taste like water from a poisoned spring'.[3] Parliament proceeded to thrust the King's Declaration aside.[4] On 25th February 1663 Lord Roberts submitted proposals designed to legalize the King's wish—though precisely excepting any indulgence to Roman Catholics—as embodied in the Declaration, but this proposal was dropped.[5] The Commons firmly indicated that the King's wish could not be granted, particularly stating that the Declaration of Breda was 'not a promise in itself, but only a gracious declaration of Your Majesty's intention to do what in you lay, and what Parliament should advise Your Majesty to do'. In reply, the King asserted that he had been 'much misunderstood'. The Commons declared that the King's proposals were inconsistent with the law established and would be a ground 'for

[1] Gould, pp. 460-8.

[2] Soon after the passing of the Act of Uniformity the bishops had issued their 'Articles of Enquiry and Visitation' for their respective dioceses, as a natural process towards securing uniformity in the parishes, though stringency of application varied in different dioceses (Stoughton, III.284-6).

[3] *Rel. Bax.*, I.430. Baxter recognized the subtlety of the proposal. 'All were averse to having anything to do with the Indulgence or Toleration of the Papists.' Under Philip Nye, however, the Independents expressed themselves content.

[4] For an account of Parliamentary proceedings in the Commons, see Gould, pp. 468-77.

[5] *L.J.*, XI.482-4.

increasing sects and sectaries' in the land. For the King, therefore, this was a temporary defeat.[6]

In no mood to relax the laws, Parliament now proceeded to a counter-attack. The bishops might be trusted to uphold the law by dealing with any infringement of it by ministers of the Church, but, in addition, the drive for uniformity must be strengthened in regard to those who were nonconforming separatists. Though it was assumed that the laws of Elizabeth's reign regarding conventicles[7] had come again into operation with the Restoration, and though the Act of Uniformity made it plain that no exception was allowed, it was deemed necessary to provide 'further and more speedy remedies against the growing and dangerous practice of seditious sectaries and other disloyal persons'.[8] There was news of private meeting in various places and some rumours as to treasonable plots.[9] Such information provided an incentive for further action. The clergy presented a petition of protest against 'the strange race of men who laboured to throw off the yoke of government both civil and ecclesiastical', and asked for stricter laws against Anabaptists who were accused of proselytizing, together with increase of fines for non-attendance at church.[10]

In view of this, Parliament introduced in March 1664 and passed in May the 'First Conventicle Act',[11] which aimed at crushing completely all centres of sedition. It recognized the Act of Elizabeth as still in force and now provided that no person of sixteen or upwards should be present at any assembly of five or more, under pretence of religion, 'in other manner than is allowed by the Liturgy'. Every such offender, for the first offence should be imprisoned not exceeding six months, or be fined five pounds; for the second offence an imprisonment not exceeding six months, or pay ten pounds; for the third be transported to any foreign plantation (Virginia and New England excepted),[12] the goods of the offender to be sold to cover the costs of transportation. Payment of one hundred pounds would discharge from such imprisonment and transportation, and the fine be

[6] *C.J.*, viii.442-3. [7] 35 Eliz. I. [8] 16 Car. II, c. 4.

[9] Stoughton, III.302-4. In October there was the 'Farnley Plot' in Yorkshire (Ibid. pp. 307-8).

[10] Wilkins, *Concilia Magnae Brittanniae*, IV.580.

[11] Gould, pp. 477-88.

[12] If they had been sent to Puritan colonies there would have been some compensation for banishment.

appropriated for repair of churches and highways. Escape subjected the victim to death. Any who allowed a meeting in house or outhouse, in woods or grounds, incurred the same penalties as those attending. For refusing to take the oath Quakers were to suffer transportation. Two classes of persons were to receive special treatment. Noblemen in the first two categories were to pay double fines, and in the third to be tried by their peers, the penalties being undefined; persons with an annual income from land of £5, or estate value £50 were not to be sent to prison. Upon any jailer who allowed a prisoner to leave the jail there was a penalty of ten pounds. The Act was to continue in force for three years.

Clearly this Act was aimed at lay people, and it seems to have passed the two Houses with little discussion: it was regarded as 'the greatest discountenance the Parliament had yet given to all factions in religion'.[13] The Act was to take effect on 1st July and was executed with severity.[14] It might be supposed that such measures against Nonconformists were drastic enough,[15] but things went farther still. Sheldon, now Archbishop of Canterbury,[16] used his authority under the Act to demand episcopal information concerning unlawful meetings and the conduct of ejected ministers.

In 1665 London was stricken by the Plague and during the spring and summer the deaths steadily increased.[17] The richer people fled into the country: the poorer remained amidst overcrowded conditions. Many clergy remained in their parishes and cared for their flocks; some fled, however, and the ejected Nonconformists took possession of some of these vacant pulpits and began a pastoral ministry in the city parishes.[18] Whilst these

[13] Clarendon, *Hist.*, p. 1115.

[14] *C.S.P.D.* (1664, 30th September, 18th November; 1665, 3rd and 15th July). See also *Broadmead Records* (ed. 1865), pp. 53-5.

[15] In 1665 a Bill was introduced into the House of Lords, with the approval of the King, which would have allowed Protestants and Catholic Nonconformists to purchase liberty of worship by graduated monetary payments. It failed, but it increased bitterness against Roman Catholics (Clarendon, *Hist.*, p. 1130).

[16] Sheldon had been consecrated in June 1663 following the death of Juxon.

[17] In the first week of July 1665 deaths numbered 1,000; in one week in September, 10,000.

[18] *Rel. Bax.*, III.2: 'Divers nonconformists . . . resolved that no obedience to the laws of any mortal man whatsoever could justifie them for neglecting of men's souls and bodies in such extremities.' Cf. Richard Baxter: *An Apology for the Nonconformist Ministry* (1681), p. 101; *A Second True Defence of the Meer Nonconformist* (1681), 'Historical Preface'. Baxter produced a broadsheet, *Short Instructions for the Sick, especially who by contagion or otherwise are deprived of the presence of a faithful pastor* (1665), which was intended to be pasted on the walls of the house (*Rel. Bax.*, I.121).

Nonconformists were risking their lives in the City, Parliament, meeting in Oxford, was passing an Act for their further distress. Passed in October 1665, this Act was entitled: 'An Act for restraining Nonconformists from inhabiting Corporations.'[19] It is more commonly spoken of as 'The Five Mile Act'. It required all persons 'in holy orders or pretending to be', who had not taken the oath and made the declaration under the Act of Uniformity, to take the following oath:[20]

I do swear that it is not lawful, upon any pretence whatsoever, to take arms against the King; and that I do abhor that traitorous position of taking arms by his authority against his person, or against those that are commissioned by him, in pursuance of such commissions; and that I will not at any time endeavour any alteration of government, both in Church and State.

All ministers failing to take this oath were forbidden to come—except as travellers—within five miles of any corporate town or any place where they had been accustomed to officiate. For offence against the Act a penalty of £40; a further section provided that unless the minister frequented 'divine service established by the laws of the kingdom' he should also incur the same fine and not be allowed to exercise any teaching function. Two county magistrates could commit a persistent transgressor to prison for six months.

The Act of Uniformity had banished nonconforming ministers from parish pulpits; the Conventicle Act had broken up those congregations which had gathered since St Bartholomew's Day, 1662; now these persons were forced into exile and distress.

Following the Great Fire which devastated the City in the following year, 1666, Nonconformists fulfilled a ministry similar to that during the year of the Great Plague. The ejected ministers came forward to occupy the vacant places, resolved that amidst the ruins they would preach until they were imprisoned. In temporary structures, when parish churches were in ruins, they ministered to the congregations.[21]

[19] 17 Car. II, c. 2. Gould, pp. 488-90.

[20] This is sometime styled 'The Oxford Oath'.

[21] *Rel. Bax.*, III.162. This applied both to Presbyterians and Independents.

II

In 1667 Clarendon fell from power and his place was taken by a small group more favourable to the design of Charles towards toleration. Some change of attitude seemed likely. In October, Sir Robert Atkins prepared a Bill for comprehension as a healing measure by which Presbyterian ministers who subscribed the Articles concerning the Christian faith and practice should be allowed to preach; no one should be denied the Lord's Supper if not kneeling, and no minister should be compelled to wear the surplice or use the sign of the cross in baptism; the word 'consent' was to be left out of the form of subscription. But the Bill was never printed, and so this scheme of comprehension came to nothing.[22]

A second scheme went farther. In February 1668 the proposal was made by Sir Orlando Bridgman and supported by Sir Matthew Hale. On the episcopal side Dr Wilkins, Bishop of Chester entered into negotiations with the Presbyterians represented by Baxter, Dr Manton, and Dr Bates. The basis of the scheme[23] was the Declaration of Breda, and there were to be provisions for Nonconformists other than Presbyterians to build their own places of worship, and to worship in their own way provided they registered and made certain monetary payments. The bishops were against it and Parliament, suspicious that here was another instance of possible attempt to procure dispensing power for the King, was also against introducing anything permissive into the legal situation.[24] The Commons moved towards the idea that the King should issue a Proclamation for stricter exaction of existing laws. Any scheme of comprehension, therefore, could not possibly survive in this situation; indeed the direction of opinion in Parliament was towards still more severe measures, and the expiry of the Conventicle Act—which had been passed in 1664 for three years only—gave the opportunity. In April 1668 a Bill providing for its continuation was passed by the Commons, but there was delay. Parliament was prorogued successively until October 1669. In September the King had

[22] Bodleian Library (Barlow MS.). Printed in H. Thorndike, *Works*, V.302.

[23] *Rel. Bax.*, III.23-5.

[24] Ibid. III.36: 'How joyfully would . . . the Nonconformist ministers of England have yielded to these terms, if they could have got them. But, alas! all this labour was in vain.'

granted audience to a few Presbyterians under the leadership of Dr Manton, Baxter being absent through illness. In the meantime Archbishop Sheldon had discovered that nonconformity was expanding.[25] In the light of this he prevailed upon the King to issue a Proclamation commanding that the laws against the Nonconformists should be pressed. Many congregations were broken up. Baxter was put in Clerkenwell prison for preaching, but the mittimus being found irregular he was released; Tavener, another Nonconformist, was sent to Newgate for teaching a few children without taking the oath.[26]

Before the spring of 1670 Parliament passed the Second Conventicle Act,[27] which was not a precise reproduction of the First Act, and in its penal demands was less severe, but more likely to gain its end because magistrates under penalty of monetary fine were instructed not to neglect their duties; if any doubt existed as to conventicles the law should be most stringently applied; further, to informers it awarded one-third of the collected fines. The fine for attendance at a conventicle was for the first offence five shillings; for second and subsequent offences ten shillings; nothing was said in the Act about imprisonment. The fine was to be levied on the offender's goods, and if, through poverty, the worth of these proved insufficient, the fine could be levied at the discretion of the magistrate on some other person present, though the whole sum for one person was not to exceed ten pounds. The preacher was to be fined ten pounds for the first offence and twenty pounds for the second. The most sinister phrase declared that 'if any doubt should arise concerning the meaning of any part of this Act' it was to be determined in the sense that was the most contrary to conventicles, 'it being the intention of the House to suppress them in the most effectual manner possible'—and there could be no reversal of a decision.

Andrew Marvell described the Act as 'the quintessence of arbitrary malice'. Nevertheless, even in this situation there were gleams of light which suggested that there was some leaning

[25] For the return of episcopal visitations, see G. Lyon Turner, *Original Records of Early Nonconformity under Persecution and Indulgence*, p. 31: 'There are divers conventicles and other seditious meetings in Westminster . . . where great numbers of evil-affected persons frequently meet.' In London, Calamy's congregation numbered 100; Manton's 100; Dr Annesley's 800; Caryl's 500. In Canterbury there were said to be 500 Independents (Stoughton, III.385-7; *C.J.*, IX.108.)

[26] *Rel. Bax.*, III.130.

[27] 22 Car. II, c. 1; Gould, pp. 491-9.

towards the idea of toleration which some day would find expression more fully.

III

In the year following the passing of the Second Conventicle Act Dissenters in England suffered as perhaps never before. Yet there were those about the Court who were urging the King to exercise his prerogative in the direction of toleration. To some of the London ministers who came to him he declared that he was against persecution, and that in the near future he hoped to assert his authority.[28] By December 1671 it was expected that a proclamation was but a matter of time.[29] The Declaration of Indulgence was issued 15th March 1672.[30] Asserting his love for the Church of England, and observing that penal legislation against nonconformity had proved itself incapable of gaining its end, he suspended this legislation and proceeded positively. A number of places were to be permitted 'for the use of such as do not conform to the Church of England, to meet and assemble in order to their public worship and devotion', and both places and 'teachers' must be certified; Roman Catholics might meet only in their houses and without any claim to 'teacher' or 'place'; preaching in allowed places must disavow all sedition or anything 'to the derogation of the discipline or government of the Established Church'.

It was another bid by the King for disciplinary power. This Declaration seemed to raise a new hope for the Nonconformists, though some were hesitant because there was at least some benefit allowed to Roman Catholic dissent, and they felt that it was hopeless to expect any relief from Parliament; for twelve years they had endured persecution in varying degrees and had experienced alternating hope and despair. Some disliked the limitation of the terms of the Indulgence to specific places and ministers;[31] yet the Presbyterians sent a deputation to the King,

[28] *Rel. Bax.*, III.87.

[29] *C.S.P.D.* (1671), pp. 562-3.

[30] Robertson, pp. 42-4; Bate, *The Declaration of Indulgence*, pp. 76-8.

[31] M. H. Lee, *Diaries and Letters of Philip Henry* (1882), p. 250: 'The danger is, lest ye allowing of separate places help to overthrow our Parish-order which God hath own'd and beget divisions & animosityes amongst us which no honest heart but would rather should be heal'd. . . . Wee are put hereby to a Trilemma, either to turn flat Independents, or to strike in with ye conformists, or to sit down in former silence & Sufferings, till the Lord shall open a more effectual door.'

and the Independents through Philip Nye and John Owen, realizing that there was no possibility of their comprehension in the national Church, did likewise.[32]

Petitions for licences poured in rapidly from all parts of the realm, and the places for which they were requested were very varied in character. Some asked to use large public halls, vacant churches, and unendowed chapels; but for the most part private houses,[33] and other buildings such as barns and outhouses. Meeting-houses began to spring up.[34] The licences were of three varieties—for particular places, for preachers in particular places, and for 'teachers in general and at large', who might preach in any of the places so registered. Within ten months the total number reached 3,500,[35] though at first there was refusal, probably on the ground that to give too great provision for nonconformist services would find disfavour with the Anglicans.[36] The lists of preachers and places show much light upon the strength of nonconformity in various countries. They show that the south-eastern and the western corners of England were the great strongholds of dissent. Presbyterians were strongest in London, and in Lancashire and Yorkshire; Congregationalists and Independents in their old home—East Anglia, round London and in Bedford and Gloucestershire. Of the two hundred Baptist licences more than eighty were in Kent, Somerset, Lincoln, Wiltshire, and Norfolk.

The offer of licences made no difference to the Quakers; even under earlier persecution they had never ceased, and now they continued with even greater vigour, and their increase became the subject of complaint.[37] Though without licences magistrates refused to prosecute, because by the Declaration the King

[32] For the text of Dr Owen's address, see Bate, *The Declaration of Indulgence*, pp. 92-4. For other addresses to the King, see Bate, App. V.

[33] Ibid. pp. 94-5.

[34] In Lancashire seventeen are recorded (Stoughton, III.299). Several London merchants united to establish at Pinner's Hall a 'lecture' for select preachers.

[35] For complete list see Bate, *The Declaration of Indulgence*, App. VII. Appendix VI gives drafts of the three forms of licence issued. Denomination is stated in each case. Bunyan's Licence was for 'the Howse of Josias Roughed, for the use of such as . . . are of the Perswasion commonly called Congregationall' (E. Offor, *The Works of John Bunyan* [1854], III.24). In Vol. II of the *Diaries*, Oliver Heywood's Licence is shown in facsimile (p. 17).

[36] Bate, p. 96. A bishop writing to Sir Joseph Williamson: 'These licensed persons increase strangely. The orthodox poor clergy are out of heart. Shall nothing be done to support them against the Presbyterians who grow and multiply faster than the other.' (Stoughton, III.400; *C.S.P.D.* [1672], p. 589).

[37] *C.S.P.D.* (1672), p. 450.

himself was to deal with offenders. But on the basis of the Declaration itself George Whitehead was allowed to plead the cause of the Quakers before the King in Council. On 29th May 1672, thus ten days after the Indulgence, a letter was sent to all Sheriffs requiring details of all Quakers in their prisons; on 3rd September the King's pardon was granted to four hundred and seventy-one Quakers.[38] This pardon included also some who were not Quakers, for on the advice of the Quakers themselves, other dissenters asked that their names might be included in the general pardon, amongst them John Bunyan, whose first book had been directed against the Quakers, and who now, after nearly twelve years imprisonment, owed his liberty to their help.

It is worth noting that the first public nonconformist ordination service since 1662 took place in a house in Manchester, in October 1672.[39] This indicates the attempt to make a more formal provision for the future, and the closer contacts of Presbyterians and Independents is shown by the fact that ministers of both persuasions took part in the service.

Despite the Indulgence, however, it was still possible for Nonconformists to suffer hostility at the hands of both magistrates and ecclesiastical authorities.[40]

It was not to be expected that the King's Declaration would pass without challenge, and some Nonconformists were apprehensive for the future.[41] Further it was not likely that when Parliament met again they would acquiesce in such exercise of the royal prerogative. There was a constitutional issue as to the rightness of the King's decision, and despite the King's protest[42] it was increasingly felt in some quarters that the faith of the King was leaning in a Romeward direction. Though the Roman Catholic was given less liberty than others, to some that little seemed too much.

On 7th March 1673 the Declaration was cancelled: the King had come to his final defeat. Nevertheless there were numerous

[38] The Pardon is printed, with an index of names in George Whitehead, *Christian Progress* (1725), pp. 350-66. Cf. Braithwaite, *The Second Period of Quakerism*, pp. 82-5.

[39] Halley, *Lancashire: Its Puritanism and Nonconformity* (1872), p. 412; Drysdale, *History of Presbyterianism in England* (1889), p. 397.

[40] Bate gives examples (pp. 101-3).

[41] Henry, *Diaries*, p. 253. 'Some think by accepting of y^{em} wee give ye King a power above the lawes.... Others think twill end in a severe Tax upon licens'd meetings.... Others in a Massacre, it being now known where such people may bee mett with....'

[42] *C.J.*, IX.246. 'I shall take it very ill to receive contradiction in what I have done. And I will deal plainly with you: I am resolved to stick to my Declaration.'

impulses 'for the ease of tender consciences', and this was indicative of a more generous view of the principle of toleration for the dissenters. Some even ventured to suggest the claim of Roman Catholics to toleration. The Commons resolved to bring in a Bill 'for the ease of His Majesty's Protestant subjects that are dissenters in matters of religion from the Church of England'. Though this was defeated by the Lords, it reveals the advance of more liberal ideas, the first by the Commons since 1660. The same impulse was at work outside Parliament. This will to toleration accounts in part for the greater breadth in contemporary Parliamentary debate; it was important that the support of nonconformity should be enlisted against any Romanizing tendency. On 27th February the Commons initiated the groundwork for a Relief and Comprehension Bill, which, passed on 17th March, permitted Nonconformists who would take the Oath of Allegiance and Supremacy and subscribe to the doctrinal Articles of the Church of England to meet for worship without penalty, and Nonconformist preachers to have licences under the same terms. A possibility for comprehension, yet this Bill foundered on the differences between the two Houses, the Lords desiring a clause which would allow for the King's dispensing power.[43]

On 28th February the Commons resolved that all Roman Catholics should be deprived of civil and military office—the prelude to the Test Act with its demand that any person holding civil or military office must take the Oath of Allegiance and Supremacy, must receive the Lord's Supper by Anglican rite, and declare against transubstantiation.[44] This Act received royal assent on 29th March 1673. Immediately there was a declaration of Roman Catholicism from James, the King's brother and heir to the throne. Although intended against Roman Catholics, by this Act a new disability was placed upon all Nonconformists, and was a reversal to the old order.

IV

For some two years the King took no steps for the recall of the licences granted under his Indulgence. Thus Nonconformists

[43] *L.J.*, XII.576, 579, 580; *C.J.*, IX.271-81. For details of debates see Bate, Ch. 6; Stoughton, III.409-17.

[44] Gould, pp. 499-507.

were at liberty to pursue their ministry.[45] But the work of informers was widespread and the bishops were impatient and vexed.[46] The penal laws were still in existence,[47] though in some places the magistrates refused warrants and resisted the temptation to persecute. Meetings were disturbed, yet the Nonconformists still continued to hold them.[48] There was talk of comprehension, and actual attempts were made. The Earl of Orrery approached Baxter in 1673[49] 'professing that he met with many great men that were much for it', including Morley, Bishop of Winchester, 'who vehemently professed desire of it'. Baxter was asked to draw up 'the terms and means which would . . . satisfy the nonconformists so far as to unite us all against Popery'. Baxter hesitated but eventually agreed. All that came of it was a paper of 'strictures' written by Morley.[50] In 1675 Baxter was told that Dr Tillotson and Dr Stillingfleet wished for a meeting in order to discuss possible accommodation, 'encouraged to it by some Lords both Spiritual and Temporal'. At the request of his brethren Baxter drew up 'An Act for the Healing and Concord of His Majesty's Subjects in matters of Religion', but again the attempt came to nothing.[51]

It is worthy of note that on the Anglican side there was an occasional approval of some scheme of comprehension. In 1675 Herbert Croft, Bishop of Hereford, published as 'An Humble Moderator', *The Naked Truth*, in which he advocated liberty as to ceremonies and a revision of the Prayer Book; he contended for parity of the ministry and that confirmation and ordination might, where necessary, be administered by priests as well as bishops. The tract concluded with an admonition to Nonconformists exhorting them to return to the Church. It was published anonymously.[52]

The King was now slowly moving away from his policy by

[45] M. H. Lee, *Letters and Diaries of Philip Henry*, pp. 262-3. 'It is suppos'd wee are to take no notice of any th. but may plead our licences till revok'd. In ye present juncture . . . I have given up all to the will of God & am in this further confirm'd by w^{t} ye Parl. did, that tis now it seemes their Opinion, that tis fit wee should have liberty to preach, at least for a year & if ye Quarter-sessions grant it.'

[46] *Rel. Bax.*, III.104. Baxter had a conversation with Dr Gunning in May 1672.

[47] *Rel. Bax.*, III.103. Nathaniel Heywood, of Ormskirk, had thirty-four warrants out against him in the period January to April 1673. *Life*, p. 26-7.

[48] Bate, p. 138; Stoughton, III.430-1.

[49] *Rel. Bax.*, III.109-13.

[50] Ibid. III.156: 'The event showed that my incredulity was not without cause.'

[51] Ibid. III.158-60.

[52] *The Naked Truth, or the True State of the Primitive Church*, by An Humble Moderator (1675).

which he had frequently attempted accommodation. In October 1674 he summoned the bishops to procure their advice. In the following January they gave him their counsel, which concerned the most effectual way of suppressing Popery, and also that he should 'take effectual care for the suppression of conventicles, and whereas they support themselves by the pretence of licences and authority from him, he would publicly declare that the licences were since recalled, and that they had no authority and encouragement from him'.[53] They thought it well that any declaration he might make in this way should end with 'some little door of hope' for dissenting Protestants.[54] On 3rd February 1675 the King issued an Order in Council declaring that

> the laws which were made for the preservation both of Church and State should be put into execution with more care and diligence than of late they have been . . . and doth therefore order . . . that effectual care be taken for the suppression of conventicles . . . and no conventicle hath any authority, allowance or encouragement from His Majesty.[55]

Archbishop Sheldon also ordered his bishops to enquire once again as to the numbers of popish recusants and other dissenters in their dioceses.

So all royal authority for the liberty of Nonconformists was now taken away, and the King's order weighed heavily upon both ministers and congregations. But dissent had gained momentum. The episcopal returns revealed that many left the national Church upon the Indulgence, and now had become Nonconformist. Also many who had long cherished the hope of comprehension set it aside and created non-Anglican congregations, a considerable number of which still exist. Nonconformity had really laid its foundations too deeply to be eradicated.

V

From about 1675 the attack upon the Roman Catholics steadily increased. James, Duke of York, and heir to the throne, was known to be of that religious persuasion, and steadily the atmosphere of suspicion intensified. In Parliament there were repeated attempts to challenge this issue. In the autumn of 1678 the disclosure of the 'Popish Plot' set forward by Titus Oates

[53] *C.S.P.D.* (1673-5), pp. 550-1. [54] Bate, p. 140. [55] Ibid. p. 146.

brought matters to a state of panic. It was openly declared that the only ground of security was the exclusion of James, and measures to achieve this became the centre of debate for the next two or three years, and these were focused upon a Bill of Exclusion, first introduced in 1679. A Bill to shut out Roman Catholics from Parliament had been passed in 1678.

During the earlier part of this period the penal laws against Nonconformists were again set in motion, and a new chapter of persecution began. The emergence of the Roman Catholic scare shifted the attention, and a temporary abatement of hostility against Nonconformists set in. It became evident to some that to equate Nonconformity and Roman Catholicism as dangerous to the nation was absurd, not least because Nonconformity had proclaimed its anti-Roman attitude.[56]

Strangely enough the idea of comprehension emerged once again. In 1680, on 18th November, a Bill appeared in Parliament[57] which after some debate was dropped. Another Bill founded on the principle of toleration proposed to exempt Protestant dissenters 'from the penalties of certain laws' also collapsed at its final stage through not being brought for royal assent.[58] Being foiled in this measure the Commons passed a resolution to the effect that the policy of persecution of Nonconformists was against the best interests of the realm.[59] This indicates the presence of a more lenient attitude.[60]

[56] It is not without significance that the Corporation of Bristol, 'lamenting that at this time more heats and animosities should be fomented among us', drew up a paper asserting that 'differences among ourselves' afforded the Jesuits 'a fairer prospect of bringing us under the tyranny of Rome', and regretted that any Anglican 'who had any moderation towards dissenting Protestants should be considered ill-disposed to that Church or to the Throne'; and further declared that 'a hearty union among all Protestants is now more than ever necessary to preserve us from our open and avowed enemy' (*C.S.P.D.*, September I; Stoughton, IV.22.)

[57] Just prior to this a conference had taken place between John Howe on one side and Dr Tillotson and Dr Stillingfleet on the other and there may have been some connection. On 2nd May 1680 Stillingfleet had preached a sermon in London on 'The Mischiefs of Separation', and had spoken of the Dissenters as 'schismaticks who had rent the Church in twain'. Yet in his *Irenicum* (1659) he had shown no form of Church-government to be *jure divino*. On receiving a copy of the sermon, Howe declared he would defend the Dissenters' cause, and wrote a noble reply: '*A Letter out of the Country to a Person of Quality in the City* . . . (Rogers, *Life of Howe*, pp. 143-5, 183-7, 191-2.)

[58] Burnet (I.495) says that by the King's order the Clerk to the Crown withdrew the document from other Bills presented for royal assent, because it limited toleration to Nonconformists.

[59] *C.J.*, IX.704, 10th January 1681.

[60] It may be noted that the notorious Duke of Buckingham, from whatever motives, offered to be leader of the Nonconformists' cause at Court, and invited Howe to discuss this, but the letter declined saying 'that the Nonconformists being an avowedly

These incidents show how 'Nonconformist fortunes depended upon far other things than the merit of Nonconformity itself.[61]

But the respite was only a passing phase. In this period of embittered politics, a distinct change occurred in the circumstances of Nonconformists from 1681. There was rumour abroad that revolutionary activity was brewing against the throne, and it was believed that Nonconformists were involved.[62] Their anti-Catholic attitude combined against them. They had now been forsaken by Charles and as no Parliament met, any voices on behalf of leniency were silenced. The King was concerned only to secure the royal position for his successor. The reaction began to sweep violently over the Dissenters,[63] and in terms of disloyalty to the throne and a desire for a revival of republicanism.

Complaints arose as to the failure to exercise the penal statutes against the Nonconformists. Spies and informers were now at work again, and the Council ordered magistrates to proceed to the suppression of conventicles,[64] and warrants and arrests began once more.[65] Some of those arrested died in prison.[66] Persecution of Quakers in Bristol went to the length of putting children into the stocks and the thrashing of boys.[67] In the same year the Baptists suffered severely.[68] Not in one place alone, however, was this persecution to be met—in varying degrees it was widespread. Only an occasional voice was raised against it, yet unable to accomplish any mitigation.[69] The closing years of Charles II's reign were calamitous for the Nonconformists, not only on the ground of their religious convictions but because of the political

religious people, it highly concerned them . . . to choose someone who would not be ashamed of them, and of whom they might have no reason to be ashamed'. This ended the matter. (Rogers, *Life of Howe*, pp. 180-1.)

[61] Clark, II.102.

[62] For the plot against Charles, involving Stephen College, who was probably a Nonconformist at some time, and was made the scape-goat of the affair, see Stoughton, IV.43-7.

[63] For indication of the anti-Nonconformist attitude, see *C.S.P.D.* (1681), *passim*, but there seems no proof of any Nonconformist plot.

[64] E.g. Middlesex; Reading, Plymouth (Neal, IV.507).

[65] E.g. Stoughton, IV.50-6, 68-72, 79-60; Calamy *Continuation*, pp. 137-40.

[66] E.g. Thomas Delaune, a Baptist schoolmaster (Whitley, *H.B.B.*), and Francis Bampfield, a Baptist minister (Underwood, *H.E.B.*, p. 114).

[67] Besse, i. p. 66; Braithwaite, Ch. iv.

[68] *Broadmead Records*, *passim*.

[69] Clark quotes the case of Samuel Bold, Vicar of Shapwick, in Dorset, who in *A Plea for Moderation towards Dissenters* declared: 'You may turn the places of our worship into prisons, if you please, but you cannot by these means make the Dissenters a willing people in the day of your power. The members of the Church must be volunteers, not pressed men' (II.104).

course which they felt it was their duty to follow: they were regarded as standing for constitutional liberty against despotism; they had supported the opposition in the last three elections—'which alone', wrote John Howe in 1689,

and not our mere dissent from the Church of England in matters of religion, wherein Charles II was sufficiently known to be a prince of great indifferency, drew upon us, soon after the dissolution of the last of those parliaments, that dreadful storm of persecution, that destroyed not a small number of lives in gaol, and ruined multitudes of families.[70]

On 1st February 1685 Charles II died. Evelyn summarizes the tragedy of his reign:

Certainly never had King more glorious opportunities to have made himself, his people, and all Europe happy, and prevented innumerable mischiefs, had not his too easy nature resigned him to be managed by crafty men.[71]

His reign ended amidst scenes of depravity,[72] and there is ample evidence to make it clear that he died in a state of reconciliation with the Church of Rome.

VI

It was not to be expected that the coming of James II would bring any mitigation to the Nonconformists, but rather the opposite. The prospects were full of foreboding, for they had already suffered much. Furthermore some of the great leaders of Nonconformity had passed from the scene. In illustration of the temper of the Government we may recall that Baxter, now an old man, much older than his years, was brought before the infamous Judge Jeffreys, the charge being the publication of his *Paraphrase of the New Testament* (1685). He was fined five hundred pounds and since he could not raise the amount was committed to prison, where he remained eighteen months.[73] In this year it was the old story of harassings and exile, fines and imprisonments.

[70] *The Case of the Protestant Dissenters Reprinted and Argued* (1689). It may be noted that, by a strange inconsistency, Charles allowed asylum for Protestant refugees from France, who had suffered under Louis XIV. This probably invigorated the suffering Dissenters in England (Stoughton, IV.74-7).

[71] *Diary*.

[72] Ibid.

[73] An account of Baxter's. See J. M. Lloyd Thomas, *The Autobiography of Richard Baxter* (Everyman edn, 1925), Appendix I. The notes prepared by Baxter for his defence, but which he was not allowed to offer, are preserved in the Baxter MSS. (Treatises), I.ff. 2-13, VII.215-19.

There is no doubt about the intentions of the new King. He was determined to establish the Roman Catholic faith throughout the land, and to do it openly. He attended Mass, ordered all clergy to cease denunciation of the Catholic Faith, and the Test Act notwithstanding, he placed Roman Catholics in places of high office, and in university posts. The Court of High Commission was restored. It was not long before the attitude of Parliament became one of active criticism, and after Stuart fashion, James prorogued the Parliament which had challenged him. He determined to strengthen his position, and to use the Nonconformists as possible allies, though with no particular regard for their views.[74] He was only concerned to use them as pawns in the political game. On 4th April 1687 James therefore issued a Declaration of Indulgence,[75] whereby by direct royal command, the Test Act, which prevented Roman Catholics from entering Parliament, together with all penal laws against Nonconformists were set aside. It differed from Charles II's Indulgence of 1672 in that it was without conditions, no licence being required, and 'free and ample pardon to all nonconformists, recusants . . . for all crimes and things by them committed or done contrary to the penal laws, formerly made relating to religion and the profession and exercise thereof' was to be given.[76]

It was clear to the more discerning that sooner than the Roman Catholics should be persecuted, James was willing that the Nonconformists should go free at least for the time being; in order to secure his own party from oppression, he was ready to extend relief to others. Some Nonconformists regarded the Declaration as a door of hope for the future, and favourable addresses were presented by Independents, by Baptists and Presbyterians, in some cases in extravagant terms.[77] Oliver Heywood wrote:

[74] It was largely, however, owing to James's friendship with William Penn (as previously with his father, Admiral Penn) and with Robert Barclay, that the King viewed the Quaker petition for release in favourable light, and granted their release (Braithwaite, pp. 117-19, 125. See W. Penn's *A Persuasion to Moderation to Church Dissenters*, [1685].)

[75] For text see Gee and Hardy, pp. 641-4; Bettenson, pp. 407-10.

[76] Whilst the Roman Catholics were naturally pleased with the Declaration, members of the Church of England were alarmed at this exercise of arbitrary power, and saw the possibility of a destruction of Protestantism, though others approved. Addresses of thanks were given to the King, though with much caution. A great number of pamphlets, both Anglican and Puritan and Roman in origin came from the Press (Stoughton, IV.118-19; Whiting, pp. 542-4).

[77] Stoughton, IV.120-2.

It begets displeasure in men of the Church of England, contentment in some Dissenters, jealousies in others, who suspect a design therein, and however it may prove, it becomes us thankfully to accept this immunity, to improve opportunities for service and give God the glory of all.[78]

But some of the more discerning Nonconformists, such as Baxter, Howe and Bunyan, steadfastly resisted the temptation to offer any thanks to the King. It may be noted that under the impulse of the Declaration some Nonconformists, who had withheld their Nonconformity, withdrew from the Church and joined Nonconformist congregations.[79]

Disillusionment, however, was not long in coming. Further instalments of Roman Catholics in university appointments showed clearly the direction in which things were moving swiftly. In April 1688 the Declaration was proclaimed again,[80] and with the order that it should be read in the pulpits of the churches, the bishops to be responsible for seeing that it was done. Seven bishops refused and presented a petition to the King, who charged them with misdemeanour. Though the judges were divided in their verdict the jury released them, to the immense delight of the nation generally. This incident had deep-seated effects; the nation now clearly realized the situation.

The days of James II's rule were swiftly coming to an end. On 30th June 1688 the day of the acquittal of the seven bishops, seven members—'the immortal seven'—of the Whig party took the step, perilous because it implied treason, of inviting William of Orange to come to England.

It is not necessary to compass the details of the following months. William arrived in England on 5th November 1688 and James left

[78] *Diaries.* Under the liberty provided he built his chapel at Northowram in 1688. It was in that year, however, that he wrote: 'Though Dissenters had liberty, yet we know it was not out of love for us, but for another end, for we heard the King say he was forced to grant liberty for the present to those whose soul he abhorred.'

[79] Evelyn, *Diary*, 10th April 1687. In Deptford 'there was a wonderful concourse of people at the Dissenters' meeting-houses in this parish, and the Parish Church left exceeding thin. What this will end in, God Almighty only knows, but it looks like confusion, which I pray God avert.'

[80] This second pronouncement of the Declaration brought few congratulatory addresses, and the Nonconformists in particular declined. 'We are absolutely . . . for liberty by a law, but we are utterly against letting Papists into the government, and of this the King had often had, or should have a clear understanding and be fully possessed with it, that he may not have any colour afterwards to say we deceived'—Entry Book (1688, 9th June), Morice MSS. (quoted Stoughton, IV.149).

these shores in flight some six weeks later. On 21st December an address was presented to William by a hundred clergy, together with certain Nonconformist ministers, the company led by Compton, Bishop of London, who in his speech made reference to the four Nonconformist brethren, 'at which words the Prince took particular notice' of them. A few days later other Nonconformists presented a further address to the King.

We should now observe that out of the growing animosity to the policy of James II, a new relationship between the Church and the Nonconformists had emerged. Amongst the visitors to the Seven Bishops in the Tower were some ten Nonconformist ministers. 'When Church and Parliament and country came to take stock of the situation, they found themselves owing to Nonconformity a debt which must be honoured and for which toleration was the *minimum* that could be offered in discharge'.[81]

It was natural that under the new reign the Nonconformists should look for an early settlement of their position, but for the time being they were to suffer disappointment. On 25th February 1689 a Bill was introduced for a repeal of the Corporation Act, but through party complications it was set aside.[82] Similarly, arising from the King's Speech of 16th March, in which, whilst standing firm against the Roman Catholics, he expressed his wish 'to leave room for the addresses of all Protestants that are willing and able to serve', he showed his desire for some alteration in the Test Act. But though there were some of the Upper House who were willing to agree, and would have abolished the sacramental test, the majority were against the proposal.[83]

Though the Test Act and the Corporation Act were to remain unrepealed for a century and a half longer, Parliament was moving definitely in the direction of affording substantial relief to Nonconformists.

Once again the idea of comprehension emerged—for the last time. On 11th March 1689 a Bill described as 'An Act for uniting their Majesties Protestant Subjects' was introduced to the Upper House by the Earl of Nottingham. It was a bold measure.

[81] Clark, II.114.

[82] *C.J.*, X.74.

[83] Despite this defeat it was suggested that a clause should be inserted the purpose of which was to render the celebration of the sacrament in a Nonconformist meeting-house as legally equivalent to the celebration in a parish church (Stoughton, V.76).

Candidates for ordination were now to make the following declaration:

I, *A.B.*, do submit to the present constitution of the Church of England. I acknowledge that the doctrine of it contains all things necessary to salvation, and I will conform myself to the worship and government thereof as established by law, and I solemnly promise in the exercise of my ministry to preach and practice according thereunto.

An ordained Presbyterian minister was not to receive reordination, but submit to imposition of hands of a bishop. The declaration required by the Act of Uniformity of 1662 was no longer necessary. Except in Royal chapels, and in Cathedrals and Collegiate churches, the surplice also was now unnecessary; no communicant was compelled to kneel at the sacrament; no minister was compelled to use the sign of the cross in baptism; and god-parents could be dispensed with. The Bill urged the appointment of a commission to revise the Liturgy and canons, and to consider alteration in ecclesiastical jurisdiction, particularly regarding the removal of scandalous ministers. The Bill provided that the commission should consist of thirty bishops and priests, but the Whigs in the Lords required that some members should be laymen, an amendment which on voting had equal numbers for and against.[84] It was suggested by the Commons that for discussion of these matters Convocation should be recalled. The commission for revision of the Prayer Book met frequently but their labours came to nothing. Convocation met in November, but showed itself opposed to any concessions to Nonconformists, and so the Comprehension Bill was dropped. Calamy declared that if it had gone through

two-thirds of the nonconformists would have conformed, which being done, and at the same time a liberty continued to such as could not be comprehended, would have been greater service to religion than can easily be imagined.[85]

Mainly because it implied 'equality' between Churchmen and Nonconformists comprehension had failed entirely. On 28th February 1689 a Bill was introduced by the Earl of Nottingham into the Lords. It passed both Houses without difficulty, and

[84] A copy of the Bill was printed for the first time in *Report of Her Majesty's Commissioners* . . . (Parliamentary Papers [1865], Appendix 47-8); Dale, pp. 470-1.
[85] Calamy, *Abridgement*, I.448.

received royal assent on 24th May 1689. It bore the title: 'An Act for exempting their Majesties' Protestant Subjects dissenting from the Church of England from the Penalties of Certain Laws.'[86] It is usually styled The Toleration Act, 1689. To an examination of this we shall return later on.

[86] Wm. & M., c. 18. Gould, pp. 507-16; Gee & Hardy, pp. 654-64.

CHAPTER SIX

'PERSECUTED BUT NOT FORSAKEN'

IN recounting in previous chapters the story of Nonconformists during the thirty years from the Restoration of Charles II in 1660 to the Act of Toleration in 1689, we had a partial glimpse at the sufferings of those who refused to conform. It is now a fitting place to give more detailed consideration to this aspect of the story.

It is very necessary to hold the situation in perspective, for exaggeration is easy. We have already observed that in some few instances the ejected ministers possessed private means, and in others by the generosity of friends they were supported. There were also occasional instances of attempts at accommodation upon the part of those incumbents who were returned to their benefices,[1] though Kennett is too sweeping when he states: 'There was a great regard paid to the ejected and silenced ministers by the patrons of the Churches which their nonconformity left vacant.'[2] Some few found a place in professional life, and there were cases where, in more remote places, ministers continued to preach for years without disturbance.

The fact remains, however, that there were cases of extreme distress, and as the penal acts against Nonconformists became enforced, these increased greatly, and touched large numbers who had not been ejected from parish churches, but, nevertheless were open to the penalties imposed upon all who refused to conform.

To those who suffered, the measures taken against them were naturally regarded as cruel and vindictive; to the authorities who held the theory that uniformity was the basic essential alike for the welfare of Church and State, such Nonconformity amounted to civil disobedience, and therefore merited punishment. 'It was idle to expect the Cavalier Parliament to innovate on what had been the theory and practice of every previous Government, the Commonwealth included; and that while it was intelligible that

[1] E.g. Samuel Fisher, ejected from Thornton-on-the Moor (Halley, pp. 368-9).
[2] *Register*, p. 938.

the Nonconformists should obey a higher authority, and break the law, it was equally intelligible that they should be punished for doing so.'[3] The fact still remained, however, that in multitudes of cases the punishment which was meted out was entirely unwarranted by the laws of common humanity.

The pattern of persecution reveals great variety and shows that the penal laws were not consistently applied or uniform in severity. As in the early Church centuries it was sporadic but often intense.

The motives behind it were also varied. Apart from the basic theory of the unity of Church and State, it was sometimes an assertion of personal rights upon the part of an incumbent, as for example when Quakers refused to pay the appointed tithes. Sometimes there lay behind it motives that were social and political rather than religious. 'Men who for years had suffered severely suddenly found themselves in a position to repay their persecutors in kind . . . for twenty years the vials of bitterness had been filling; now they poured out without restraint on any who could be held responsible for the indignities suffered in the past.'[4] Certainly the motive of 'malignity' and of revenge was sometimes at work in the persecution of dissenters. In the later period, when the party spirit ran high, and Nonconformists used their influence in the Whig interest in elections, opponents turned to the penal laws in revenge.[5] Sometimes it was the rough vengeance of the crowd beginning in sport, but ending in tragedy, to which the Dissenters were exposed. The motive of gain was sometimes present, for informers were prepared to go to any lengths for their own profit.[6]

On occasion the persecutors, reluctant to proceed against Dissenters, acted under external pressure from neighbouring justices or ecclesiastical authorities or persistent informers who pressed for action.[7]

At the foundation of much persecution lay a deep-rooted fear. The events of the years prior to the Restoration were still remembered, and in every meeting of dissenters the authorities were

[3] *C.R.*, Intro., p. lix.

[4] Cragg, p. 33; cf. Baxter, *Cain and Abel Malignity* (1689); P. Henry, *Diaries*, p. 309.

[5] J. Whiting, *Persecution Exposed* (1715). The Conventicle Act enforced against Quakers 'in a way of revenge, since our Friends have appeared in the late election for such members of Parliament as they believed would most approve themselves just men for the general good of their country' (p. 33).

[6] Besse, *Sufferings*, *passim*; O. Heywood, *Diaries*, III.211.

[7] Cragg, pp. 34-5; *Broadmead Records*, pp. 90-1, 130; *Rel. Bax.*, III. § 185, 328.

prone to see the preparation of some incipient plot, and 'therefore crave the extirpation of them all'.[8] The more extreme groups of Dissenters certainly were antagonistic but the fear of the authorities was altogether out of proportion to the extent of any danger in this respect.[9]

Whilst an individual Dissenter might be taken as he walked abroad, or was within his own home, it was in the place of meeting that he was most likely to encounter persecution along with his fellow-worshippers, and this was not seldom accompanied by violence, on the part of the assailants.[10] In some instances meeting-houses were destroyed.[11] The privacy of homes was invaded,[12] and, on occasion, by force.[13]

Anxious that their ministers should not fall prey to the authorities, some congregations prepared secret hiding-places into which escape might be quickly effected, but when dispersed from their meeting-houses and they gathered in woods and fields escape proved more difficult, especially under sudden surprise from ambushed troops. In some instances worshippers lost their lives.[14] Even the occasion of a funeral was no protection, for it was regarded as a gathering of Dissenters.[15]

Once under arrest a Dissenter might be placed in prison without appearing before a magistrate; if no justice of the peace was available he might be put under house arrest or lodged in a tavern; sometimes a whole congregation was locked in their meeting-house for hours. Magistrates varied considerably in their attitude towards the Dissenters, some dealing more kindly

[8] Baxter, *The English Nonconformity* (1690), p. 26; Cragg (p. 35) quotes Bridgman's definition of a conventicle as 'a meeting together to plot against the King and State'; also (p. 265) Bishop Ward's comment on ejected ministers at Exeter as those 'who lie gnawing at the root of government and religion'.

[9] Cragg, p. 35; Ellwood, *Life*, p. 78. 'He the justice urged upon me that an insurrection had been lately made by armed men, who pretended to be more religious than others; that that insurrection had been plotted and contrived in their meeting-house where they assembled under colour of worshipping God; that in their meeting-house they hid their arms, and armed themselves, and out of their meeting-house issued forth in arms, and killed many: so that the government could not be safe unless such meetings were suppressed.'

[10] *Broadmead Records*, pp. 105-6, 135, 138; Ellwood, *Life*, pp. 92-3; [E. Pearse] *The Conformist's Plea for the Nonconformists*, pp. 52-3.

[11] In Bristol five meeting-houses were wrecked. *Broadmead Records*, *passim*.

[12] Calamy, *Continuation*, I.245-6. A group of friends accidentally increased their number by a child who entered in order to escape from a dog; the house was immediately invaded by informers and constables. The minister was fined £20 for preaching and £20 on his house as an unlawful conventicle; each person was fined five shillings and the house was ransacked.

[13] *Broadmead Records*, p. 273.

[14] Ibid. pp. 241, 247, 249, 257-8.

[15] Ellwood, *Life*, p. 140; Besse, *Sufferings*, *passim*.

with the culprit, and on occasion might rebuke the over-zealous informer, or ignore the clerical pressure upon him to act more severely. On the other hand, some were impatient, and in case of Quakers were entirely without understanding of the position regarding the 'plain speech' and the refusal to remove the hat was regarded as contempt of court and as a studied insult; on occasion the temper of the magistrate became venomous and violent. In some instances prisoners had the fortune to be taken under mittimus that was defective, and so the charges were dismissed—a situation which shows the incompetence of the legal arrangements. Frequently a Dissenter was sent to prison to await trial by a higher court, and if he failed to secure a trial he was returned to prison and might be retained indefinitely. At the trial itself the prisoner might be confronted with scorn and vindictiveness,[16] though on some occasions greater consideration might be shown.[17] It sometimes occurred that dialogue between the justices and the accused would open up, and the discourse soon turned to the argument from Scripture, often to the discomfort of the justices themselves. The most notorious example of violence is that of Baxter's trial before Judge Jeffreys, which was a complete travesty of justice.[18]

Sentences might involve indefinite imprisonment; even banishment or death, though the more severe sentences probably difficult to enforce were seldom imposed, and were probably used for intimidation. The method of fines was a great source of distress, and many were brought to destitution. It is impossible to make any exact calculation but Quaker records form some indication of the enormous amount.[19] Failure to pay the fines

[16] Cragg, p. 47: 'A justice willing to relieve the tedium by a practical joke might clap a Quaker's hat on his head, and when the prisoner's conscience forbade its removal, punish him for contempt of court. A man more openly malicious would fill the hat with water before replacing it on the owner's head while a man with still more venom and even less regard for the proprieties of the court-room would heap it full of filth. As he scoffed at the predicament of the prisoner, a justice might administer the oath to a Quaker who had been seized by virtue of an obsolete warrant.'

[17] E.g. the case of Thomas Horrocks, of Malden, Essex. Calamy, *Continuation*, pp. 469-50 *et passim*.

[18] See *supra*, p. 82. In a letter to Matthew Sylvester, Dr Tillotson describes the occasion: "Nothing more honourable than when the Rev. Baxter stood at bay, berogued, abused, despised; never more great than then. . . . This is the noblest part of his life, and not that he might have been a bishop' (Baxter MSS [Letters], IIf. 76-7; Powicke, *Life*, II.294).

[19] Cragg states that in Suffolk, in May 1663, fines against Quakers for absence from worship reached £33,000; in Bristol they amounted to £16,440 (p. 270). It is also reported that fines from Bristol Nonconformists were expected by the authorities to reach £100,000.

imposed resulted in distraint of goods, often at the pressure of the informer, who profited thereby; often the value of the goods was far in excess of the fine imposed.[20] It was often discovered, however, that it was easier to take the goods than to sell them, for people refused to buy. It is only fair to say, however, that many justices recoiled from this procedure, only the more unscrupulous pressing for such action. Finally, folk often reimbursed the sufferers; sometimes on hearing of a warrant for distraint, coming to fetch the best goods into their own houses for safety.

The role of the informer was the most sinister of all forces at work against the Dissenters—'the shame and scourge of his country'.[21] Every evil device seems to have been employed by these men, though on occasion magistrates would warn them of their unscrupulousness beyond what the law allowed.[22] Thomas Ellwood challenged two local informers by legal proceedings so that he thereby 'ended the informing trade in these parts in the county of Bucks . . . discouraging all others from attempting the like enterprise there ever after'.[23]

II

All groups of dissenters had some share in the afflictions of these years. Space will not allow of more than a few instances of these sufferings, but every denominational history has its own record of persecution.[24] But it was the Quakers who suffered more widely and more severely than the rest.[25] Their refusal to compromise to take an oath, their insistence upon retaining the hat in court, its removal being the sign of honour to God alone, their 'plain speech', and above all to hide themselves from attack together with their readiness to challenge the authorities made them prone

[20] Cragg, p. 58; cf. Baxter, *The English Nonconformity*, Preface, dated 28th September 1683. 'Nine ministers are now in Newgate, and many more in other places, and almost all of them mulct and fined in far more than ever they were worth. Their goods and their books taken by distress. . . . I myself was distressed of all my goods and books on five convictions before ever I heard of any accusation or saw a proof. So is it with many others and more . . . and all this for our nonconformity.'

[21] [E. Pearse], *The Conformist's Third Plea* . . . pp. 11-12; *Fourth Plea*, pp. 15-16; Samuel Bold (*A Sermon against Persecution*), an Anglican rector, described them as 'the pests of society'.

[22] Cragg, pp. 61-2.

[23] Ellwood, *Life*, pp. 178-9.

[24] Drysdale, *History of Presbyterians in England*, pp. 381-416; Whitley, *A History of British Baptists*, pp. 103-60; Underwood, *A History of the English Baptists*, pp. 89-116; Dale, *A History of English Congregationalism*, pp. 423-58.

[25] Braithwaite, *The Second Period of Quakerism*, [ed. 1961], pp. 21-114.

to greater sufferings. It is true, however, that whilst there was a determination to remain loyal to the truth, there were some who avoided sufferings that otherwise might have befallen them by taking a careful calculation of risks and unwillingness to court disaster unnecessarily. The Quakers kept careful records of their sufferings, and these not only indicate the extent of persecution amongst themselves, but also give some conception of the full extent of the Nonconformist affliction, seeing that all other sufferings must be added to these.

In Besse's *A Collection of the Sufferings of the People called Quakers* (1753) the indexes show 12,406 names for England and Wales, but it is quite likely that the total number of Quakers suffering during the Restoration period considerably exceeded 15,000. Probably some 450 died under their afflictions.[26] The following quotation from Robert Barclay's *Apology* (1775) is eloquent:

Of this excellent patience and sufferings, the witnesses of God, in scorn called Quakers, have given a manifest proof: for . . . they went up and down, as they were moved of the Lord, preaching and propagating the Truth in market-places, highways, streets and public temples, though daily beaten, whipped, bruised, haled and imprisoned therefore. And when there was anywhere a church or assembly gathered they taught them to keep their meetings openly, and not to shut the door, nor do it by stealth, that all might know it, and those that would might enter. And as hereby all first occasion of fear of plotting against the government was fully removed, so this their courage and faithfulness . . . did so weary out the malice of their adversaries that oftentimes they were forced to leave their work undone. For when they came to break up a meeting, they were obliged to take every individual by force, they not being free to give up their liberty by dissolving at their command; and when they were haled out, unless they were kept forth by violence, they presently returned peaceably to their place. Yea, when sometimes the magistrates have pulled down their meeting-houses they have met the next day openly upon the rubbish and so by innocency kept their possession and ground, being properly their own, and their right to meet and worship God being not forbidden to any. So that, when armed men have come to dissolve them, it was impossible for them to do it, unless they had killed everyone; for they stood so close together that no force could move anyone to stir, until violently

[26] Ibid. pp. 115-16. Statements compiled at various times show the following: Fifth Monarchy imprisonments (1661), 4,257; in prison after the Quaker Act (October 1662), about 1,300; in prison at the time of the Pardon (1672), about 500; in prison August 1685, about 1,000; in prison, March 1685, 1,460.

pulled thence; so that when the malice of their opposers stirred them to take shovels, and throw the rubbish upon them, there they stood unmoved, being willing, if the Lord should so permit to have been there buried alive, witnessing for him. As this patient but yet courageous way of suffering made the persecutors' work very heavy and wearisome unto them, so the courage and patience of the sufferers, using no resistance, nor bringing any weapons to defend themselves, nor seeking any ways revenge upon such occasions, did secretly smite the hearts of the persecutors, and made their chariot wheels go heavily. Thus after much and many kinds of sufferings patiently borne . . . a kind of negative liberty has been obtained: so that at present for the most part we meet together without disturbance from the magistrate.[27]

The experiences, then, of those who suffered in prison, form a tragic record. Of course there were exceptions. Baxter's first imprisonment was not marked by serious distress;[28] Oliver Heywood was reasonably treated in York Castle;[29] Philip Henry, in Chester Castle, declared that he and his companions were 'better accommodated . . . than we could have expected', though he also states that a price had to be paid for it.[30] But generally speaking conditions were very different indeed. Overcrowding was common, often unavoidably so owing to the outbreaks of sudden persecution involving large numbers. Ellwood gives a vivid picture of conditions:

In the night we all lodged in one room, which was large and round, having in the middle of it great pillars of oaken timber. . . . To this pillar we fastened our hammocks at the one end, and to the opposite wall on the other end, quite round the room . . . three stories high, one over the others: so that they who lay in the upper and middle row of hammocks were obliged to go to bed first, because they were to climb up to the height by getting into the lower. And under the lower rank of hammocks by the wall sides, were laid beds upon the floor, in which the sick and such weak persons as could not get into the hammocks lay. And indeed though the room was large and pretty airy, yet the breath and steam that came from so many bodies, of different ages, conditions and constitutions packed up so close together, was enough to cause sickness amongst us. . . . For there were many sick and some very weak, though we were not long there, yet in that time one of our fellow-prisoners, who lay in one of the pallet beds, died.[31]

[27] Barclay, *An Apology for the True Christian Divinity* (10th edn), pp. 481-2.
[28] Baxter, *A Breviate of the Life of Margaret . . . wife of Richard Baxter* (1681), p. 113; *Rel. Bax.*, III.50-1.
[29] O. Heywood, *Diaries*, IV.114. [30] P. Henry, *Letters*, p. 340. [31] *Life*, p. 107.

Summer weather made conditions more trying and in the winter there could be even greater misery, for often there was neither fuel nor candles. George Fox tells of his experiences in Lancaster Castle in 1664, where the smoke was so intense

it stood as dew upon the walls and sometimes it was so thick I could hardly see the candle when it burned . . . so that I was almost smothered. . . . Besides it rained upon my bed, and many times when I went to stop out the rain in the cold winter season my shirt was as wet as muck with the rain. . . . [32]

Similarly when in Scarborough Castle in 1665, Fox was on the side of the sea and open to the storms.

The wind drove in the rain so forcibly, so that the water came over my bed, and ran about the room, that I was fain to skim it up with a platter. And when my clothes were wet I had no fire to dry them; so my body was numbed with cold, and my fingers swelled that one was grown as big as two.[33]

Sometimes worse conditions prevailed. At Leominster it was usual for the prisoners to be

shut up . . . in a little close nasty hole where they were forced to lie on straw, and sometimes so crowded, that they could not lie down together; besides they were forced to ease their bodies in the same place, which for want of cleaning was become so loathsome that those who came to speak with them through the hole of the door could hardly bear the stench for a few minutes. Here there were sometimes kept twelve or fifteen of them together several days and nights.[34]

At Launceston, in 1656, Fox and his fellow-prisoners were confined in the Doomsdale—

a nasty stinking place, where they used to put murderers after they were condemned; . . . the excrement of the prisoners had not been carried out. So that it was all like mire, and in some places to the top of the shoes in water and urine. . . . At night some friendly people of the town brought us a candle and a little straw; and we went to burn a little of our straw to take away the stink. The thieves lay over our heads and the head gaoler in a room by them over our heads also. It seems the smoke went up under the room where the gaoler lay: which put him into such a rage that he took the pots of excrement from the thieves and poured them through a hole upon our heads . . . till we

[32] *Journal* (3rd edn), p. 374. [33] Ibid. p. 379. [34] Besse, Abstract (1738) II.211.

were so bespattered that we could not touch ourselves nor one another. . . . Moreover he railed at us most hideously, calling us hatchet-faced dogs.[35]

It was a natural consequence of such conditions that health of the prisoners should suffer serious deterioration. Fevers and epidemics of smallpox brought their toll of life. Calamy tells of Richard Flavel, who was imprisoned in London in 1665, and who died of the plague in Newgate; of thirty-eight committed with him, nine died in prison.[36]

But it was in mental and spiritual sufferings that the deepest distress occurred. To stand firm to the dictates of conscience could bring a Dissenter into an acute dilemma. An example of this is seen in a familiar passage from John Bunyan's *Grace Abounding* (1666).

I found myself a man and compassed with infinities. The parting with my wife and poor children hath often been to me in this place as the pulling the flesh from my bones; and that not only because I am somewhat too fond of these great mercies, but also because I should have often brought to my mind the many hardships, insults and wants that my poor family was like to meet with, should I be taken from them, especially my poor blind child, who lay nearer to my heart than all I had besides. . . . O I saw in this condition I was as a man who was pulling down his house upon the head of his wife and children: yet thought I, I must do it, I must do it.[37]

Such a *crie du cœur* must have been frequently uttered in many a soul.

Further, again and again there was the inner conflict of spirit arising from a sense of injustice. Resentment was a natural reaction against such vindictiveness. 'Take heed of giving way to secret wishes of hurt to your adversaries, or of reproachful words against them; take heed of hurting yourselves by passion or sin, because others hurt you by slanders or persecutions.'[38] So wrote Richard Baxter in counsel to those who were to suffer for conscience' sake. In the conquest of self lay the secret of victory in the cause of Truth.

Throughout all the innumerable records of the sufferings of these Nonconformists during this period there is displayed an unmistakable conviction of the purpose of God and of the divine

[35] Fox, *Journal*, (3rd edn), pp. 172-3. [36] Calamy, *Account*, p. 328.
[37] Op. cit. pp. 327-9. [38] Baxter, *A Christian Directory* (1673), I.48.

grace as sufficient for any calamity. This was the ground of Bunyan's assertion, which could be paralleled in many an instance. 'If I were out of prison today I would preach the Gospel again tomorrow by the help of God.'[39] Such a sense of the Divine Presence enabled Thomas Browning, of Desborough, Northamptonshire, ejected in 1661 and imprisoned in Northampton gaol, to write in a letter to his congregation written from his prison:

The cup of affliction for the Gospel is sweeter the deeper; a stronger cordial the nearer the bottom: I mean death itself. . . . I tell you, if you knew what Christ's prisoners, some of them, enjoyed in their jails you would not fear their condition but long for it. . . . If men have nothing against you but in matters of your God, rejoice and triumph in all your persecutions. . . . There is no shadow like the shadow of God's wings: therefore keep close to God.[40]

[39] Bunyan, *A Relation of the Imprisonment of Mr John Bunyan.* [40] Palmer, II.219-21.

CHAPTER SEVEN

TOLERATION AND DECLINE, 1689-1750

I

As we have already observed the spirit of toleration towards Dissenters had been at work long before the Toleration Act of 1689. Comprehension as a principle had been found unworkable. The Act of Uniformity had totally failed to produce uniformity and extinguish dissent. The Nonconformists not only remained unreconcilable and unsubdued, but at the end of twenty-five years were more numerous than ever. Such a situation could not remain unobserved. A growing respect for Dissenters; a recognition of the fact that they represented an important group of citizens of value in the emerging political party-system; the economic necessity of preserving useful members of the community in the interests of national prosperity; the recognition that truth cannot be the exclusive possession of one side; the greater understanding of the claims of reason[1]—all these factors acted as solvent forces upon the idea that persecution of men for religion was a justifiable procedure.[2]

Until the barriers of Anglican intransigeance could be broken through there was no prospect of any degree of toleration for Nonconformity. On this issue the polemical warfare was constant in innumerable treatises and pamphlets, and the Nonconformists proved themselves equal to arguing their own position. Their own most immediate defence was that they were neither seditious nor rebellious.[3] Uniformity was unattainable and national safety did not require it, as was evidenced by the religious situation in the

[1] Cf. F. Kenworthy, 'The Toleration Act of 1689', in *T.U.H.S.* (October 1939): 'The influence of Socinianism upon the growth of tolerance though indirect is greater than is usually acknowledged. Though few of those among the liberal Anglicans, or the nonconformists who read Socinian works, adopted the theology of Socinus, they caught his habit of applying reason to religion, and he who exercises reason is led also to exercise tolerance' (p. 21). Cf. H. J. McLachlan, *Socinianism in Seventeenth-century England.*

[2] For full discussion of these factors see Cragg, *From Puritanism to the Age of Reason* (1950), pp. 219-24.

[3] E.g. J. Owen, *A Peace Offering in an Apology and Humble Plea for Indulgence and Liberty of Conscience* (1668); *Indulgence and Toleration Considered* (1687); J. Howe, *Case of Protestant Dissenters Represented and Argued* (1689).

United Provinces.[4] Not only had the Quakers made defence of liberty of conscience by their numerous writings,[5] but 'by exhausting the malice of the justices virtually won for the Nonconformists the right to maintain their own forms of worship'.[6]

It should also be observed that within Anglicanism there were those who were convinced of the futility of the policy of repression. The early Latitudinarians, Falkland, Hales, and Chillingworth, in the first half of the seventeenth century, had expressed a liberal spirit; the Cambridge Platonists (whose works were mainly published after 1660) had stood for toleration by lifting the whole matter of religion into the higher sphere beyond controversy and bitterness, and asserted the vital relation between religion and moral values. The policy of Anglicanism during the years following 1662 took little or no account of these groups; but the spirit of these men became reflected in the more liberal-minded Anglicans[7] who brought their own contribution towards the movement, which, on its religious side, culminated in the Act of Toleration.

But these were not the only elements out of which the Act of Toleration emerged in 1689. The motive was in fact, largely, if not mainly political.

> When toleration came, it came in a form determined by political considerations and not by enthusiasm for religious liberty arising from noble motives; . . . circumstances made it clear that political expediency was really on the side of at any rate political toleration.[8]

For this reason the Act 'fell so far short of the best aspirations of the supporters of toleration and why some of its most ardent advocates received from it so little advantage'. The immediate cause was a fear of the re-establishment of Roman Catholicism in England. The policy of James II failed, but his acts of tyranny brought unanticipated results. The following estimate of the position is sound:

[4] Sir W. Temple, *Observations of the United Provinces* (1672); cf. Cragg, *From Puritanism to the Age of Reason*, pp. 212-13.

[5] E.g. I. Pennington, *Concerning Persecution* (1661); W. Penn, *The Great Case of Liberty of Conscience . . . defended* (1671), and *Three Letters*.

[6] Cragg, *From Puritanism to the Age of Reason*, p. 221.

[7] E.g. H. Croft, *The Naked Truth* (1675); [E. Pearse,] *The Conformist's Plea for the Nonconformists* (1681), followed by a *Second*, *Third* (1682), and *Fourth Plea* (1683); G. Burnet, *Exhortation to Peace and Unity* (1681).

[8] A. A. Seaton, *The Theory of Toleration under the Later Stuarts* (1911), p. 234.

James failed—but his tyrannical acts had unexpected results. They brought together Dissenters and moderate Churchmen on the fundamental issues of Protestantism and Constitutionalism. It is to be noted that while the Dissenters had naturally taken advantage of the Declarations of Indulgence of 1672 and 1687, for the most part they were unwilling to do so. They recognized that while they profited from them, the benefits conferred were unconstitutional. Their fear of Roman Catholicism was united with their inherent desire for constitutional liberty, so that they preferred to wait for their freedom until it could be given with consent of Parliament. For their part, the Churchmen at last realized that it was to their own interests that the dissenters should be given relief from persecution. Not only was the spirit of the age against all attempts to enforce a rigid uniformity of doctrine and discipline within the church upon everybody, but the essential Protestantism of the country was threatened. The alternatives before them were either to come to some agreement with the Dissenters so that they might unite against James, or to witness the forced reimposition of Catholicism upon the country.[9]

This position is clearly manifest in the 'Articles' of Archbishop Sancroft to the bishops of the Province of Canterbury on 16th July 1688, when he urged them to instruct their clergy in their dioceses

to have a very tender regard to our brethren the Protestant Dissenters: that upon occasion they visit them at their houses and receive them kindly at their own, treating them fairly whenever they meet them, discoursing calmly and civilly with them, persuading them (if it may be) to a full compliance with our church, or at least that whereto we have already attained, we may walk by the same will, and mind the same thing: and in order thereunto, that they take all opportunities of assuring them that the bishops of the Church are really and sincerely irreconcilable enemies to the erroneous superstitions, idolatries and tyrranies of the Church of Rome, and that the very unkind jealousies, which some have had of us to the contrary are groundless . . . and that they warmly and most affectionately exhort them to join with us in daily fervent prayer to the God of all peace for an universal blessed union of all reformed churches both at home and abroad against our common enemies.[10]

So in a very real sense the Toleration Act was a remedy designed to meet an emergency in which both Church and State were involved.

[9] F. Kenworthy, in *T.U.H.S.* (October 1939), pp. 22-3.
[10] T. Brice, *Life of Dr John Tillotson* (1752), pp. 165-6.

It is important to note carefully the terms of the Act.[11]

The penal acts against Nonconformists were not repealed by the Act—the Corporation and Test Acts still remained in force. But freedom was allowed now as to rites and ceremonies of the Church, though not from its doctrines. All dissenting ministers were required to subscribe to the Thirty-nine Articles[12] (excepting the 34th, 35th, 36th, and part of the 20th, i.e. those concerning traditions of the Church, the Homilies and the consecration of bishops and priests). The Oaths of Supremacy and Allegiance were still required. The Baptists were not required to subscribe to the article on infant baptism; also the Quakers were allowed to substitute a promise and declaration without oath, whilst expressing their belief in the doctrine of the Trinity and the divine inspiration of the Scriptures. All dissenting ministers who subscribed must be registered and anyone attending a Nonconformist place of worship could be called upon by a magistrate to take the oaths, and if he refused could be imprisoned 'without bail or mainprize'. No dissenting meeting should be held behind locked doors, and Dissenters were still required to pay their tithes. So the restrictions of the Act pressed upon two classes of people who were entirely excluded from its benefits—Roman Catholics and anti-Trinitarians.

It will be seen that the toleration thus granted by the Act was limited and conditional. There was a certain admission of the rights of conscience in matters of worship, but freedom of civil status was not granted. It still remained impossible for Nonconformists to hold office under the Crown or in civil life, and universities remained closed against them.

II

At this point it is suitable to attempt some estimate of the numerical strength and geographical distribution of English Dissent.[13] At the time of the Restoration Dissent was vigorous in London, and in the country was also considerable though variable as to its distribution. As to its numerical strength no definite assertion is

[11] Gould, pp. 507-16; Gee and Hardy, pp. 654-64.

[12] Baxter drew up a brief 'Explication' of these terms, *Richard Baxter's Sence of the Subscribed Articles of Religion* (1689), 'which he gave in at the time of the subscription in which many of his brethren censured with him'.

[13] For elaboration of this aspect see E. Bebb (*Nonconformity and Social and Economic Life*, 1660-1800 [1935], pp. 30-45), to whose summary we are indebted.

possible, for the followers of the ejected ministers must have varied greatly. It is not possible to discover the number of those who obtained licences under the Indulgence of 1672; there are inaccuracies in existing records, and further, the Quakers did not take out licences, which was also the case with some Nonconformists. Yet some picture of the distribution is available. Dissent showed strongly in the south-eastern and south-western regions of England. The Presbyterians were strong around London, in the West Region, and in Lancashire and Yorkshire, but weak elsewhere. The Independents were strong in East Anglia, Bedfordshire, Gloucestershire, and London. The Baptists centred mainly in Kent, Somerset, Wiltshire, Buckinghamshire and Sussex, Lincolnshire and Norfolk.[14] The position can be more exactly estimated in 1689 when a numerical return of Conformists, Nonconformists and Papists was made to William III. The number of Nonconformists is given as 108,676—in proportion to Conformists of one to nearly twenty-three. Remembering the fear of persecution it is at least likely that the numbers might be larger.[15] It is certain that from 1672 to the end of the century there was a rapid expansion of Nonconformity.[16]

In addition to the above there were the Quakers, of whom no statistics were kept. About 1661 there were some 6,000 to 8,000 adult male Quakers and the total number of the men, women and children may be put at from 30,000 to 40,000 out of a population of some five millions.[17] In the period 1670-9 the figures would be about 40,000, perhaps rather more than that number. These figures suggest that the Society did not increase in size after the Toleration Act,[18] owing mainly to the large emigrations to America, where there were many thousands of Friends by the close of the century.

During the last quarter of the seventeenth century the number of Nonconformists may be fairly estimated at more than 150,000 and probably nearer 250,000, in addition to which there were the

[14] Bate, Appendix VII. Bebb (op. cit.) lists licences in England to *persons* as follows: Presbyterians 872, Congregational and Independent 374, Baptist and Anabaptist 203—making a total of 1,457. For *places:* Presbyterians 861, Congregational and Independent 268, Baptist and Anabaptist 69—Total 1,269. Cf. A. G. Matthews, *C.R.*, Intro., p. xv.

[15] *C.S.P.D.* (1693), pp. 448-50.

[16] Bebb, op. cit., Appendix I.

[17] Braithwaite, *The Beginnings of Quakerism* (1923), p. 513.

[18] Braithwaite, *The Second Period of Quakerism* (edn 1961), pp. 458-60.

Quakers.[19] The last years of the century witnessed the consolidation of Nonconformity.

Although the Quakers still continued to protest against tithes and other Church dues, generally speaking the Nonconformists readily took advantage of the Act of Toleration. Nearly one thousand chapels were built within the twenty years that followed, the majority being Presbyterian, the Baptists probably coming next in number, and the Independents a good third. 'Plain looking, square or oblong buildings of stone or brick with stone facings and high-pitched roofs which expressed the character of dissent and often enshrined behind their bareness a spirit of unearthly beauty' were erected.[20]

In London the neglected Halls of the City Companies became available and by alteration were adapted into places for Nonconformist worship. In some cases it was still felt wise to screen the buildings and meeting-houses from view, and so they were erected in secluded places. In the provinces the same process went forward. Places of worship were put under trust-deeds, usually in general terms and without provisions as to articles of faith or reference to a particular ecclesiastical standard. Amongst the Presbyterians in particular, ordinations became numerous. Prior to the Revolution any such had been privately conducted, but now they emerged into more public view.[21] The examination of an ordinand was thorough, and the filling of vacant pastorates was only after careful enquiry. The theological training of candidates for the ministry had been a constant anxiety during the years of stress; this matter now became more disciplined and effective under the new opportunity, though not without difficulty and even interference from the authorities.

Under the new régime the Quakers also benefited. The policy which had stood out against the conditions of worship allowed by the Indulgence of 1672 was now altered, and they obtained some 230 licences within two years of the passing of the Act.[22]

From these considerations we see how very speedily Nonconformity made outward advance after 1689.

[19] Bebb, op. cit. p. 35.

[20] F. J. Powicke, in *Essays Catholic and Congregational*, ed. Peel (1931), pp. 301-2; Stoughton, V.279. See also Wilson, *History and Antiquities of the Dissenting Churches in London*.

[21] Stoughton, V.283-4.

[22] Parliamentary Papers (1853), lxxviii.164, Brit. Mus.

III

It is convenient at this point to consider briefly the rise and importance of the Dissenting academies.[23] The Act of Uniformity effectively excluded Dissenters from Oxford and Cambridge. One of the resources of the ejected ministers was teaching, partly to secure maintenance, but also that they might afford their own sons and those of other Nonconformists the nearest approach to university education. Most of them were men of learning; some of the ejected had been tutors at Oxford or Cambridge. However, such were under oath not to teach *tamquam in universitate* elsewhere than in the two universities.[24] Despite the fact that it was contrary to the law, places of teaching sprang up widely, and by 1689 at least twenty academies existed. After the Toleration Act funds were organized to help the training of students for the dissenting ministry. The early academies were usually domestic foundations often in the houses of their founders. In the middle of the eighteenth century another pattern developed, more closely resembling a modern theological college.

The academies were not confined, however, to the teaching of divinity, but their studies included philosophy, mathematics, natural science and political philosophy, the purpose being to provide a liberal education for all classes of students. The standard generally was at least equal to that of the universities, and the result was that 'the stream of learning and the currents of thinking were kept in movement'.[25] Dr W. A. Shaw asserts that 'the strong claims of the Dissenting Academies to recognition rests on the high standards of academic education which they maintained during a century in which the English Universities were nearly as palsy-stricken as the Church'.[26]

The movement of the earlier academies from place to place was due mainly to persecution of their founders. That of Richard Frankland,[27] founded at Rathmell in 1669, had six migrations;

[23] The term 'academy' in this connection had its origin in Calvin's establishment at Geneva in 1559 of the first university without association with papal authority. Instead of using the term *universitas* he entitled it *academia*, recalling 'the olive grove of Academe' where Plato taught at Athens (A. Gordon, 'Early Nonconformity and Education', in *Essays Biographical and Historical* [1922], p. 70-1).

[24] This was the so-called 'Stamford Oath', dating back to 1334.

[25] Gordon, op. cit. p. 201.

[26] 'Dissenting Academies', in *Encyclopaedia of Education*.

[27] More than 300 students were trained in this academy between 1669 and 1698, most of them for the Christian ministry (Calamy, *Continuation*, p. 287).

that of Thomas Doolittle founded in 1672 at Islington not less than five.

The extent of their influence during the seventeenth and eighteenth centuries may be seen when it is remembered that more than three hundred names of students have found their way into the *Dictionary of National Biography*.[28] In the light of this fact alone it will be clear that the Nonconformist academy rendered a service of the highest importance to English education. In the words of Alexander Gordon:

> The immediate work of the Nonconformist academies was to fit and equip men for public duty, not in the ministry alone, but in all professions: it was to make them thinkers—not closing their minds with fixed opinions, but opening their intelligence and giving them an impetus towards the acquirement of further knowledge. . . . Far more was this their aim than to make them Nonconformists. . . . Small wonder that many who were not Nonconformists were ready to avail themselves of an education thus conceived and thus pursued. Nor need we grudge that infusion of new blood into the order of institution of religion, for which the Anglican church stands indebted to able and conspicuous men, made what they were, in the obscurity of the Nonconformist Academy. It was not Oxford, it was Tewkesbury that matured the mind of Butler.[29]

As already indicated, before the Revolution, the men who had founded these academies were subjected to persecution. In a sermon in 1685, Robert South urged his hearers 'to employ the most of this your power . . . to suppress utterly and extinguish, those private, blind, conventicling schools or academies of grammar and philosophy set up and taught secretly by Fanatics here and there all the kingdom over'.[30] Even under the new liberty granted to Dissenters by the Act of Toleration there was still strong episcopalian antipathy. In 1703 Samuel Wesley attacked the academies with considerable vigour, in a small pamphlet which led to a serious and prolonged controversy.[31]

[28] For a full account of Dissenting Academies see I. Parker, *Dissenting Academies in England* (1914); and H. McLachlan, *English Education under the Test Act* (1931), which contains a list of 72 academies.

[29] Op. cit. pp. 84-5.

[30] R. South, *Sermons* (edn 1737), V.45.

[31] *A Letter from a Country Divine, concerning the Education of Dissenters in their Private Academies in several parts of the Nation. Humbly offered to the Grand Committee of Parliament for Religion.* The letter was written about 1690, and surreptitiously printed without Wesley's consent. For details of the provocative circumstances out of which it arose see L. Tyerman, *Life and Times of Samuel Wesley* (1866), pp. 270-82. A sense of humour on Wesley's part could have prevented the writing of the unfortunate letter.

He complained that by these institutions men were being seduced from the Church; that the memory of 'the Blessed Martyr King Charles' was dishonoured; that they endangered the success of the two universities; that those who taught were violating the oath of graduation. A warfare of pamphlets continued for four years. In a sermon in 1709 before the Lord Mayor of London, Dr Sacheverell declared that these institutions were a national peril, and that 'Atheism, Deism, Tritheism, Socinianism, with all the hellish principles of Fanaticism, Regicide and Anarchy were taught in them'.[32]

The Tory party believed that the destruction of the academies would be an end of dissent. It would mean that the next generation of Dissenters would have no educated ministry; the sons of wealthy merchants who supported the dissenting interest would go to the universities and become loyal churchmen; the conventicles would be the home of the poor and ignorant.

On 12th May 1714 a Bill was introduced into the Commons 'to prevent the growth of schism and for the further security of the Church of England as by law established'.[33] No person was to keep school or seminary unless he declared that he conformed to the Liturgy of the Church of England and obtained an episcopal licence, which could only be obtained if the certificate could be produced stating that within the previous year he had received the Sacrament according to Anglican rite. To teach without this authority incurred a three-months' imprisonment. Further, if after obtaining such licence the teacher attended any worship other than Anglican he would also be imprisoned for three months and no longer be allowed to teach. If, in teaching, there was the use of any other than the catechism as in the Prayer Book, the licence would be void and the penalties would be incurred.

It will be clear by the terms of the Bill that it was not aimed merely at the academies. It was intended to prevent Dissenters having their own children taught by Dissenters under any circumstances. Both a petition by the Dissenters to the House of Lords that their case should be presented by counsel,[34] and a motion that they should have their own schools, but that children of parents who were not Dissenters should be excluded were

[32] H. Sacheverell, *Perils of False Brethren*, p. 15.
[33] Robertson, pp. 110-2. [34] L. J., XIX.704, 709, 710-11.

defeated. Three amendments were carried. The licence could be dispensed with in the case of a tutor employed by any nobleman to teach his family; for any tutor only giving instruction in reading, writing, arithmetic and mathematical learning; the imposition of penalties to be taken away from magistrates and given to a supreme court. The Act was to take effect from Sunday 1st August 1714. On that morning Queen Anne died. The situation changed with the accession of George I, and the Act was never enforced. It stood, however, as a reminder of the danger from which Nonconformity had escaped. The year 1714 had all but taken from Dissenters what 1689 had given.

IV

For a brief time we must retrace our steps. William III died on 8th March 1702. During the last years of his reign the attitude of the High Church[35] and Tory party had grown more bitter against Dissenters. Under Queen Anne most of the Whig statesmen who had served under William were replaced by Tories, and in the Parliament which assembled in October their number was double that of the Whigs. With her passionate defence of the Church of England, Anne looked upon Dissenters with utmost disfavour. This political situation and the ecclesiastical attitude foreshadowed the recrudescence of anti-Nonconformist feeling from both sources.

In December 1702 a Bill was introduced to the House of Commons to prevent what was regarded as an evasion of the Corporation and Test Acts, under which no person could hold office under the Crown or in civic life without receiving the Sacrament. There were some Dissenters who qualified themselves for such official position by conforming to this requirement. It was maintained that by this practice the most sacred service of the Church suffered degradation.[36] The deeper reason for opposition was political. If Nonconformists were excluded from municipal corporations these would send Tory members to Parliament. These were the motives behind the Bill against 'occasional conformity'.

The practice had long been regarded by moderate Dissenters

[35] This term should not be misunderstood. It signifies the party within the Church fanatically jealous for her prerogatives: it does not imply any Romanizing tendency.

[36] Bishop Hoadly, *Works*, II.522: 'To make the celebration of this institution . . . is debasing the most sacred thing into a political tool and engine of State.'

as reasonable and lawful.[37] The majority of Presbyterians and some Congregationalists practised it; but the Baptists were so rigid against it as to exclude from membership any who participated. Sir Thomas Abney, a member of John Howe's church, had qualified in 1701 for the office of Lord Mayor of London by conforming and this aroused the anger of Defoe.[38] Moderate Churchmen, such as Burnet, regarded the practice as softening the hostility of Dissenters to the Church, and making the position of the Church itself more secure.[39] Not alone, but the bitterest of all others in his vituperation, Dr Sacheverell denounced the practice, and his cry, 'The Church in danger', rang through the land. Nonconformists were as vermin fit for extermination, and an outbreak of hostility resulted in destruction and wrecking of meeting-houses, and of the houses of those known to be sympathetic to Nonconformity. Persecution of Dissenters again raised its evil head.

Of all publications at this time the strangest was from the pen of Daniel Defoe, though issued anonymously. Its purpose was the very opposite of that indicated by its title, *The Short Way with the Dissenters*. Angered by the continual invectives of Sacheverell, Defoe tried the policy of ridicule by this little satire urging the total suppression of Dissent.

> This is the time to pick up this heretical weed of sedition . . . that has so long poisoned the good corn. . . . If one severe law were made, and punctually executed, that whoever was found at a conventicle should be banished the nation, and the preacher be hanged, we should soon see an end of the tale: they would all come to Church.

As soon as the writer's real intention was discovered, the High Churchmen were indignant; the pamphlet was publicly burnt, and Defoe fined £200, and sentenced to stand in the pillory and be imprisoned. This strange weapon in the interests of the Nonconformist cause did not commend itself to the graver sort, who

[37] J. Howe, *Some Considerations . . . concerning Occasional Conformity of Dissenters* (1701): 'In 1662 most of the considerable ejected ministers of London met and agreed to hold occasional conformity with the now re-established church; not quitting their own ministry or declining the exercise of it as they could have opportunity' (p. 33).

[38] Defoe, *An Enquiry into the Occasional Conformity of Dissenters in Cases of Preferment* (1697), written in criticism of Sir Humphrey Edwin, a Congregationalist, who not conforming had gone in state to 'a nasty conventicle, Pinners Hall'.

[39] *History of my Own Times* (quoted Dale, p. 488): 'I think the practice of occasional conforming, as used by the dissenters, is so far from deserving the title of a vile hypocrisy, that it is the duty of all moderate dissenters, on their principles to do it.'

feared that greater hostility might result. Defoe had been trained in the dissenting academy at Newington Green, *circa* 1676-81.[40]

Such then was the temper of the time. In its original form the Bill provided that if anyone who held office attended a Dissenting service he should forfeit his place and be fined £100 for the offence and £5 for every day he ventured to continue; he could not hold any other office until conformity for a year had been proved to the satisfaction of the magistrates; if on reappointment he repeated the offence the penalties were to be doubled. The real purpose was not merely to protect the Sacrament from profanation, but to strengthen the Tory interest in the House of Commons.

Carried by a large majority in the Commons it was resolutely opposed in the Lords, largely through the leadership of Archbishop Tenison and Bishop Burnet. After conference between the two Houses the Bill was dropped. In 1703 it was brought in again, in modified form, but again it did not pass. In 1704 a third attempt was made and again it fell through. The elections of 1705 gave the Whigs a majority in the Commons, and the Bill was set aside for some years. With the return of a large Tory majority in the elections of 1710, the Bill was again raised in modified terms, and in 1711 became law.[41] Attendance at a Dissenting meeting involved a fine of £40. The Act was intended to present Nonconformists with the choice of either abandoning their Nonconformity or abandoning all chance of servicing the State or the civil order—in the hope that the former would be the choice made. It was an indirect way of trying to repeal the Toleration Act of 1689. It was to prove a policy of relentless pressure.

V

Despite the new opportunities which the Toleration Act presented to the Nonconformists their advance was hindered by some lack of agreement in both denominational and theological issues.

It is true that there were some attempts at closer association. In 1690 Presbyterian and Independent ministers in and about London[42] entered into what was termed 'The Happy Union',

[40] Op. cit. pp. 18, 21.
[41] 10 Anne, c. 6; Robertson, pp. 107-10.
[42] Already ministers of Somerset, Wiltshire and Gloucestershire had agreed upon an accommodation together with a Common Fund, and had offered their 'Minutes' for use in London. A. Gordon, *Freedom after Ejection* (1917), p. 155.

following the establishment of a Common Fund for poor and disabled ministers, a year earlier. They drew up a document under the title *Heads of Agreement*,[43] which showed clearly that some modification had taken place in the views of both groups before the Restoration. The Presbyterians had now abandoned the idea of parish presbyteries and provincial synods and had come nearer to the concept of 'the gathered church'; the Independents now ceased to stress the duty of Church members to formal covenants, and allowed ruling authority to pastors and elders. The 'Preface' declares:

It is incumbent on us . . . to reduce all distinguishing Names to that of UNITED BRETHREN; to admit no uncharitable jealousies, or censorious speeches.

This 'Happy Union' came, however, to an early end by the close of 1694, and from the Common Fund the Independents withdrew.

A further and more lasting impulse towards closer union emerged in the early years of the eighteenth century. The Presbyterian, Baptist and Independent ministers living in and about London had already formed themselves into three separate 'Boards', for the promotion of their several interests, but on some occasions had acted together.[44] On 11th July 1727 it was resolved to form an organization that should include all ministers of the three denominations living within ten miles of London for the maintenance and extension of civil and religious liberty: its title —'The General Body of Protestant Dissenting Ministers of the Three Denominations residing in and about the Cities of London and Westminster.' It is still in existence and still retains the ancient privilege of personal access to the Sovereign.[45]

Returning now to 'The Happy Union', the reason for the disintegration referred to above was a theological disagreement occasioned by a volume of sermons preached by Dr Tobias Crisp, nearly fifty years earlier, and now reprinted by his son. The theological position of these discourses was strongly Calvinist, even to the point of being antinomian. Dr Daniel Williams

[43] For the *Heads of Agreement* and the compromise involved thereby, see A. Gordon, *Cheshire Classics* (1919), pp. 111-12; cf. Dale, pp. 475-9. The movement was initiated by John Howe and received the support of 'some fourscore ministers'.

[44] This unity of action was expressed as early as March 1702, when representatives of the three denominations presented an Address to the Throne.

[45] G. F. Nuttall, *The General Body of the Three Denominations: A Historical Survey* (1955); Dale, pp. 496-8.

attacked the theology of Crisp, and was supported by many Presbyterians, but most Independents were against Dr Williams. The controversy increased in bitterness and Dr Williams was accused of Socinianism. 'It was a fight between *ultra* and moderate Calvinists, the *ultras* being Congregationalists who posed as vindicators of the pure ancient Gospel. . . . Perhaps the saddest consequence was that . . . it began the habit of identifying the name Presbyterian with heretic.'[46]

It was also upon theological issues that a serious twofold cleavage took place among the Baptists in the early years of the eighteenth century. Amongst the General Baptists an impulse towards Socinianism had been steadily developing for nearly half a century through the teaching of Matthew Caffyn; the Particular Baptists suffered division from an extreme Calvinism which developed antinomian tendencies. In addition this section of Baptists became divided in a dispute about congregational singing of psalms and hymns, arising from the publication of Benjamin Keach's hymn-book in 1691,[47] though this also affected the General Baptists.

The Quakers also suffered religious decline. Their leaders, George Fox and Robert Barclay, passed from the scene. The main problem, however, lay in the question of organization to which course Fox had turned in his later years, thereby producing controversy. The Story-Wilkinson criticism of the introduction of 'discipline' as being a departure from the original Quaker belief in the sufficiency of the 'Inner Light' had resulted in their condemnation at the London Yearly Meeting in 1677. This appeared as a separating influence, 'which presented the Quakers to the world as a divided people, whose inward law led them into divided camps': it formed the background of later Separatist movements which extended into the early eighteenth century. The vividness of the first Quaker ideal became dimmed, though for refusal to pay tithes they still suffered for what they believed was the cause of Truth.[48]

We see, then, that round the whole circle of the Nonconformist groups there was some measure of decline owing to departures from the first ideals which had illuminated each in its earlier

[46] F. J. Powicke, in *Essays Congregational and Catholic*, ed. Peel (1931), p. 304.
[47] Underwood, pp. 124-34.
[48] Braithwaite, *The Second Period of Quakerism*, pp. 469-82, 494.

days. It is probably true to say that Dr F. J. Powicke's criticism of Congregationalism at this period is applicable to all the constituent groups of English Nonconformity, though in varying degrees:

There was little or no grasp on the thought of a church as constituted by the living Spirit of Christ in the midst, but there was a fanatical grasp on the supposed form of sound words and a form of worship removed as far as possible from the Prayer Book, while, with this there went a pharisaical rancour which poisoned the springs of brotherly love.[49]

VI

With the accession of George I in 1714, the House of Hanover brought a new security for the English Throne, though for a time the future was uncertain. James, the Young Pretender, made a bid for the succession, but this Jacobite rebellion was broken, and he fled to France. Arising out of the High Church and Tory antipathy to the new régime, popular feeling became violent, and expressed itself against the Dissenters. Meeting-houses at Oxford, Birmingham, Bristol, Norwich, Reading and Wrexham and elsewhere were burnt, and in Staffordshire the outrages were exceptionally violent.[50] From the beginning Nonconformists were staunch supporters of the House of Hanover, and under the new order they confidently expected some extension of their rights and liberties.

When the political danger had passed, some two hundred members of the House of Commons met to consider the possibility of a parliamentary bill for redress of Nonconformist grievances. Throughout the country there came a growing demand for the repeal of the Occasional Conformity Act and the Schism Act of Anne's reign, and also of the Corporation Act and the Test Act of the reign of Charles II. In view of this, late in 1718, a Bill was introduced into the Upper House 'for strengthening the Protestant interest'.[51] In the course of the debate the clauses in the Bill relating to certain parts of the Corporation and Test Acts had to be deleted; but the Bill passed both Houses and received royal assent in February 1719. It secured at least partial relief.

[49] In *Essays, Congregation and Catholic,* ed. Peel, p. 303.
[50] These outrages occasioned the passing of the Riot Act (I Geo. 1, 2, c. 5), which made it a felony to damage any building used for religious worship.
[51] *L.J.*, XXI.24.

In an attempt to prevent Dissenters making further pressure, and yet to show that their support was valued, Walpole arranged in 1723 that a grant from the King's Purse—the *Regium Donum*—should be paid half-yearly 'for the use and behalf of the poor widows of dissenting ministers', the fund to be administered by representatives of the Presbyterians and the Independents. Though it was in no sense a State endowment, this proved unacceptable to the more radical Nonconformists, especially as time went on. By 1736 the feeling grew that this hampered the freedom of Dissenters, and at a meeting of the 'Three Denominations' it was declared that acceptance was inadvisable. Although the motion was defeated, objections grew and eventually (though not until 1851) the *Regium Donum* ceased.[52]

In 1727, in the year of accession of George II, the first Annual Bill of Indemnity was passed for relieving Dissenters from the penalties of the Corporation and Test Acts,[53] but this was somewhat ineffective, for it only applied to those who 'through ignorance of the law, absence or unavoidable accident' had failed to qualify; those who failed on conscientious grounds were not covered. The Act applied only to those in office; it did not help any candidate. The King was known to have a more generous view and evidence of this came when, in 1733, an ecclesiastical prosecution against Philip Doddridge for keeping 'an unlawful academy' at Northampton was stopped by his intervention. 'During my reign there shall be no persecution for conscience' sake.'[54]

In November 1732 the ministers of the 'Three Denominations' strengthened their positions by bringing together laymen as well as ministers from all churches within ten miles of London, for defence of civil rights of Dissenters. These became known as the Dissenting Deputies.[55] Their struggle for the rights of Dissenters was to prove a long one.[56] 'This was the first attempt of nonconformity to combine for purposes of self-defence: it marks a distinct

[52] Dale, pp. 521-3, 524-6.

[53] Geo. II, i. This measure was repeated annually to 1828, when the Acts themselves disappeared from the Statute-book.

[54] Doddridge, *Correspondence and Diary* (1829), III.139-40.

[55] B. L. Manning, *The Protestant Dissenting Deputies*, 1952.

[56] An illustration of this was concerned with the office of Sheriff in the City of London, where under the Corporation Act requiring the taking of the Sacrament in parish churches, the Corporation imposed heavy fines upon those who refused. Nonconformists were deliberately elected and upon refusal were fined, the proceeds being devoted to the cost of the new Mansion House. Litigation lasted from 1748 to 1767, when the Lord Justice ruled that Nonconformists had the right to decline. B. L. Manning, ibid. pp. 119-25.

stage in the struggle for civil and religious liberty.'[57] Throughout the eighteenth century the Dissenting Deputies showed great courage and energy in defending Dissenters whose legal rights were violated.

VII

During this period, an important theological controversy arose: it centred in a series of meetings in Salter's Hall, during the early months of 1719.[58] A dispute had occurred in Exeter where three Presbyterian ministers claimed the right to express their belief in the Trinity in purely scriptural phrase and refused to be bound by a non-scriptural definition. The cry was raised that their views were Arian. The London ministers had already been informed of the controversy and about a hundred and fifty met to discuss the position. It was generally agreed that a letter of advice should be forwarded to Exeter. A Congregationalist minister, proposed that every minister present in the meeting should, as a testimony to his own faith, subscribe the first of the Thirty-nine Articles on the doctrine of the Trinity, together with the fifth and sixth questions in the Westminster Confession. This immediately divided the company, and the motion was opposed on the ground that it was the imposition of a human creed, and that such imposition was against the basic principle of Protestant dissent. The motion was rejected—by seventy-three to sixty-nine votes—the Congregationalists voting with the majority and the Baptists divided by ten to nine. The minority resolved themselves into a distinct body, thus creating two assemblies. That of the 'non-subscribers' was mainly Presbyterian; that of the 'subscribers' included most of the London Congregationalists. Separate 'Advices for Peace' were sent to Exeter, but too late to be of use. Unfortunately the proceedings did not end with this. Recriminations occurred and a paper war involving some seventy pamphlets was carried on. The charge of Arian opinions was fastened upon the non-subscribers. Certainly opinions akin to Arianism spread among the dissenting Churches, as also in the Church of England, and amongst the Presbyterians there was most rapid advance; as time went on these developed into Socinianism and Unitarianism.

Not a few historians have drawn certain conclusions arising out

[57] Dale, p. 519.

[58] Ibid. pp. 528-39; Skeats and Miall, *History of the Free Churches of England, 1688-1891* (1891), pp. 236-48.

of the Salter's Hall meeting. Dr F. J. Powicke has effectively argued that three things often asserted are not true.[59] It is not true that more Presbyterian ministers alleged to be Arian were, as a rule less evangelical in their preaching than the Independents; it is not true that alleged Arians were to blame for emphasizing the moral aspect of Christianity, rather was it their glory, for many had come to realize that if the Church preached a faith which had no vital relation to moral righteousness it was dead; nor is it true that Presbyterian Churches, said to be tainted with Arianism, withered away under its influence, a 'stock charge' frequently asserted against them. The fact is that the so-called Arian Churches did not die out in greater measure than the orthodox.[60]

> The simple truth is that many an orthodox church died of its own orthodoxy. . . . The Evangelical Revival would have worked out far better for the future of religion in England if a reasonable response to the light of truth represented by the maligned Arian movement could have been conjoined with a reasonable respect for tradition as represented by a true orthodoxy. Christian love, in the ascendant, would have opened a way to this, but Christian love was absent, as is so often when most needed.[61]

VIII

'The most depressing twenty years in English Christianity in the eighteenth century were those between 1730 and 1750.'[62] Isaac Watts speaks of 'the decaying interest of religion and the withering state of Christianity at this day'.[63] Of the decline in religion 'it is not in one denomination, but in all that symptoms of the decline appear'.[64] Such a situation is repeatedly affirmed. Socially manners and morals were degenerating and contempt for religion was widespread. There was decay of 'the dissenting interest'; wealthy dissenting families forsook the meeting-house; sons of eminent Nonconformists who had suffered for their Nonconformity passed over to the Church; congregations in many cases showed decline, and sometimes became extinct. At least fifty dissenting

[59] In *Essays, Congregational and Catholic*, ed. Peel, p. 306. Cf. *T.U.H.S.*, Vol. I, 'Apology for the Nonconformist Arians of the Eighteenth Century'. See also J. H. Colligan: *The Arian Movement in England* (1913) and *Eighteenth-century Nonconformity* (1915).

[60] F. J. Powicke in *Essays, Congregational and Catholic*, pp. 306-7, gives detailed statistics.

[61] Ibid. p. 304.

[62] J. H. Colligan, *Eighteenth-century Nonconformity*, p. 90.

[63] *Works*, IV.63.

[64] Clark, II.197.

ministers entered the Church between the years 1714 and 1731.[65] The serious disquiet is indicated by the number of pamphlets issued about this time.[66] The Quakers were disturbed and found it necessary to send serious exhortations to those who were lukewarm.[67] Naturally there were some who, disturbed by the religious apathy, sought for a remedy. In 1731 a number of laymen formed 'The King's Head Society', out of which grew the Lime Street Lecture, for propaganda of the faith, and also the establishment of the King's Head Academy for a more thorough training of the ministry.[68]

Although there is undoubted evidence of decline within Nonconformity nevertheless it should be remembered that during these years there came forth the hymns of Isaac Watts and Philip Doddridge, who may be taken as respective of the best Dissent of the period. In 1745 Doddridge produced a classic of personal religion: *Rise and Progress of Religion in the Soul.*

[65] Anon., *Some Observations on the Present State of Dissenting Interest* (1731).

[66] E.g. Gough, *An Enquiry into the cause of the Decay of Dissenting Interest* (1731); Doddridge, *Free Thoughts on the most Probable Means of reviving the Dissenting Interest* (1730); Watts, *An Humble Attempt towards the Revival of Practical Religion among Christians* (1731); Taylor, *Spiritual Declensions* (1732).

[67] Braithwaite, *The Second Period of Quakerism* (edn 1961), pp. 631-8.

[68] Dale, pp. 558-9.

CHAPTER EIGHT

REVIVAL: THE AGE OF WESLEY

I

OF the condition of England in the first half of the eighteenth century there is ample evidence.[1] In 1692 a Society for the Reformation of Manners had been established, but its influence had declined and by 1730 it had ceased to exist. In spite of its outward refinement society was corrupt and its vices were flagrant, regarded as almost an indisputable qualification for entry into fashionable life. Immoderate drinking, gambling and sexual immorality were taken as a matter of course. Drunkenness was a feature of all classes, in town and country alike, and it resulted in degrading and repulsive orgies. In such a low state of morals it is not surprising that crime was widespread. Punishment was barbarous—there were over two hundred and fifty offences for which the death penalty could be inflicted—and thousands flocked to the hangings at Tyburn, where special seats were provided for more wealthy spectators. Transportation as a penalty resulted in shipment of large numbers to criminal centres in Australia. The brutality of the age is illustrated in its sports. Baiting of bears and bulls and cock-fighting formed favourite village pastimes; prize-fighting with bare fists resulted in severe injuries for the contestants. The lot of children tells its own tragic tale. The London Bills of Mortality show that in this period three out of four children, born of all classes, died before their fifth birthday; plagues swept through the homes of all alike. Illegitimacy was rife, and unwanted children were ruthlessly destroyed.[2]

The Church of England was in a state of serious decline, though this can easily be exaggerated. It suffered from the abuses of pluralism and non-residence[3] and a wide gulf existed between the

[1] G. M. Trevelyan, *English Social History* (1944); L. E. Elliott-Binns, *The Early Evangelicals: a Religious and Social Study* (1953); J. H. Whiteley, *Wesley's England: A Survey of Eighteenth-century Social and Cultural Conditions* (1938); J. W. Bready, *England before and after Wesley* (1938); M. L. Edwards, *John Wesley and the Eighteenth Century* (1933).

[2] J. W. Bready, op. cit. p. 142.

[3] It has been estimated that more than half the incumbents of English parishes in the eighteenth century were absentees. N. Sykes, *Church and State in England in the Eighteenth Century*, p. 217.

higher and lower clergy, the latter poorly paid and without security, all of which resulted in a lowering of spiritual vitality. There was widespread scepticism regarding religion. The complaint uttered by Bishop Butler in 1736 reflects the attitude of many persons at this time:

Christianity is not so much a subject of inquiry: but it is now, at length discovered to be fictitious, and accordingly . . . set up as a principal subject of mirth and ridicule as it were by way of reproach, for its having so long interrupted the pleasures of the world.[4]

Fifteen years later, in 1751, he emphasized his convictions:

It is impossible for me . . . to forbear lamenting with you the general decay of religion in this nation; which is now observed by everyone and has been for some time the complaint of all serious persons. The influence of it is more and more wearing out of the minds of men: . . . the number who profess themselves unbelievers increases, and with their numbers their zeal. . . . For as different ages have been distinguished by different sorts of particular error and vice, the deplorable distinction of our own is an avowed scorn of religion in some, and a growing disregard to it in the generality.[5]

Allowing for all the danger that accompanies generalities of statement one thing is without doubt: the common people throughout England were poor, illiterate, and uncared for.

Moreover, the English Church was 'uncapable of making any appeal to those who lived sordid lives in the growing towns, and who could only be roused from their brutality and squalor by some vigorous and emotional call'.[6]

As we have already observed the decline of Dissent from the stirring quality of its original ideals had rendered it unequal to the task of spiritual deliverance of the mass of the people.

It was in the midst of this situation that a new spiritual impulse emerged. The Evangelical Revival began, and the new movement was to change the face of England, bringing not only the spread of the Gospel, but a new vigour into both the English Church and English Dissent. Its influence was to penetrate into every phase of life and eventually to reach out to all parts of the world.

[4] *The Analogy of Religion.*

[5] *A Charge to the Clergy . . . of Durham* (1751), §§ 1, 2. Cf. the comment of Montesquieu: 'In England there is no religion, and the subject if mentioned in society, exacts nothing but laughter.'

[6] L. E. Elliott-Binns, *The Early Evangelicals*, pp. 99-100.

It is never easy to define precisely the origins of any great movement, but in regard to this movement one fact is without question.

The revival of the eighteenth century, which came as a breath from the Spirit of God into a hopeless and fainting world, can only be accounted for, from a human point of view, by that instinct for God which never quite dies away in the hearts of men. It certainly owed nothing to human organization, and when it came, it came almost without observation or expectation.[7]

The principal source of the movement is to be found in the life and work of John Wesley (1703-91); he stood and stands alone. But two other sources of influence contributed to the development of this impulse of spiritual revival. There was the Calvinist movement of which George Whitefield (1714-70)[8] and Selina, Countess of Huntingdon (1707-91) were the leaders; also the important group of Evangelicals who remained within the Church of England.[9] Throughout these groups, despite differences of theology and method, there was a common element. The word of W. E. Gladstone concerning the last of these groups applies to them all:

The main characteristic of the Evangelical school was a strong, systematic, outspoken and determined reaction against prevailing standards both of life and preaching. It aimed at bringing back, on a large scale, and by an aggressive movement, the Cross and all that the Cross essentially implies, both into the teaching of the clergy and into the lives as well of the clergy as of the laity. . . . They preached Christ largely and fervently where, as a rule, he was but little and coldly preached before. But who is there that will not say from his heart: 'I therein do rejoice, and yea, will rejoice?'[10]

Our concern in these pages is with the first two of these groups.

II

Turning now to the Methodist movement it has been customary for some to date its rise in 'The Holy Club' at Oxford in 1729;[11]

[7] Ibid. p. 117.
[8] See *infra*, pp. 128-30.
[9] For further study of this group see: Elliott-Binns, op. cit.; Horton Davies, *Worship and Theology in England: From Watts and Wesley to F. D. Maurice, 1690-1850* (1953); G. W. E. Russell, *A Short History of the Evangelical Movement* (1915).
[10] Quoted G. W. E. Russell, op. cit. p. 11.
[11] For an account see L. Tyerman, *The Oxford Methodists* (1873).

others would give the beginning of field-preaching in 1739 as its real beginning. But most would affirm that it began with the experience of John Wesley—and his brother Charles—in May 1738.[12] Yet we may trace the springs of the movement in the formative influences that lie beneath that experience. 'Methodism was definitely indebted to the Reformers, to Pietism, to Moravianism and to mysticism, and all these connexions and cross connexions carry us far back into the history of the Church in earlier days.'[13] The 'religious societies', first formed in the seventeenth century, were known to Samuel Wesley,[14] and in John Wesley's *Journal* there is frequent reference to his contact with them. It was on 1st May 1738 that Wesley inaugurated his first society in London.[15]

John Wesley was born in 1703 in the Rectory at Epworth, in Lincolnshire. His ancestry is interesting. Both his grandfathers and one great-grandfather were among the ejected ministers in 1662. His father received education at the Newington Green Academy for the Dissenting ministry, but after two years he left to enter Exeter College, Oxford, a decision reached partly by a growing uneasiness about Dissenting principles and practice, and partly by the desire to go to Oxford, influenced by the anticipation of Dr John Owen that degrees in the University would become open to Nonconformists in the near future. Samuel Wesley soon became a convinced and eager conformist. Susanna Wesley was the daughter of Dr Samuel Annesley, a leader amongst the ejected ministers of London; she was a woman of unusual ability, and seems to have had some leanings towards Socinianism which at that time was found in Dissent; probably influenced by young Samuel Wesley she also passed over into the Anglican fold. John Wesley, reared in the Epworth household—which probably represented the English Church of the eighteenth century at its best—declared himself to be a loyal son of that Church throughout all his lifetime. Nevertheless Puritan Nonconformity was part of the spiritual inheritance of the Wesley household.

[12] For an excellent analysis of this experience, see H. Bett, *The Spirit of Methodism* (1937), Ch. 1.

[13] For elaboration of these influences see Bett, ibid. pp. 40-63. For the particular influence of Moravianism, see C. W. Towlson: *Moravian and Methodist* (1957); for that of mysticism (especially William Law) see E. W. Baker, *The Herald of the Evangelical Revival* (1948); J. B. Green, *John Wesley and William Law* (1945).

[14] S. Wesley, *A Letter concerning the Religious Societies* (1699).

[15] J. Wesley, *Journal*, in loc. See J. S. Simon, *John Wesley and the Religious Societies*. This society was not Moravian as sometimes is supposed. See *Journal*, I.458 note.

At the age of eleven John entered the Charterhouse School, Westminster, where he remained six years. In 1716 his brother Charles joined him, and for four years they were in London together. In 1720 John entered Christ Church, Oxford, his brother following him six years later. In 1726 John was elected a Fellow of Lincoln College; for a short time he held a curacy at Wroote, in his father's Lincolnshire parish, but in November 1729 he returned to Lincoln College to take up tutorial work. It was after his return from Wroote that he became the recognized leader in a little group in the University, already known as 'Methodists' because they 'agreed together to observe with strict formality the method of study and practice laid down in the statutes'. A regular study of the Greek Testament, strict devotion to prayer and the Church seasons, a systematic visitation of the sick and poor and those in prison formed the commitments of its members. The 'Holy Club' owes its place in history solely to the after-deeds of three of its members—Whitefield, and the two Wesleys. In October 1735 John and Charles Wesley set out for Georgia to convert the settlers and the Indians in the colony—of immense importance in the experience of Wesley, yet as a mission it proved a failure. To quote his own words: 'I who went to convert others was never myself converted.' This journey brought him into contact with the Moravians, and later through their leader Peter Böhler, Wesley was led at last to spiritual peace. The occasion of 24th May 1738 was a day which marks (in the words of Lecky) 'an epoch in English history'. It was in a 'religious society'—an Anglican and not Moravian—in Aldersgate Street, London, that the illumination came to both brothers. Once more the now classical words may be quoted. Listening to a member reading Luther's *Preface to the Epistle to the Romans*—

About a quarter before nine, while he was describing the change which God works in the heart through faith in Christ, I felt my heart strangely warmed. I felt I did trust in Christ, Christ alone for salvation; and an assurance was given me that he had taken away *my* sins. . . .[16]

This was the moment of a new beginning—the point at which the direction of Wesley's life-work was determined. Henceforth, for half-a-century he had but a single aim:

[16] *Journal*, I.475-6.

One point in view is to provide so far as I am able, vital practical religion, and by the grace of God to beget, preserve and increase the life of God in the souls of men.[17]

The magnificent way in which he fulfilled this ideal is known of all men and upon the details it is not necessary for us to linger.[18] His *Journals* together with his *Letters* and *Sermons* and treatises tell the story, which may be summarized in the following passage:

In the heat of summer, in the snows of winter; exposed to discomfort of all sorts and dangers not a few, by day or night; along roads infested with robbers, so bad that three days was a fair allowance for a ride from London to Bristol; losing his way on the mountains, detained at the ferries for hours, overtaken by the dark when there was no shelter but the nearest hovel; through the length and breadth of England, Scotland and Ireland, John Wesley journeyed, never travelling less that 'four thousand five hundred miles in a year'; reading as he went; writing as he rested, tracts and polemics, or abridging the best literature for his people; preaching everywhere, whether the people were anxious to hear him or had been kindled into a furious mob that sought his life, indifferent whether it were to half a dozen in some tiny room, or to the thousands that thronged around him on Moorfields or Kensington; with the care upon him of all his churches, and the numberless detail neither relinquished nor overlooked, which the affairs of a growing society involved.[19]

Of permanent significance for the development of the Methodist movement was the influence of Charles Wesley (1707-88).[20] For many years the two brothers worked closely together, but in the later years Charles retired from his regular itineraries and settled down at Bristol, and after 1771 in Marylebone, London, ministering mainly to the London societies. But it is as 'the sweet singer' of Methodism that his supreme contribution lies. In the words of F. L. Wiseman:

Long hence, when probably the standard works of the elder brother are read only by the preachers, and the organization which he built up

[17] J. Wesley to Samuel Walker, of Truro, 3rd September 1756 (*Letters*, III.192).

[18] Of the many studies of Wesley, see J. S. Simon, 5 vols (1921-7); L. Maldwyn Edwards, *John Wesley and the Eighteenth Century* (1933), *The Astonishing Youth* (1959); M. Piette, *John Wesley in the Evolution of Protestantism* (E.Tr., 1937); W. L. Doughty, *John Wesley, Preacher* (1955); V. H. H. Green, *The Young Mr Wesley* (1961): C. E. Vulliamy, *John Wesley* (1954), Ingvaar Haddal, *John Wesley* (E.Tr., 1961) (a Norwegian study).

[19] H. B. Workman, *Methodism*, p. 39.

[20] See *Journal of Charles Wesley* (2 vols) 1849; F. Baker, *Charles Wesley as Revealed by His Letters* (1948). Dr Baker has a definitive edition of the Letters (some 3,000) in preparation.

has so modified as to show but little trace of its original form, the hymns of Charles Wesley will continue to permeate the Methodist Church with the gracious leaven of its primitive experience.[21]

These hymns declare the personal experience of religion; they proclaim the universality of salvation; they bear witness to the reality of divine assurance and perfect love; they emphasize the significance of the sacraments of the Church.[22] Although it is probably true that many of these—it is said that in all Charles composed more than six thousand hymns—have long since become invested with a certain unreality, due partly to their strange allegorism and undue subjectivity, the fact still remains that 'the very genius of the Evangelical Revival is in their burning lines'.[23] To this rich inheritance of song from the soul of Charles must be added the stately translations from the German hymns done by John Wesley.

Wesley's determination that for him the world was his parish not only explains much of his success, but was also the ground of antagonism against him. Throughout England religion was parochial in pattern. At first the Wesleys proclaimed their gospel from Anglican pulpits, where the goodwill of the incumbents could be obtained. But there was sometimes the implication that the ordinary preaching from the pulpit was inadequate. The new declaration in terms of personal appeal differed from the read discourse. Further, those flocking to hear were beyond the capacity of the buildings, and the more decorous churchgoers became scandalized. All this steadily mounted to a bitterness which resulted in the churches being closed against the preachers. George Whitefield—an Oxford friend of the young Wesleys—had already achieved great results by open-air preaching, as early as February 1739, and it was he who reconciled Wesley to this hitherto untried way.

Arising inevitably out of the success of his labours, Wesley was faced with the problem of organization, and for the purpose he had unique genius, which resulted in some measure of autocratic rule. This was bound up with his convictions as to conformity to the Anglican Church he so dearly loved. So emerged

[21] *New History of Methodism*, I.242.

[22] J. E. Rattenbury, *The Evangelical Doctrines of Charles Wesley's Hymns* (1949), *The Eucharistic Hymns of John and Charles Wesley* (1948); H. Bett, *The Hymns of Methodism* (1945); B. L. Manning, *The Hymns of Wesley and Watts* (1942).

[23] Bett, op. cit. p. 169.

the Methodist Societies, with their inner companies of 'bands' and 'classes', the leader of each exercising pastoral care over his small group; 'watch-night services' and 'covenant services' developed. But there were larger developments. The growing requirements necessitated ultimately an order of 'helpers' and 'local preachers'; it became essential that some of the former should become 'itinerants'. So the 'circuit system' emerged. The exclusion from parish churches necessitated the erection of new buildings and this process went on rapidly. In 1744 the first 'Methodist Conference' met to arrange for the preachers' 'stations' and for the general conduct of affairs. 'In five years all characteristic features of Methodism had been developed.' Throughout his lifetime Wesley held supreme control. He possessed a rare skill in moulding into institutions the religious enthusiasm which could easily have faded away. In the words of Dr Workman:

> Nothing is more remarkable than the fact that such a man was driven into irregularity in spite of himself. But his very irregularities were a proof both of his administrative genius and of the intensity of his convictions. . . . He was less concerned with the means provided he deemed them righteous, than with the end. . . . He subordinated everything, training, instincts, prejudices, to the accomplishment of his great object, or rather to the fulfilment of his imperative call. . . . With him the supreme need was the interests of the Kingdom of God: all else, however dear or desirable in itself, became secondary.[24]

III

It is here that the relationship between Wesley and the Church of England becomes an important issue, which needs close examination.

There is ample evidence in Wesley's own affirmations that he had no intention whatsoever of separating from the Church of England. He purposed that his own work and that of his fellow-labourers should be supplementary to the Church he so deeply loved. Yet he was impelled, step by step, and in part due to the opposition he had to face, to develop an organization which sooner or later must become a separate unit, and that in terms of a complete breach with the Church of England. The elements of dissent were contained within his most important decisions. 'The Methodists were the new Puritans, and by the same combination of forces that we saw at work in an earlier age were

[24] *Methodism*, p. 59.

driven to become separatists'.[25] It would appear that at least in the beginnings of the movement Wesley did not realize the full implications.

> Not without cause has he been likened to a rower whose face is set one way, but whose stream and effort alike carry in an opposite direction. In spite of his passionate devotion to the Church of his father, he plunged into acts and deeds which were logically bound to end in the separation he dreaded.[26]

In *The Sunday Services of the Methodists*, which was Wesley's revision of the *Book of Common Prayer*, there are such significant changes that one writer has declared that 'where the suggestions meet the demands made by the Presbyterians in 1661 Wesley follows them, but where they depart from those demands Wesley does not follow them'.[27] Further, in his abridgement of the Thirty-nine Articles, 'the alterations are exactly the kind of changes that would be made by any evangelical Dissenter today if he had to revise the *Book of Common Prayer*'.[28] Again when Wesley describes the Church 'in the proper sense', as 'the congregation of English believers', and defines 'the catholic or universal Church' as 'all the persons in the universe whom God hath so called out of the world', he brings the Methodist societies into line with those earlier Separatists who had affirmed the principle of 'the gathered Church'.

The growing needs of the Methodist societies led Wesley to build up an organization that resembled the Presbyterian rather than the episcopal system,[29] and he certainly approximated to a Presbyterian position as to the ministry when in 1748 he declared his approval of Lord King's *Account of the Primitive Church*, and discovered that bishop and presbyter were essentially of the same order. From that point he came to regard himself as a 'bishop' in the New Testament meaning of the term. To his brother Charles he wrote:

[25] W. B. Selbie, *Nonconformity*, p. 176.

[26] H. B. Workman, op. cit. pp. 60-1.

[27] F. Hunter, 'Sources of Wesley's Revision of the Prayer Book in 1784-8', in *W.H.S. Proceedings*, XXIII.123-4. Cf. Bett, *The Hymns of Methodism*, pp. 67-8.

[28] Bett, ibid. pp. 68-9.

[29] Cf. Wesley's word to Samuel Bradburn: 'As soon as I am dead the Methodists will be a regular Presbyterian Church.' S. Bradburn, *The Question 'Are the Methodists Dissenters?' fairly examined*, p. 15.

I firmly believe I am a scriptural ἐπίσκοπος as much as any man in England or in Europe; for the *uninterrupted succession* I know to be a fable, which no man ever did or can prove.[30]

Yet by a strange inconsistency he adds:

But this does in no wise interfere with my remaining in the Church of England: from which I have no more desire to separate than I had fifty years ago.

It was under this conviction regarding the ministry that we find him ordaining his preachers for the work of the ministry, first for America, then for Scotland, and then for England. He was not prepared to allow his people to be deprived of the sacraments because Anglican bishops were unwilling to ordain his preachers.[31]

Despite his protests—and still more strongly those of his brother Charles—as to his unwillingness to leave the Anglican Church, the Methodists were being built into an organization with its own special features, and 'principles of Church government that were nearer to Edinburgh than Canterbury'.

Whilst it must be admitted that Wesley and his followers suffered some measure of clerical opposition to their labours, it is sometimes assumed that the advance of Methodism was frustrated and hindered by episcopal action. Speaking generally this was not so. In a letter dated 8th September 1785 Charles Wesley wrote to his brother:

I do not understand what obedience to the Bishops you dread. They have let us alone, and left us to act just as we pleased, for these fifty years. At present some of them are quite friendly towards us, particularly towards you.[32]

The simple fact is that the bishops themselves were faced with a really difficult problem so far as ordination of Methodist preachers was concerned. The situation has been clearly stated in recent words:

The Church had a surfeit, not a shortage, of ministers, and the number of candidates admitted to Holy Orders was in excess of the benefices

[30] *Letters*, VII.284, 19th August 1785.

[31] The whole question of Wesley's ordinations has been recently examined in E. W. Thompson's *Wesley: Apostolic Man* (1957), in which it is argued that Wesley acted in *conscious* opposition to the regulations of the Church of England, convinced that he was under a divine vocation, and that his divine mission justified his action. On the subject of separation from the Church, see A. W. Harrison, *The Separation of Methodism from the Church of England* (1945).

[32] T. Jackson, *Life of Charles Wesley* (1841), II.396.

and curacies open for their possession in the unreformed Hanoverian Church. Few individual bishops could contemplate the ordination of the growing *corpus* of Methodist lay preachers. Nor could they conceive the innovation of creating new orders of lay evangelists, working in co-operation with and 'supplying the deficiencies of the parochial clergy'.[33]

The real position was that the bishops had taken no steps 'to establish a corporate policy'. In the later words of Newman:

> The English Church of that day ... saw that there was excellence in the Methodistic system; it saw that there was evil; it saw there was strength, it saw there was weakness; it praised the good, it censured the faulty; it feared its strength, it ridiculed its weakness: and that was all. It had no one, clear, consistent *view* of Methodism as a phenomenon; it did not take it as a whole—it did not meet it; it gave out no authoritative judgement on it; it formed no definition of it. It had no line of policy towards it; it could speak but negatively, as going *too far*; or vaguely, as wanting in *discretion* and *temper*. Whereas it, on the contrary, defective as it was, was a living acting thing, which spoke and did, and made progress amid the scattered, unconnected and inconsistent notions of religion which feebly resisted it.[34]

It was in 1787 that Wesley licensed his chapels and preachers under the Toleration Act, so as to avoid the penalties of the Conventicle Act. Thus the Methodists became Dissenters in the legal sense.[35]

Wesley came to realize that ultimately separation was inevitable.

> Such a separation I have always declared against: and certainly it will not take place (if it ever does) while I live. But a kind of separation has already taken place, and will inevitably spread, though by slow degrees.[36]

That the complete breach did come is a fact of history, though for a long time many Methodists of the older school of thought were

[33] N. Sykes and E. G. Rupp in *Conversations between the Church of England and the Methodist Church: An Interim Statement* (1958), p. 11.

[34] J. H. Newman, *Essays, Critical and Historical*, pp. 404-5. This passage was written by Newman whilst he was still an Anglican, and the occasion was a review of a life of Selina, Countess of Huntingdon, published in the *British Critic* (1840). For the source of this I am indebted to Monsignor H. Francis Davis of Birmingham University.

[35] This legal protection did not always prove effective because, as some Methodists attended parish church services, some justices refused to regard them as Dissenters; this injustice, in two instances, produced a complaint from Wesley, in letters to William Wilberforce, July 1790. *Letters*, VIII.231.

[36] *Works*, XIII.230.

unwilling to recognize it, and to place the Methodist Church as unquestionably one of the Free Churches of England. The situation is well summed up by Dr Rigg:

> Looking at the whole evidence, it appears undeniable that . . . Wesley not only pointed but paved the way to all that since has been done, and that the utmost divergence at this day is but the prolongation of a line the beginning of which was traced by Wesley's own hand. . . . Wesley himself led his people into the course which they have since consistently pursued. It is at the same time no less undeniable that separation was the necessary result of Wesley's work, because the Church of England failed to make any provision . . . for the incorporation of Methodism within its own system.[37]

At the time of Wesley's death there were some sixty thousand members in the Methodist societies.

IV

George Whitefield (1714-70)[38] was brought into touch with the Wesleys in the Holy Club in Oxford, and in 1736 preached his first sermon in Moorfields, in London. Though only twenty-two his success was immediate and extraordinary. After a year in Georgia he returned to London, soon to find the doors of the churches closed to him. He then took the bold step the impact of which on the future of the Revival cannot be exaggerated. It was on 17th February 1739 that Whitefield preached out of doors on Kingswood Hill, near Bristol, to some two hundred colliers. Within days the congregation had grown into thousands. This new venture aroused bitter opposition and within a year some fifty pamphlets were published against him. As we have seen, it was Whitefield's call to Wesley and the latter's response that began the field-preaching of Methodism. Whitefield raised his voice in proclamation of the gospel in England; and in Wales, as a helper of Howell Harris, the great apostle of the religious revival there;[39] and in America, crossing the Atlantic no less than

[37] *The Churchmanship of John Wesley*, p. 109.

[38] R. Philip, *The Life and Times of the Rev. George Whitefield* (1838); L. Tyerman, *The Life of the Rev. George Whitefield* (1876); A. D. Belden, *George Whitefield, The Awakener* (1930). An excellent and complete edition of Whitefield's *Journals* has recently (1961) been published by the Banner of Truth Trust.

[39] Clark, *History of English Nonconformity*, II.235: 'In Wales he left upon the reviving religion of his times so strong an impress that "Calvinistic Methodism" became one of the Principality's most prominent varieties of religious life.'

thirteen times. Sir James Stephen has estimated Whitefield's work:

> If ever philanthropy burned in the human heart with a pure and intense flame embracing the whole family of man in the spirit of universal charity, it was in the heart of George Whitefield. He loved the world that hated him. He had no preferences but in favour of the ignorant, the miserable, the poor. In their cause he shrank from no privation, and declined neither insult nor hostility.[40]

After thirty restless years he died in America on 30th September 1770. His funeral sermon was preached by John Wesley, at Tottenham Court Road Chapel, the visible symbol of his preaching power.

The position of Whitefield was very different from that of Wesley. The latter was an Arminian in theology; the former—probably influenced by Jonathan Edwards, the Calvinist leader of revival in America. This fact secured for Whitefield some theological sympathy with Dissenters, who in some places opened their meeting-houses to him when the use of the Anglican pulpits was denied to him. Scornful of convention he followed his own line quite fearlessly. The theological differences between Wesley and Whitefield were basic, and soon led to divisions within the Methodist camp. Controversy between the two leaders developed, but without serious rancour; yet each went his own way.

Two 'Tabernacles'—in Moorfields and Tottenham Court Road—were erected in London as preaching centres whenever Whitefield was in England, and these he invested with Nonconformist status when he procured licences for them under the Toleration Act. The friendliness between Whitefield and the Dissenters made it easier for his converts to find spiritual home in the already existing Dissenting chapels.

In England, a number of churches somewhat loosely connected, indirectly owed their origin to Whitefield. The title by which they became known was that of 'The Countess of Huntingdon's Connexion'. The bond that held them together was the common acceptance of Anglican doctrines interpreted in an evangelical spirit, and also the common use of the Anglican prayers. It was under the direction of Selina, Countess of Huntingdon,[41] that

[40] *Essays in Ecclesiastical Biography* (1860), p. 387.

[41] Anon., *The Life and Times of Selina, Countess of Huntingdon*, 2 vols (1890). Dr A. Victor Murray, President Emeritus of Cheshunt College, Cambridge, has a new '*Life*' in preparation.

they were created into a unity. At first they were set up as within the Church of England, and the Countess herself had no intention of separation therefrom, but a legal decision compelled their recognition in 1781 under the Toleration Act, as dissenting chapels. 'So I am to be cast out of the Church now, only for what I have been doing for these forty years in speaking and living for Jesus Christ.'[42] Upon the Methodist movement she looked favourably from the beginning, and both Wesley and Whitefield were her intimate friends, but being Calvinist in her theology she was particularly drawn to the latter, to whose appeal for support in the work of evangelizing she gave ready response, both by her influence and her wealth. For the future ministry of her 'Connexion' she established a Training College at Trevecca,[43] later removing to Cheshunt, in Hertfordshire, and now transferred to Cambridge. That men went forth from it without episcopal ordination did not suggest to her a breach with the Church she loved. The story of the Connexion in this respect runs parallel to that of the Methodist movement under Wesley, though the Countess saw more swiftly than did Wesley that separation would be involved. Many of her congregations established by Whitefield became Congregationalist though the process is somewhat imperceptible.[44]

V

It is important to make some estimate of the impact of the Methodist movement, which exerted an influence far beyond the eighteenth century. In his excellent book, *The Spirit of Methodism*,[45] Dr Henry Bett suggests a fourfold contribution of which the following is but a brief summary. First, the *religious* contribution. In matters now taken for granted, but not recognized in 1738, when in almost every sense religion was counted deplorable, Methodism expounded the meaning of 'conversion'. Therefore it proclaimed the significance of personal religious experience, as something deeper than external religion that was often little more

[42] Anon., *The Life and Times of Selina, Countess of Huntingdon*, 2 vols (1890). II.315.

[43] Fletcher of Madeley was appointed its first President, but his Arminian views compelled him to resign.

[44] Whitefield had registered his chapels as 'places of worship for nonconformist congregations calling themselves Independent'.

[45] This study is perhaps the best exposition of the whole ethos of the Methodist movement.

than 'a sort of moral Deism'. Methodism declared the evangel of divine forgiveness bringing peace to the soul.

The religious contribution of Methodism was therefore the recovery of the evangelical witness and the evangelical experience—the spiritual fact that real penitence, real faith, a real surrender of the heart and life to Christ brings an assurance of the pardon and peace of God from which a sense of wonder and joy naturally spring, and which leads directly to an intimacy of religious fellowship, and a zeal of passionate evangelism.[46]

Secondly, the *theological* contribution. Methodism brought 'a revolution in theological practice'. It 'shifted the ultimate authority in religion to the last place and the right place—to religious experience'. Theologically it stood for 'the witness of the Spirit'—'in the appeal to experience as against dogma'. In so doing Methodism 'carried forward the work of the Reformers to its legitimate and logical conclusion'. Further 'Methodism made an end of Calvinism for all practical purposes'. It declared a gospel of free grace with 'undistinguishing regard' for a 'world' Christ suffered to redeem.[47] In addition Methodism gave a new emphasis to the concept of holiness: 'Holiness means loving God and loving men'; not mere sinlessness, but every part of life a sacrifice unto God.

Thirdly, a *literary* contribution. In the hymns of the Wesleys there is 'the noblest body of devotional verse in the English language . . . entirely different in style as well as in substance from the poetry of the period', and thus anticipating the Lyrical Revival by some fifty years. The prose writings of John Wesley were unique in their 'simple, vigorous and idiomatic English'. It was Augustine Birrell who spoke enthusiastically of Wesley's *Journal* as 'the most amazing record of human exertion ever penned or endured'.

Fourthly, there is the *social* contribution. Some of the titles of Wesley's tracts indicate its extent: *Thoughts upon Liberty* (1772); *Thoughts concerning the Origin of Power* (1772); *Thoughts upon the present scarcity of Provisions* (1773); a series of brief pamphlets entitled: *A Word to a Smuggler; A Word to a Swearer; A Word to an Unhappy Woman; a Word to a Drunkard*—all for popular distribution. Prison

[46] *The Spirit of Methodism*, pp. 100-28.

[47] Ibid. pp. 153-5. Dr Bett italicizes words in the hymn, 'Father whose everlasting love' (*M.H.B.* No. 75.) indicating this universal emphasis of the Gospel.

reform, the abolition of slavery, Christian education, charity schools, orphan children were all deep concerns for Wesley.[48] 'Methodism gave to multitudes of ordinary Englishmen a degree of culture that they would certainly have never acquired apart from it.'

VI

It remains to indicate the impact of this impulse of spiritual revival in the eighteenth century. It has been stated that the Dissenters, in comparison with the Church of England at the beginning of the century were as one to twenty-two; at the end the proportion was one to eight. Probably these figures are not correct, but there is no doubt as to the great increase in the strength of Nonconformity between 1700 and 1800. If the figure for 1800 is only approximately correct, it still does not include the Methodists as they did not regard themselves as Nonconformists. The number of Dissenting congregations also naturally increased.[49]

The influence of the Revival reached Dissent both directly and by the raising of the temperature of the whole of religious life in the country. The more direct influence came through the preaching of Whitefield, the Wesleys and their helpers, but it should be remembered that there were movements of the Spirit independent of these, examples of which may be seen in the evangelical ministries of Risdon Dorracott, in Somerset, between 1741 and 1759; of the Baptist pastor Benjamin Beddomes, at Bourton-on-the-Water, for some fifty years from 1740 to 1795. The solvent forces at work in the spiritual experience of Robert Hall, Senr (1728-91), and Andrew Fuller (1754-1815), in the latter case leading up to his work, *The Gospel Worthy of All Anticipation* (1785) were spontaneous in their origin, and welcomed 'after the winter of hyper-Calvinism'.

Nevertheless the Methodist movement had a distinct influence upon the Dissenters. At first there was an aloofness arising out of mutual suspicion. Despite his Nonconformist ancestry, Wesley had a distinct dislike for Dissent and was particularly out of favour with the Baptists and Quakers. With few exceptions the majority of Dissenting ministers were strict Calvinists and viewed

[48] It is true that some of the Methodist leaders of the early nineteenth century stood aloof from social movements, e.g. Chartism, but the disturbances and secessions in the later period did much to correct the balance. See *infra*, p. 146.

[49] Dale records that in 1772 the congregations in England belonging to the 'Three Denominations' numbered 1,092; fifty years later they numbered 1,583 (p. 580).

him with disfavour because he was an Arminian. Politically he was a Tory whereas most of the Dissenters were Whigs or Radicals. The situation was different in regard to Whitefield because of his Calvinist position.

For some time the Congregationalists regarded the new movement with distrust. When Philip Doddridge took part in Whitefield's meetings he was severely criticized by his brethren, though he remained impenitent. Steadily, however, suspicion cleared away as churches began to catch the flame.

Their ministers were beginning to preach with a new fervour . . . the religious life of their people was becoming more intense. A passion for evangelistic work was taking possession of church after church, and by the end of the century the old meeting-houses were crowded; many of them had to be enlarged, and new meeting-houses were being erected in town after town and village after village in every part of the kingdom.[50]

Many congregations founded by Whitefield, though distinguished for a time as 'Calvinistic Methodist', gradually became Congregational churches though the process was often imperceptible.[51] It should also be observed that Congregationalists were strengthened by secessions from Anglicanism. The change of churchmanship in a parish formerly under an evangelical incumbent might cause many to leave the parish church and become Congregationalist. In the case of Henry Venn, of Huddersfield, and that of Samuel Walker, of Truro, their removal led to the formation of a strong Independent Church by their former hearers. Contact with the Revival brought modification of both doctrine and polity; there was a change in the character of Congregationalist preaching, the creation of new forms of service, and new religious activity. Thus in 1776 a society was formed in London called the *Societas Evangelia* for the purpose of 'extending the Gospel in Great Britain by itinerant preaching', and in 1778 it established an academy for training evangelists.[52]

Of the two groups of Baptists, the Particular Baptists were the slowest to yield to the impact of the revival, partly because of the strictness of their views as to 'closed communion', and partly because of their strong Calvinist theology. But renewal was most marked in the group known as the General Baptists. About 1741,

[50] Dale, p. 585. [51] Ibid. pp. 587-92. [52] Ibid. p. 593.

in Leicestershire, David Taylor, a servant in the household of the Countess of Huntingdon began to preach, and one of his converts was Samuel Deacon (1714-1812), a wool-comber; societies were formed in the villages around after the Methodist pattern. In Yorkshire, Dan Taylor, the son of a Yorkshire miner was drawn to the Methodists by the Wesleys and Whitefield, and sometime listened to the preaching of William Grimshaw, of Haworth. Later, embracing Baptist conviction, he came into touch with the evangelical movement in Leicestershire. In 1770 a new body of General Baptists was formed—the 'New Connexion' of General Baptists declaring that their design was 'to revive experimental religion or primitive Christianity in faith and practice'. This new body was 'a child of the Methodist revival, and manifested two Methodist characteristics; strong evangelical zeal and strong corporate piety'.[53]

Although it falls beyond the scope of our present study, we may note that the influence of the Revival on Nonconformity was more marked in Wales than in England. As we have seen the chief figure was Howell Harris (1714-73), but with him were Daniel Rowland (1730-90), and William Williams (1717-91) of Pantycelyn; very swiftly under their preaching the movement spread. Encouraged by Whitefield, the movement in Wales, however, was parallel to, rather than the result of, the revival in England. The new impulse penetrated Independent and Baptist congregations.[54]

Further illustration of this new spiritual influence upon Nonconformity is seen in the rise of fresh foundations for ministerial training, partly because the increase in the number of churches required it, and partly because some of the older institutions had come to manifest Socinian tendencies. The majority of these new academies were Congregational, but at Newport Pagnell there was a representation of both Anglican and Dissent in both management and students, John Newton, the evangelical clergyman of Olney, being its founder, and William Bull, a Congregational minister, its first head. The first Baptist academy, created probably in 1690, was now enlarged.

Through this revival a new philanthropic spirit emerged in

[53] Underwood, *History of the English Baptists*, pp. 151-9.

[54] T. Rees, *History of Protestant Nonconformity in Wales* (1853), Ch. 5; G. T. Roberts, *Howell Harris* (1951).

Nonconformity as seen in the spread of Sunday-schools, the work of prison investigation under John Howard who began his work in 1773, and the emergence of the missionary impulse as seen in the conviction of William Carey, Baptist pastor at Moulton, Northamptonshire, in 1787.

VII

There were, however, two Dissenting groups—the Presbyterians and the Quakers—which remained largely untouched by the revival movement, though it cannot be denied that each had an important contribution to make during this period.

The Presbyterians call for first mention. As we have already seen it was over the question of ministerial subscription that the English Presbyterians began to become more fragmentary. Arian and Socinian[55] ideas were charged upon those who refused to subscribe. It should be noted again that this tendency was found within the Church of England as well as amongst the Dissenters. Those Presbyterians who cherished the older faith tended to pass over into Congregationalism; those who remained and who were advocates of the new school of critical enquiry were fortunate in having a number of very able men who could present the doctrinal issue with clarity and vigour, though it still is true that some congregations suffered decline under the stress of withdrawals. In the Presbyterianism of this period there were the names of Richard Price (1723-91), Joseph Priestley (1733-1804), Samuel Chandler (1693-1766), Andrew Kippis (1763-84), George Walker (1734(?)-1807)—all of whom were Fellows of the Royal Society—and John Taylor (1694-1761),[56] bearers of distinction in theology, literature, and science. An Anglican vicar, the Rev. Theophilus Lindsey (1723-1808), after the failure of a petition to Parliament for the relaxation of terms of subscription, resigned his living in 1773, and the following year, in London, opened a Unitarian chapel, and thus 'first organized Unitarian Dissent as a working force in the religious life of England'. In 1791 together with Thomas Belsham (1750-1829) Priestley and Lindsey founded 'The Unitarian Society for Promoting Christian Knowledge and

[55] E. A. Payne, *The Free Church Tradition in England*, p. 83: 'As these labels have often been wildly and abusively used, it is perhaps better to speak of the increasing tendency to question the principle of subscription to the ancient creeds and formulas, and to study both the New Testament and the history and doctrines of the Church from a critical standpoint.'

[56] For details of these, see *D.N.B.*, in loc.

the Practice of Virtue by the Distribution of Books'. The Rules contained the first public profession of belief in the proper unity of God, and in the simple humanity of Jesus in opposition both to trinitarian doctrine and the ancient Arian formula. It is not surprising that they stressed the importance of the education of the ministry, and at least a dozen academies contributed students of the more liberal view. These 'Rational Dissenters', to whom we owe much on the intellectual side in terms of the spirit of fearless enquiry into divine truth, remained unaffected by the revival.[57]

The contacts between the Revival and the Quakers were but few. Although Whitefield received kindness from individual Friends and Wesley had esteem for such, there is no evidence that, taken as a whole the Quakers were deflected from their normal course. The emotional excitement sometimes associated with the new uprising would hardly commend itself to those whose principle was to follow 'the Inner Light'. Further, the recent development of 'organization' within the Quaker movement had brought some measure of uncertainty, and indeed decline in the movement, and this was the problem with which the Quakers were preoccupied in this period. Yet towards the end of the century an evangelical tendency developed and 'the formative leaders . . . who pointed the line of march in this general direction were for the most part born in other folds and nurtured outside the Quaker atmosphere'. Such an example is Stephen Grellett (1773-1855).[58]

In one matter the Quakers made distinctive witness, namely, concerning the problem of slavery. As early as 1743 John Woolman (1720-72) had begun his protests in America. A few years later the London Quakers publicly exposed the evils of the system, and in 1774 it was declared that any Friend having dealings with the slave trade should be expelled. In 1781 the Quakers presented a petition to Parliament, and in 1783 formed a small group to organize public opinion; this group became the nucleus of the later opposition associated with Granville Sharpe, Thomas Clarkson, and William Wilberforce. It was to the latter that Wesley wrote on 24th February 1791:[59]

[57] For further study, see Drysdale, pp. 519-42; E. Wilbur, *A History of Unitarianism* (1952); J. H. Colligan, *The Arian Movement in England* (1913).

[58] F. Baker, 'Methodism and the Society of Friends', *London Quarterly and Holborn Review*, XVII-XVIII (1948-9); R. M. Jones, *The Later Periods of Quakerism*. I.284ff.

[59] *Letters*, VIII.264.

Unless the divine power has raised you up to be as *Athanasius contra mundum*, I see not how you can go through your glorious enterprise in opposing that execrable villany, which is the scandal of religion, of England, and of human nature. Unless God has raised you up for this very thing, you will be worn out by the opposition of men and devils. But if God be for you who can be against you? Are all of them together stronger than God? O be not weary of well doing! Go on, in the name of God, and in the power of his might till even American slavery (the vilest that ever saw the sun) shall vanish away before it. . . . That He who has guided you from youth up may continue to strengthen you in this and all things is the prayer of, dear sir,

Your affectionate servant,

JOHN WESLEY.

There was growing Nonconformist support for the movement for abolition, but the Quakers were the pioneers of the struggle for emancipation.

CHAPTER NINE

THE NINETEENTH CENTURY: THE ERA OF EXPANSION

As we have seen, a declining Nonconformity in the eighteenth century was revitalized before that century closed by the influence of the Methodist movement as part of the Evangelical Revival, thus preparing for the renewed advance which came in the nineteenth century. All this was upon the background of far-reaching changes. The Industrial Revolution had brought vast social and economic upheaval; the American Revolution in the last quarter of the eighteenth century had altered the whole situation across the Atlantic, bringing new concepts of liberty; the French Revolution had raised the cry of Liberty, Equality and Fraternity, bringing expectancy and uncertainty in Britain, though followed by the reactionary terrors and the ensuing Napoleonic struggle. After 1815 there was a period of exhaustion and poverty.

This general situation was one factor in the delay for Nonconformist advance; yet some political leaders were being compelled to give attention to the claims of religious liberty. Whilst Burke stood steadfastly against any legislation that might be more liberal in this direction, Fox firmly upheld the liberal cause. Pitt leaned in the direction of a more liberal approach, but was cautious and restrained.

I

The struggle for the recognition of Nonconformity falls into two stages. The first consisted of various attempts to repeal the disabling legislation; the second was marked by a movement towards securing equality with the Established Church.

Towards the end of the eighteenth century three attempts were made to lift the burden of the Test and Corporation Acts. In March 1787 a Bill was introduced following a seemly favourable interview with Fox and Pitt. But strong opposition secured its defeat. Lord North spoke of these Acts as 'the great bulwark of the constitution'; Archbishop Moore had declared that the majority of the bishops were agreed that the Acts should be retained. In 1788 followed a similar defeat, though by a smaller majority. In 1790 Fox appeared as champion of the Nonconformist cause, but again without success. Some asserted that the Dissenters had too strongly favoured the French Revolution.

After these three defeats there was a temporary suspension until 1812. By this time the political panic concerning the French situation had subsided, but in popular opinion there was still hostility, and the cause of liberty for Nonconformists was still suspect.

In 1789 Lord Stanhope had failed in his attempt to secure the repeal of the Acts punishing people for non-attendance at Church, and in 1792 Fox proposed a removal of the Acts which made denial of the Trinity a penal offence, though in fact these were in practice obsolete. That they should no longer, however, have even nominal legal sanction indicates a liberalizing tendency.

Yet in many parts of the country there was hostility. Magistrates, believing Dissenters to be disloyal, revived the Conventicle Act and people were fined for attending meetings; some suffered damage to property and were boycotted. The Quakers made renewed attempts to have distraint for tithe recognized as an adequate penalty when voluntary payment was refused so that imprisonment should not be superimposed in addition, but these were rejected. All this resurgence tended to stimulate the power of Nonconformist resistance ready to seize an opportunity. 'Nonconformity had its hand upon the sword . . . it was refraining from the actual stroke.'

It was when Lord Sidmouth in 1811 put forward a Bill, the effect of which would have been to reduce the number of licences under the Toleration Act, that the opportunity arose. The Bill suggested that before a licence could be procured the minister of a settled congregation must produce a testimony from six householders belonging to the Church: the same requirement was demanded from those whose ministry was itinerant and at once this created a problem. The aim was to strike a blow at the rapidly advancing Methodism.[1] He declared that he purposed to save Dissenters from themselves—from preachers who were 'cobblers, tailors, pig-drivers, and chimney-sweepers', who were claiming certificates. Nonconformity was roused throughout the country; multitudes of petitions following meetings of the 'Three

[1] Maldwyn Edwards, *After Wesley* (1935), pp. 75-82.

Denominations', the Dissenting Deputies, and the Methodists, reached the Government, and the measure was dropped. Now came a Nonconformist offensive. After the defeat of Sidmouth's Bill the 'Protestant Society for the Protection of Religious Liberty' was formed, and with the Dissenting Deputies it entered upon further challenge by campaigning for the repeal of the Five Mile and Conventicle Acts. By 1812 a parliamentary proposal under Lord Castlereagh for a repeal of these Acts became law virtually without opposition.[2] It became known as 'the New Toleration Act'. Quakers were no longer required to take the oaths; the number of persons who might meet in an unregistered building was increased from five to twenty; oaths under the Toleration Act were only necessary if demanded in writing by a magistrate; any outside disturbance of Nonconformist worship incurred penalty of a fine.

In the following year, 1813, the Acts against Unitarians were similarly set aside.[3] It may also be noted that 1813 saw a small advance as to the Catholic relief, English Catholics being put on a level with Irish, as to holding of civil and military office.

All these incidents reveal the fact that Nonconformity was not merely on the defensive but on the attack.

Further battles lay ahead. In 1828, under the proposal of Lord John Russell, a Bill was read for the repeal of the Test and Corporation Acts, with their serious disabilities for all non-Anglicans. With a majority of forty-four on its first division, opposition was dropped; the new Archbishop Howley, just enthroned, together with other bishops, declared that the tests must go, and the Bill received royal assent on 9th May 1828.[4]

Thus within thirty years of the beginning of the century all the *direct* disabilities of Nonconformists were abolished;[5] but indirect penalties remained. The repeal of these Acts was due partly to the general spirit of secular toleration, which arose out of the revolution in the closing years of the previous century, and also to the increase of the intrinsic power of Nonconformity itself together with the growing respect in which Nonconformists were held, and a recognition of their value to the social and political order.

[2] 52 Geo. III, c. 155; Dale, pp. 576-7.

[3] 53 Geo. III, c. 40. See R. M. Montgomery, 'A Note on Acts of Parliament dealing with the Denial of the Trinity,' *T.U.H.S.*

[4] 9 Geo. IV, c. 17; Robertson, pp. 184-7.

[5] In the next year, 1829, Roman Catholic emancipation was also achieved—not least with a view to avoid civil war in Ireland.

The second stage of the struggle was for the removal of the lesser, but not insignicant, disabilities from which Nonconformists still suffered, for these laws and regulations remained which were framed on the assumption that the Church of England was the only Church of the realm. It was fundamentally a struggle for equality of privilege.

Before 1836, as civil registration did not exist, Nonconformists could not have the registration of births unless they applied to the parish incumbent for 'christening'; similarly Nonconformist marriages were only legally valid if performed in the parish church.[6] Two Acts passed in 1836 removed these grievances.[7] It was not until 1852 that the process of reforming the Burial Laws began with an Act[8] dividing public cemeteries into consecrated and unconsecrated portions; in the latter the Nonconformists could conduct funeral services with their own rites. Prior to this the only public burial places in England were the graveyards of the parish churches under the control of the incumbents. By the Burial Law Amendment Act of 1880,[9] Nonconformist ministers were able to officiate either in churchyards or the consecrated portions of public cemeteries.

A further Nonconformist inequality related to Church rates. Ordinary justice seemed to demand release of Dissenters from the obligation of maintaining ecclesiastical buildings which they did not use, but it was to be forty years before release was secured, the first effort being made in 1834. The failure of this attempt brought into being a Church Rate Abolition Society in 1836, and some two thousand petitions were presented to the Government. A law-suit on the question of the right of Church-wardens to levy a Church-rate lasted some twelve years, and in 1853, though attempts at Bills for abolition failed, a feeling that a change was reasonable developed. The long battle ended in 1868 when Gladstone introduced a compromise which allowed the power to levy a Church-rate, but without legal machinery to compel payment.[10]

The attempt to open the national universities to Nonconformists

[6] This had been the position since Lord Hardwicke's Marriage Act of 1753 (26 Geo. II, c. 33); Robertson, pp. 135-9. This Act was not directed against Nonconformists, but was for the purpose of preventing clandestine marriages conducted by unsatisfactory clergymen—e.g. in Fleet Street Prison. The Act allowed marriage only in the parish church after the publication of banns.

[7] 6 & 7 William IV, c. 85, 86.

[8] 34 & 35 Vic., c. 26.

[9] 43 & 44 Vic., c. 41.

[10] 31 & 32 Vic., c. 109.

was for a long time unsuccessful. From Oxford, since 1581, Dissenters had been wholly excluded; subscription was required of every student upon matriculation. At Cambridge, Dissenters were allowed to matriculate, but since 1616 had been prevented from taking degrees. Such exclusion bore heavily upon Nonconformists seeking qualification in law and medicine. In 1834, petitions—one signed by sixty-three members of the Cambridge University Senate—seeking relaxation of statutes and admission of Dissenters to degrees in Arts, Law and Medicine formed the basis of a Bill which passed the Commons but was defeated in the Lords. In 1854 the Arts degree was made open at Oxford; similarly at Cambridge in 1856, and in this university extension to the M.A. degree. By the Act of 1871,[11] Oxford, Cambridge and Durham opened their doors to Dissenters for all degrees except in Divinity,[12] and Fellowships, College headships and Professorships remained closed. It should be noted that in the universities there was a progressive section which, in the interest of education, desired that all restrictions of a religious nature should be removed. It should also be remembered that a new opportunity for university education for Nonconformists was provided by the establishment of the University of London in 1836, in the framing of which Nonconformists had no small influence; in this new university, degrees were open without credal restrictions of any kind.

The most severe struggle was in regard to education—a battle that was waged 'almost without an armistice' from 1820 to 1902. Early in the century divergence between Anglican and Nonconformist ideals of education became emphasized. Andrew Bell (1753-1832), an Anglican clergyman, developed the 'monitorial' system whereby older boys instructed the younger in the school,[13] Anglican doctrine being part of the course. Joseph Lancaster (1778-1838), a Quaker, about the same time adopted a similar method and taught 'undenominational' religious instruction.[14] Both schools appealed to the public for financial support. In 1808 those schools following Lancaster's pattern were formed into the Royal Lancastrian Society, six years later becoming the 'British and Foreign Society'. Those under the aegis of Bell were

[11] 34 & 35 Vic., c. 26.
[12] Degrees in Divinity were not open to Nonconformists until 1918.
[13] *An Experiment in Education . . . in Madras* (1797).
[14] *Improvements in Education*, 1803.

organized in 1811 as 'The National Society for Promoting the Education of the Poor in the Principles of the Established Church'. By the middle of the century almost every village had its 'British' or 'National' School.

Founded upon the idea that as the Church of England was the national Church, and that therefore education must be under Anglican control, in 1820 Lord Brougham introduced a Bill which was a direct attack on Nonconformity. All schoolmasters must be Anglican communicants, and appointed by the parish incumbent, assisted by two or three parishioners. The pupils were to attend the parish church, though Nonconformist children were allowed to go with their parents to chapel. Religious instruction was to consist of Bible-reading. The Bill did not proceed beyond its second reading, and it was now clear that education must be regarded as a national issue. Later, in 1833 it was decided to allocate £20,000 from the Exchequer to be divided between 'British' and 'National' Schools proportionate to their income from public support: this meant an advantage for the National Society because it was supported by the more wealthy. In 1840 an additional £10,000 was administered for founding a college for training of teachers, the teaching to be on an interdenominational basis, much to the criticism of the more vigorous Anglicans. In 1844 Sir James Graham introduced in his Factory Bill a clause providing compulsory education for all children in manufacturing districts and such schools were to be financed by poor-rates, grants, and public subscriptions; the parish incumbent was to have all under his authority as to appointments and instructions. But the Bill was withdrawn. By 1850 the two school societies continued to do their best, but the 'National' type increased in members and endowments. Unfortunately many Nonconformists held to the opinion that education was a governmental responsibility, yet it was not its business to teach religion—a position which logically could mean exclusion of the instruction of the Christian faith from all schools. By 1870 the Nonconformists had lost their way. It was in that year that the Government passed Forster's Education Act,[15] the main provisions of which were the establishment of School Boards in districts where educational facilities were inadequate, and, on the religious side, the giving of 'undenominational religious instruction'.

[15] 33 & 34 Vic., c. 75.

Under the Cowper-Temple conscience clause, objecting parents could withhold their children, a privilege secured after much conflict.[16] Though the Bill finally proved more acceptable to the Dissenters, yet the more far-seeing realized that withdrawal of children would mean a strengthening of the Anglican content of the 'undenominational' teaching. The situation settled down, not to be disturbed until the Balfour Education Act of 1902, which threw the denominational schools along with the undemoninational upon the rates.[17] To Nonconformists this seemed to be State support for denominational interests in particular terms, despite the fact that the number of Nonconformist communicants now equalled the number of Anglican communicants in the country.

This prolonged controversy in education brought consolidation of the Anglican position and the gulf between 'church' and 'chapel' was widened, and often a spirit of bitterness prevailed.

One positive outcome for Nonconformity was a stimulus to establish its own educational foundations, both schools and training-colleges and also theological colleges.[18]

Under the stress of disabilities it is not altogether surprising that some Nonconformists took a strong stand upon the principle that the State has no authority to direct or legislate for a Christian

[16] It may be remembered that there was a fierce debate between Edward Miall, the Nonconformist protagonist, and W. E. Gladstone, the Prime Minister, the former threatening Gladstone with the withdrawal of Nonconformist support.

[17] The Bill was stoutly opposed by R. W. Dale and Guiness Rogers. A. W. W. Dale, *The Life of R. W. Dale of Birmingham*, Ch. 12.

[18] For the Congregationalists: Caterham, Surrey; Silcoates, Yorkshire; Mill Hill, London. Theological Colleges grew out of earlier dissenting academies, as in the following cases: Hackney and New College, London; Western College, Bristol; Lancashire Independent College, Manchester; Yorkshire United Independent College, Bradford; Paton College, Nottingham; Spring Hill College, Birmingham, removed to Oxford and renamed Mansfield College, in 1886. Baptist theological colleges established or refounded during the nineteenth century were Rawdon, Leeds; Bristol Baptist College; Regent's Park, London (removed to Oxford in 1928); Spurgeon's College, South London; Baptist College, Manchester. Wesleyan Methodists, with Kingswood School, Bath (founded by Wesley in 1748), as an example, established Woodhouse Grove School in Yorkshire in 1812 and the Leys School in Cambridge in 1875, together with teacher-training colleges at Westminster (1851) and Southlands (1872). Theological Colleges were founded: Didsbury, Manchester (1842); Richmond, Surrey (1843); Headingley, Leeds (1868); Handsworth, Birmingham (1881). Primitive Methodist at Hartley College, Manchester (1881); the Methodist New Connexion at Ranmoor, Sheffield (1864); the United Methodist Free Churches, Manchester (1876). The Unitarians had theological colleges in Manchester and in Oxford. Until the establishment of Westminster College (founded in London in 1844 and removed to Cambridge in 1899) the English Presbyterians sent ordinands to Scottish universities. The Quaker schools were very numerous, and an impressive list is recorded in R. M. Jones, *The Later Period of Quakerism* (1921), pp. 706-7.

Church, and therefore they argued for the disestablishment of the Church of England. In 1841 Edward Miall (1809-81) issued the first number of *The Nonconformist*, a journal in which the advocacy of disestablishment was its main aim. It was regarded not so much in terms of injustice to Nonconformists as in terms of a challenge to the true nature of the Church. In 1844 the British Anti-State Church Association was formed, taking in 1853 the title of 'Society for the Liberation of Religion from State Patronage and Control'. It is now commonly referred to as The Liberation Society. R. W. Dale and Miall stood for 'a free church in a free state', whether Anglican or Nonconformist. The conflict was prolonged. In 1869 Gladstone carried disestablishment for the Irish Church but the position of the English Church remained unaltered.

II

During the nineteenth century the increasing number and the advance to greater recognition led to a development of organizations within the Nonconformist groups.

In 1813 'The General Union of Baptist Ministers and Churches' was founded though it did not prove very effective. It was reconstituted in 1831, but the special baptismal doctrine, held with varying degrees of strictness, tended to make for slow development.[19]

In the same year the Congregational Union was formed from District Associations and Churches, but there was hesitancy lest there should be the formation of anything like a hierarchy and lest the principle of Independency and the democratic idea should be challenged. A 'Declaration of Faith and Order' was issued, with a seven-fold objective, though this was in no sense to be regarded as subscription to a creed. It sought 'to promote evangelical religion' and 'to assist in maintaining and enlarging the civil rights of Protestant Dissenters'.[20] For both the Baptists and the Congregationalists the following century widened the field of service.

As we have seen, Methodism had made great advances, so that by 1815 there were nearly three times as many Methodists as at the time of Wesley's death in 1791 and they were widely distributed throughout the country.[21] After Wesley had passed

[19] Underwood, pp. 212ff. [20] Dale, pp. 686-726.
[21] Maldwyn Edwards, *After Wesley* (1935), Appendix I.

from the scene it proved more and more difficult to mould the Methodist movement along lines laid down by its founder, who had left the guiding powers in the hands of an assembly of one hundred preachers—'The Legal Hundred'—which he had named in a 'Deed of Declaration' drawn up in 1784. The laity had no place in this Conference. Although the 'Plan of Pacification', proposed by the Conference in 1795, settled the question of the administration of the sacraments to Methodist congregations, the supremacy of the preacher remained largely untouched, and the powerlessness of the laity largely unremedied. It was under Alexander Kilham (1762-98) that a secession took place in 1797, forming the Methodist New Connexion,[22] in the constitution of which lay representatives on governing bodies were given adequate place. In 1806 the Independent Methodists came into existence and this movement had its origin in a 'cottage-meeting' near Warrington, which refused to dissolve when the circuit authorities decreed in 1796 that such gatherings were not permissible; this new movement grew almost imperceptibly and had Quaker admixture; later Peter Philips (1778-1853) stamped his personality upon the movement, and stressed the view that an official paid ministry was contrary to scripture teaching.[23] The next division within Methodism arose in North Staffordshire out of the refusal of the authorities to allow open-air preaching at 'camp-meetings', the first of which was held in 1810, Hugh Bourne (1772-1852) and William Clowes (1780-1851) being the protagonists in the new enterprise. In 1812 the name 'Primitive Methodists' was given to the new movement,[24] which spread rapidly.[25] The Bible Christians arose in the West Country from similar causes.[26] The spiritual condition of Devon and Cornwall weighed heavily upon the soul of William O'Bryan (1778-1868), who, when an attempt was made to restrain his 'irregular ministry', continued his evangelistic itineraries. October 1815 saw the beginning of the new denomination, the 'master-builder' of which was James Thorne (1795-1872).

During the first fifty years of the nineteenth century the parent

[22] J. Packer, ed., *The Centenary of the Methodist New Connexion* (1897).

[23] J. Vickers, *History of Independent Methodism* (1920).

[24] H. B. Kendall, *A History of the Primitive Methodist Church*, 2 vols (1905); J. T. Wilkinson, *Hugh Bourne, 1772-1852; William Clowes, 1780-1851.*

[25] By the time of its fourth Conference in 1823 the members numbered 29,472.

[26] F. W. Bourne, *The Bible Christians, Their Origin and History, 1815-1900* (1905).

body of Methodism made great strides and had developed a powerful and compact church-consciousness of its strength and independence. The figure of Jabez Bunting (1779-1858) stands out as the virtual ruler of Methodism; but his masterfulness and his failure in later years to realize the changing times resulted in the rise of a spirit of disaffection and a revolt against clerical authority. Between 1846 and 1848 anonymous 'Fly Sheets' were put forth and James Everett (1784-1872)[27] was assumed to be the author. Out of these days of bitter controversy the United Methodist Free Churches arose in 1857.[28] From the parent body over a hundred thousand withdrew to form the separate organization.

These were serious losses but each separation became an expanding unit; whilst the dissension weakened the Methodist structure for the time being it did not destroy the evangelistic zeal of Methodism but in the long run increased it.[29]

In the thirties of this century the Quakers also suffered through internal conflict which resulted in separation. The clash was between two schools of thought, one holding firmly to the inherited Quaker faith concerning the 'Inner Light'; the other asserting 'the testimony of the Spirit of God transmitted in the Scriptures' as the only ground of salvation. Under the leadership of Isaac Crewdson, a separate group styled 'Evangelical Friends' came into existence and eventually numbered some three hundred. During this time of confusion some Friends passed over into the evangelical groups in the Church of England, and some joined other Dissenting bodies. The whole controversy points 'to a low and sluggish spiritual condition' in the Society at this period.

The vigour of Nonconformist life in this century is seen in those creative movements which led to the formation of new organizations. New religious associations included the following. The Churches of the Disciples of Christ[30] (founded in America early in

[27] R. Chew, *James Everett* (1875).

[28] O. A. Beckerlegge, *The United Methodist Free Churches* (1957).

[29] When the United Methodist Church was founded in 1907 by the union of the Methodist New Connexion, the Bible Christians and the United Methodist Free Churches, the membership totalled nearly 150,000. A small group of circuits which held aloof from the formation of the United Methodist Free Churches in 1857 became the Wesleyan Reform Union in 1859 and has still a separate existence. For a useful summary of the separatist movement in Methodism, see B. Gregory, *Sidelights on the Conflicts of Methodism* (1898); C. Davey, *The Methodist Story* (1955).

[30] A. C. Watson, *History of the British Churches of Christ* (1947). For an account of their work for Christian Unity in the present century from 1935 to 1950 see *Towards Christian Union*, ed. J. Gray (1960). For the American development see W. E. Gibson, *Religion follows the Frontier; A History of the Disciples of Christ* (1931).

the century by Thomas Campbell), with a deep concern for Christian unity, planted churches in Britain. In 1827 the Plymouth Brethren[31] came into existence as an attempt to return to primitive Christianity through a literalist biblical interpretation. In the 1820's Edward Irving[32] created a sensation in London by his preaching and by his claim to possess 'the gift of tongues and healing'; cast out by the Presbyterians, he and his friends organized the Catholic Apostolic Church which attracted many wealthy supporters. The Salvation Army,[33] which rapidly became a religious organization of international scope, had its beginnings in 1865 (though this name was not legally endorsed until 1878), and was the pioneer work of William Booth, formerly a minister of the Methodist New Connexion, though previously cut off from membership of the Wesleyan Methodist society as a 'reformer'. In his work he was magnificently aided by his wife, Catherine Booth.

The period also saw the revival of orthodox Presbyterianism in England.[34] In 1844 seventy Presbyterian congregations which had long had their affiliation with Scotland came together informally under the title, 'The Presbyterian Church in England'. In 1876 this became a formal union, 'The Presbyterian Church of England', and began missionary work at home and overseas.

III

The year 1833 is generally regarded as the beginning of the Oxford Movement in England; it was in that year that the first of the famous '*Tracts for the Times*' was issued. Few would now question the fact that by its renewed emphasis upon the doctrine of the Church, its stress upon Catholicism and tradition, and its deep spiritual devotion, it brought a new life into the Anglican Church. Nevertheless the sacerdotal and sacramentarian ideas upon which it was based, together with its insistence upon the necessity of the historic episcopate had given to it a spirit of exclusiveness. The natural result was a wider separation between the Church and Dissent. Nonconformists were regarded as

[31] 'Brethren', *E.R.E.*, II.843ff.

[32] A. L. Drummond, *Edward Irving and his Circle* (1937). 'Edward Irving and the Catholic Apostolic Church', *E.R.E.*, VII.424-8.

[33] 'Salvation Army', *E.R.E.*, XII.18-60; R. Sandall, *History of the Salvation Army*, 3 vols (1947-55).

[34] Drysdale, pp. 625-8. Also S. W. Carruthers, 1844: *A Tale of Faith and Courage* (1944).

schismatics.[35] In its early stages the movement made fierce attacks on evangelicals and appeared to be mainly concerned with the revival of ancient forms and ceremonies which Nonconformists regarded as superstitious, not least because of the challenge to long-cherished Reformation principles. It resulted in a stiffening of the Nonconformist conviction. Nevertheless there were some Nonconformists who perceived the deeper spiritual significance of the Oxford Movement.[36] Despite the growth of a much greater understanding of each other the gulf then created still remains unbridged.

Of more far-reaching effect upon the life and thought of Nonconformity—as upon all branches of the Church—were the changes wrought by the new scientific discoveries, resulting in open warfare between men of science and theologians in the middle and later decades of the nineteenth century. The first challenge came in Lyell's *Principles of Geology* (1830), with the suggestion that the earth had been evolving during vast ages, and that it was not the product of six days of divine activity. This was at once a challenge to the Creation Stories in Genesis, and also to the widely accepted biblical chronology of Archbishop Ussher. Then in 1844 came the anonymous volume, *Vestiges of the Natural History of Creation*, which gave an account of the origin of the solar system in terms of nebular hypothesis, and which denied special creation of species. In 1859, Charles Darwin produced his epoch-making work, *The Origin of Species*, advancing a theory of evolution in terms of survival of the fittest—the struggle for life in a process of natural selection. So by astronomy, geology and biology the biblical position was attacked and all this reacted upon the accepted idea of God and the Christian doctrine of redemption.

[35] *The Church Times*, the organ of the Anglo-Catholic party, seldom referred to Nonconformists without severe and often unkind criticism. Happily during recent years the attitude has greatly altered, and the paper reveals a growing understanding of the Nonconformist position.

[36] Dr W. R. Inge, Dean of St Paul's, recalling the early days when he lived in his grandfather's Yorkshire parish says: 'There was a small Wesleyan chapel in the village but half of the Methodists came to Church once on Sundays. . . . The stiffer churchmanship of the next generation drove all such pious waverers into unmitigated Nonconformity' (*Assessments and Anticipations*, p. 15). Cf. the following comments from the 1880's. A. M. Fairbairn 'honestly believed that the claims put forth in the Catholic Revival were disastrous to the highest welfare of the Church' (W. B. Selbie, *Life of Andrew Martin Fairbairn*, p. 209); but R. W. Dale wrote to Fairbairn: 'The blessing of God was in it, though we did not see it, and in a form they did not understand; in the lives and in the devotion of these men a new endowment of the Holy Spirit came into the life of England' (A. W. W. Dale, *Life of R. W. Dale of Birmingham* [1899], p. 699).

Whilst some scientific interest had been fostered in the Dissenting academies and the spirit of free enquiry predisposed some Dissenters to regard the new views with serious interest,[37] there was widespread bewilderment in all Christian communions.

It was inevitable that the scientific method should ultimately become focused upon the Bible itself. Some degree of critical approach to the Scriptures had already begun in the eighteenth century; now a new school of biblical criticism emerged in Germany under the leadership of F. C. Baur (1792-1860). Revolutionary conclusions as to the authority and dates of New Testament documents resulted in rationalist accounts of Jesus of Nazareth,[38] reducing him to a mere moralist teacher and denying his divine nature. The ultimate outcome of this challenge led to a clearer understanding of the historicity of Jesus and also of the uniqueness of the Bible, but the struggle was long and severe; undoubtedly many wavered in the faith, and others, whilst holding their faith, repudiated any principle of intellectual enquiry. This movement of critical enquiry also affected all Christian communions.

Amongst the Nonconformists probably the Unitarians were least disturbed, for the Socinian principle of free enquiry had become well established amongst them. Probably the Baptists and Congregationalists suffered most under the challenge because of their conviction that the Bible was fundamental in all aspects of Christian experience and Church life. Possibly, owing to the experimental nature of their theological position, the Methodists were less disturbed. But in all groups there was prolonged tension.[39] The transition to a critical view of the Bible was not easily or suddenly made, but slowly the new movement gained ground.

The important transitional period was between 1880 and 1895, and it may be divided into two phases of transition. Between 1880 and 1887 many of the more important leaders of the largest Nonconformist bodies were individually converted to a critical approach to the Bible. It was in the half-decade beginning late in 1887 that the full impact of

[37] In illustration of the problem at this point, see Philip Gosse (1810-88) in *Father and Son*. Gosse made important discoveries in natural science whilst still holding to his views as one of the Plymouth Brethren. For a useful account of the general problem, see Elliott-Binns, *Religion in the Victorian Era* (1936), Ch. 8.

[38] Strauss, *Leben Jesu* (E.Tr., 1847); Renan, *Vie de Jesus* (1863).

[39] For an excellent account of the whole movement, see W. B. Glover, *Evangelical Nonconformity and Higher Criticism in the Nineteenth Century* (1954).

the critical movement hit the various denominations as such. The process was one of downward penetration of ideas already accepted at the top. It took the form of a series of minor crises within the several denominations.[40]

Probably the absence of any important theological issue from the controversy over criticism mainly accounted for the fact that there was no splitting of the Nonconformists' groups along fundamentalist-modernist lines. Yet the wise presentation of the new viewpoint by many biblical scholars was also responsible for this, and perhaps to Arthur Samuel Peake (1865-1929) more than any other is the credit due, for in his constant aim to transmit the new approach in terms intelligible to the average reader he was unique.[41] This is not to minimize the valuable work of other biblical scholars. It should also be recorded that in the 1880's the Nonconformist journal, *The Expositor*, eventually became the outstanding journal of advanced biblical scholarship; widely read both by Nonconformist and Anglican ministers, it did more than any other single written agency to familiarize the ministry with the views of the critics.[42]

It is true that there were theological controversies within Nonconformity during this century, but they were of minor character. They must be noticed briefly.

In 1855 there was the 'Rivulet' controversy arising out of the hymns of T. T. Lynch, which were regarded by some as merely deistic and therefore unorthodox. In the 1870's there came the challenge to Samuel Cox (1826-93) on the question of eternal punishment and universal restoration; similarly on the question of conditional immortality the attack on Edward White (1819-98)[44] when the Leicester Conference of 1877[45] declared the principle that 'religious agreement is not dependent on agreement

[40] Ibid. p. 286.

[41] Cf. *The Manchester Guardian*, 19th August 1929: 'Perhaps it was Peake's greatest service . . . to the whole religious life of England that he helped to save us from a fundamental controversy such as that which has devastated large sections of the Church in America. . . . If the Free Churches of England have been able without disaster to navigate the broken waters of the last thirty years, it is largely due to the wisdom and patience of trusty and trusted pilots like Arthur Samuel Peake that they owe it.'

[42] W. B. Glover, *Evangelical Nonconformity and Higher Criticism in the Nineteenth Century*, p. 115.

[43] S. Cox, *Salvator Mundi* (1877).

[44] E. White, *Life in Christ*, first published in 1846, but in the third edition in 1878: 'An epoch-making book in the history of conditionalism.'

[45] Skeats and Miall, *History of the Free Churches of England, 1688-1891*, pp. 646-57.

in theological, critical and historical opinion', which raised the question of admission of Unitarianism: the 'Down-grade Controversy'[46] associated with C. H. Spurgeon, who in the confusion that accompanied the decline of the Calvinism to which he was so deeply attached, charged the Baptist denomination with having forsaken the very faith of the Gospel.

In the long run these controversies resulted in a real degree of intellectual emancipation, but at the time of their occurrence they caused much burning of heart.[47]

IV

An important feature of nineteenth-century Nonconformity was its growing concern for social righteousness and the conditions arising out of the Industrial Revolution. This is illustrated in the early part of the century in the challenge of Robert Hall (1764-1831)[48] during his ministry in Leicester to the grievous distress of the stocking-makers. Through the close contact with the industrial population it was inevitable that Nonconformity should have concern for the working-classes in their efforts for improvement of conditions of labour. Foremost in espousing this cause was Methodism, though in the first half of the century one section stood strictly aloof from such radical movements, largely because of the dictatorship of Jabez Bunting. This is illustrated in the case of a number of Methodists at Tolpuddle, in Dorset, who had formed a trade union in 1834. Their wages had been reduced from ten shillings to seven shillings a week, and in their straits they formed a Friendly Society for agricultural labourers. For this they were sentenced to seven years' transportation, and this with the warm approval of the Home Secretary. A Methodist woman journeyed to London to interview Dr Bunting on their behalf, but with no avail.[49]

This was the period of the Chartists (1838-48), who, realizing that under the Reform Bill of 1832 little or nothing had been done to alleviate the lot of the working classes, fought for parliamentary

[46] So called from an article entitled 'The Down Grade', which appeared in March 1887 in Spurgeon's monthly, *The Sword and the Trowel*. See W. B. Glover, *Evangelical Nonconformity and Higher Criticism in the Nineteenth Century*, pp. 63-73.

[47] For a detailed survey of theological movements in the latter part of the nineteenth century, see J. W. Grant, *Free Churchmanship in England, 1890-1940*, Chs. 2-4.

[48] R. Hall, *Appeal to the Public on the subject of the Frame Work Knitters' Fund* (1819).

[49] R. F. Wearmouth, *Methodism and the Working-Class Movements of England, 1800-50* (1937), pp. 265-6.

reform and manhood suffrage, sometimes acting with violence. Whilst it is true that Methodists, being antagonized by its threats of violence, generally reacted strongly against this movement, it is certain that the Chartists owed a great deal to Methodism. It framed its organization after the pattern of 'class-meetings' and open-air camp-meetings, and two of its leaders, William Lovett and Thomas Cooper, owed much to Methodist influence; also John Rayner Stephens, who suggested a policy of direct action, was a Methodist minister.[50] We may note further that when Richard Cobden and John Bright were striving to secure a repeal of the Corn Laws they were able to secure support in an assembly of some seven hundred Nonconformist ministers under the auspices of the Anti-Corn Law League.

During the first half of the century the opposition to trade unions was so fierce that few such combinations could survive, but during this period of struggle men trained in Methodist discipline and power of public speaking and possessed of unselfish idealism sustained the movement through prayer and faith. A remarkable tribute is paid by Sidney Webb to Methodism in County Durham between 1820 and 1850.

> The Ranters [i.e. the Primitive Methodists] did great work from village to village. Families were transformed and these men stood out as men of character gaining the respect of their fellows. . . . From the very beginning of the Trade Unions among the miners, of the co-operative movement among all sections of wage earners, of the formation of Friendly Societies, especially Primitive Methodists, who take the lead and fill the posts of influence. . . . it still remains true that in solid, silent membership of every popular movement in the country . . . perhaps the largest part is contributed by the various branches of the Methodist community. . . . Trade unionism was itself largely a result of the elevation of character brought about by religious conversion on individual leaders.[51]

In the second half of the century this struggle for existence was reinforced by the direct commitment to political objectives, and the movement grew rapidly.[52] Two names call for mention: Thomas Burt (1837-1922),[53] who became a Liberal member of

[50] Ibid. pp. 129-63.
[51] S. Webb, *Story of the Durham Miners* (1921), pp. 21-5.
[52] R. F. Wearmouth, *Methodism and the Trade Unions* (1954), p. 34. Note that between 1850 and 1890 no less than 1,225 Unions came into existence.
[53] T. Burt, *An Autobiography* (1924).

Parliament in 1874, was an ardent Primitive Methodist and leader of the Durham Miners' Association; Joseph Arch (1837-1919),[54] founder of the Agricultural Labourers Union had no preparation for his work except what the Primitive Methodist Chapel gave to him.

What was true of Durham county was true of other centres of industry and rural stretches—in Northumberland, Yorkshire, Staffordshire, Norfolk and other counties, and the other branches of Methodism had some share in this movement, especially the Free Methodists who were radical in origin and outlook. 'Methodism in seeking the salvation of the soul was attempting something wider than the improvement of the individual; it was working like leaven in the community.'[55]

In the nineteenth century, the Unitarians were also prominent in their concern for social welfare, though in some respects the sphere of their influence was rather different. In Manchester, Liverpool, Birmingham and other centres they had many leaders of industry, whose ideals as employers of labour reached a high ethical standard in their relations with their work-people. Yet in the wider movements of social reform they also bore distinctive witness. In matters of parliamentary reform they were important. In the movements for the abolition of slavery, womens' franchise, and in housing, they gave their support; in adult education and support of establishment of libraries they were pioneers; in the struggle regarding the Factory Acts and the Ten Hours Bill, Shaftesbury was strongly supported by the work of John Fielden, Member of Parliament for Oldham.[56] The Co-operative Movement in and around Rochdale had the allegiance of the Methodist Unitarians in the area. Further, in the formation of 'Domestic Missions' there was an attempt to secure closer contact with the actual conditions of people in the great cities of Manchester, (1833), London (1835), and Liverpool (1836).[57]

Parallel with the last-named enterprise was the foundation and

[54] *D.N.B.*

[55] R. F. Wearmouth, *Methodism and the Struggle of the Working Classes, 1850-1900*, p. 242.

[56] R. V. Holt, *The Unitarian Contribution to Social Progress in England* (1938). Fielden was one of the main figures in The Methodist Unitarian Movement associated with The Todmorden Unitarian Society. Amongst other publications he wrote *The Curse of the Factory System;* and was sympathetic towards the Chartists. His services 'were second only to those of Shaftesbury'. See H. McLachlan, *The Methodist Unitarian Movement* (1919), *passim*.

[57] R. V. Holt, op. cit.

support of Settlements by Nonconformists, such as Browning Hall, Walworth (Congregational) and Bermondsey (Wesleyan) in 1890, and similarly in other great centres of population, the purpose being to bring cultural influences to bear upon the community.

In three other aspects Nonconformity contributed to social advance during the nineteenth century.

We have already observed the first stage of the struggle against the slave trade in the previous century, in which, through the labours of Wilberforce and those associated with him, prohibition throughout the British Empire was secured by the Act of 1807. Although its protagonists belonged to the Evangelical group within the Church of England, known as 'The Clapham Sect', nevertheless, in this movement Nonconformity had its influence.[58] The further stages of the struggle, with the purpose of securing complete abolition of slavery, began in 1823, and Nonconformist support was effective. As previously, the Quakers exerted important influence, not least under the leadership of Thomas Fowell Buxton (1786-1844), who by ancestry and marriage had a close Quaker association, and who in 1823 became the parliamentary successor to Wilberforce in the struggle. In 1822 the Quakers issued an 'Address to the Inhabitants of Europe on the Iniquity of the Slave Trade', which was followed six years later by an emphatic petition to Parliament. During the years which followed financial support was given to the Anti-Slavery Society; literature was prepared for the education of the public; letters were written to slave-holders; a delegation was sent to the West Indies for purposes of investigation; an Address was prepared by William Foster for distribution in European countries, and 'under a religious sense of duty' he travelled through no less than sixteen countries bearing the message.[59] Nor must the witness of John Smith (d. 1824), a missionary of the London Missionary Society, who died in prison, and William Knibb (1803-45) of the Baptist Missionary Society, and other leading Nonconformists who denounced the traffic be forgotten. The Bill for Abolition of Slavery throughout the British Dominions received royal assent on 28th August 1833.

[58] Cf. Sir George Trevelyan, *Life and Letters of Lord Macaulay* (edn 1893), p. 45 (quoted Payne): 'Without the aid of Nonconformist sympathy and money and oratory and organization their operations would have been doomed to failure.'

[59] R. M. Jones, *The Later Periods of Quakerism*, II.825-6.

The second aspect of Nonconformist contribution to social betterment is seen in the care on behalf of children. Following the establishment of Sunday-schools by Robert Raikes, in 1780, together with the pioneer work of other evangelical Anglicans, Nonconformists established Sunday-schools widely throughout the country at the beginning of the nineteenth century. Parallel to this was the foundation of orphanages. As early as 1743 Wesley had founded the Orphan House in Newcastle,[60] a charity school in London in 1747, and a free dispensary for the sick poor in London in 1746. The nineteenth century brought the extension of this social ministry. Orphanages were established in 1832 by George Muller, belonging to the Plymouth Brethren, at Ashley Down, near Bristol; in 1867 by C. H. Spurgeon, the Baptist preacher, at Stockwell; in 1871 by Dr T. B. Stephenson, a Wesleyan minister, in Lambeth (now the National Childrens' Home); and in 1870 by Dr Barnardo, who had affiliation with the Plymouth Brethren and the Baptists, at Stepney

Thirdly, the Temperance Movement was a product of nineteenth-century Nonconformity, and in this the Methodists were the pioneers. In 1773 Wesley, concerned for the poverty of common folk, declared against the use of quantities of much-needed corn in the distilleries.[61] The Temperance Movement did not exist in the eighteenth century, and probably the early Methodists drank home-brewed ale with their meals, as was then the custom. But Wesley always insisted on the strictest temperance and forbade the use of spirits. It was in 1830 that Joseph Livesey and his friends—'The Seven Men of Preston'—took a pledge of total abstinence. Most of them were Methodist local preachers, and they began a campaign to check the evils of drunkenness. By their influence 'Bands of Hope', especially for the instruction of children, soon developed as a widespread feature of Nonconformist life and work. It is noteworthy that in 1832 the Conference of the Primitive Methodists by its own

[60] Wesley intended this Orphan House to be on the model of Franke's Waisenhaus at Halle, which he had seen in 1738. This design was never fulfilled, for although the school at Newcastle existed for some time, finally it became a preaching-place. But the title-deed made provision for a school with a master and instruction of forty poor children.

[61] J. Wesley, *Thoughts on the Present Scarcity of Provisions*. Cf. *Letters*, VIII.26: 'Distilled liquors have their use, but are infinitely overbalanced by the abuse of them: therefore, were it in my power, I would banish them out of the world.' Cf. also *A Farther Appeal to Men of Reason and Religion* (*Works*, VIII.162, and V.128-9).

resolution committed the denomination to a temperance policy and later, Hugh Bourne—'the man who fought the serpent'—one of the founders of the denomination, espoused the cause with great intensity and travelled far and wide in its support, and became largely responsible for the deep-rooted tradition in this matter which prevailed in later generations. Probably the Bible Christians were the most energetic in this temperance movement, counting such activity as only second in importance to evangelism. The United Methodist Free Churches were attracted to a legislative solution of the problem. The Wesleyan Reform Union from the beginning was enthusiastic in its labours for this cause. The Wesleyan Church, which in the earlier part of the century had stood aloof, could not remain uninfluenced, and in 1873 officially permitted 'Bands of Hope' within its churches, and slowly adult temperance societies were formed. Under two temperance reformers, Charles Garrett and Hugh Price Hughes, the work increased rapidly, and in 1899 the Wesleyan Conference defined its position in terms of a policy of moral persuasion.[62] Enthusiasm for the cause was inspired in other Churches, and in 1915 largely through the work of the Rev. Henry Carter, the Temperance Council of the Christian Churches was founded.[63]

In the light of the above developments it is not surprising to discover that from the middle of the nineteenth century Nonconformity became a political force which could not be ignored. A silent revolution was taking place, and in part it was at least stimulated by what became known as 'The Nonconformist Conscience'.[64] On the background of the democratic development within the Churches, Dissent increasingly became associated with the Liberal Party, as an instrument for securing the fulfilment of its social and ethical ideals. This political party had a prominent Quaker as its outstanding representative in the Government in John Bright.[65] The leader of the Liberal party in the Midlands was Joseph Chamberlain, a prominent Unitarian,

[62] M. Edwards, *Methodism and England* (1943), Ch. 6.

[63] For a full account, see H. Carter, *The English Temperance Movement, 1830-1899* (1932).

[64] This term arose out of correspondence in *The Times* in which Hugh Price Hughes was involved in the controversy over Parnell and the leadership of Home Rule for Ireland. One of Hughes's opponents said that he was motivated not by Christianity but by 'the Nonconformist Conscience'—an epithet which Hughes seized and made his battle-cry. Cf. H. Lovell Cocks, *The Nonconformist Conscience* (1943).

[65] E. A. Payne. 'Bright, a man of outstanding Christian character, was the first Nonconformist since William Penn to be prominent as a political leader'.

and the most influential Liberal newspaper, the *Manchester Guardian*, was under the famous editorship of C. P. Scott, also a leading Unitarian. Some Nonconformist denominational newspapers had the same political colouring in their concern for social reformation.[66] The reason for the close association of Dissent with Liberalism was twofold: the Reform Bill of 1832 had enfranchised those middle-class ranks from which Nonconformity drew considerable support; further political ideas were moving towards democracy which was the very principle upon which the Dissenting Churches were built as to their government. It is a mistaken idea, however, to assume that Nonconformity sacrificed its independence by this alliance with the Liberal position in the matter of political activity.

V

Any survey of the Nonconformity of the nineteenth century must include some notice of the extraordinary series of outstanding preachers of the period. During the earlier part of the century, among the Congregationalists were Thomas Binney, of Kings Weigh House from 1829 to 1869; John Angell James (1785-1859) for some fifty years minister of Carr's Lane, Birmingham; William Jay (1769-1853), of Angel Chapel, Bath. Amongst the Baptists was Robert Hall (1764-1831) who ministered in Cambridge, Leicester, and Broadmead Chapel, Bristol—'a great pulpit genius'. When we turn to the second half of the century great names appear more numerously. Amongst the Congregationalists were R. W. Dale (1829-95)[67] of Carr's Lane, Birmingham, who has been described as 'the finest and most spiritual nineteenth-century representative of the Nonconformist ideal'; Joseph Parker (1830-1902)[68] of the City Temple, London, a preacher of great dramatic power. Amongst the Baptists were Charles Haddon Spurgeon (1834-92),[69] who ministered for thirty years in the Metropolitan Tabernacle, London, which was built in 1861 for the accommodation of some six thousand persons; Alexander Maclaren (1826-1910),[70] of Manchester, whose fame rested on his power as an expository preacher. Hugh Price

[66] *The Christian World* (1857); *The Methodist Times* (1885); *The British Weekly* (1886).
[67] A. W. W. Dale, *Life of R. W. Dale, of Birmingham*, 1899.
[68] *D.N.B.* (A. Gordon); *Life*, G. H. Pike (1904).
[69] *D.N.B.* (A. Gordon); *Life*, G. H. Pike, 3 vols (1892).
[70] *D.N.B.* (A. Gordon); *Life*, D. Williamson and J. H. Shakespeare (1910).

Hughes (1847-1902),[71] a Methodist in West London, was a great exponent of the social implications of Christianity and an apostle of radicalism. Amongst the Presbyterians perhaps their greatest preacher was John Watson (1850-1907),[72] of Sefton Park, Liverpool, whose pen-name was 'Ian Maclaren'. Another outstanding figure in Liverpool was the Unitarian, James Martineau (1805-1900),[73] a thinker of great power and of wide vision, who after twenty-two years in Liverpool moved to London.

These names are outstanding, but in most large centres there were Nonconformist preachers who were leaders of thought and guardians of righteousness. They had a profound influence particularly amongst the middle-class population of the period, and as we shall see later, their mantle descended upon others in the early decades of the following century.

VI

'In geographic extent, in movements issuing from it and in its effect upon the race, in the nineteenth century Christianity had a far larger place in human history than at any previous time.'[74] A century earlier the Society for the Propagation of the Gospel in Foreign Parts, an Anglican foundation, had been established; similarly the Society for the Promotion of Christian Knowledge, also Anglican, and founded a little earlier in 1698, was for 'promoting religion and learning in any part of His Majesty's Plantation abroad'.[75] The beginning of Nonconformist missionary impulses, however, marked a new era in that its ideal was world-wide in scope.

The immediate cause of the origin of this missionary enterprise lay in the conviction of William Carey (1761-1834), Baptist pastor and shoemaker, who in 1792 prepared *An Enquiry into the Obligation of Christians to use means for the Conversion of the Heathen*, a work influenced by John Eliot and David Brainerd who had laboured amongst the American Indians. He presented his proposals concerning this world-evangelism in a sermon preached in Nottingham in 1792, and on 2nd October 'The Particular

[71] D. P. Hughes, *The Life of Hugh Price Hughes* (1904).

[72] *Ian Maclaren: Life of Rev. John Watson*, by W. R. Nicoll (1908).

[73] *D.N.B. Suppl.* (A. Gordon); J. Drummond and C. B. Upton (1901), *Life and Letters of James Martineau;* J. E. Carpenter : *Life of James Martineau* (1905).

[74] K. Latourette, *History of the Expansion of Christianity*, V.I.

[75] Both these societies were reinforced by the new impulse of the Oxford Movement.

Baptist Society for Propagating the Gospel among the Heathen' was founded, a name soon to be superseded by that of 'The Baptist Missionary Society'. Carey was one of the original number who went out to India. The organization of this Baptist Missionary Society is usually regarded as the beginning of modern foreign missionary enterprise.

In 1795 the London Missionary Society was founded, following a letter written by Carey. Although it drew its strength mainly from Congregationalism it was based upon a wider foundation, as is indicated by its 'fundamental principle', which is stated in its Declaration adopted in 1796:

Our design is not to send Presbyterianism, Independency, Episcopacy, or any other form of Church order and government (about which there may be differences of opinion among serious persons), but the glorious Gospel of the Blessed God to the heathen; and that it shall be left to the minds of the Persons whom God may call into the fellowship of His Son from among them to assume for themselves such form of church government as to them shall appear most agreeable to the Word of God.

The Society was supported by Presbyterians, and some Evangelical Anglicans, and its fields of service were in the South Seas, and later in South Africa and India. The inaugural sermon of the Society spoke of 'the field as the world'.

In the 1780's Thomas Coke, friend of Wesley, had been active in propagating Methodism in America and in the West Indies; until his death in 1814 on his way to the East, Coke was the leader of Methodist missions to the non-western world. From 1790 the Wesleyan Conference steadily organized its forces to assist him, and eventually in 1817-18 The Wesleyan Missionary Society was formed as the official society. According to the resources at their command the smaller Methodist groups began similar missionary enterprises: The Methodist New Connexion in China in 1859; the United Methodist Free Churches in Jamaica and later West Africa in the 1840's; the Primitive Methodists in West Africa in 1870; and the Bible Christians in China in 1885, following an appeal from Hudson Taylor of the China Inland Mission.

Thus by this enterprise there came into being in Africa, Asia and Australasia, Christian communities free and non-episcopal and it should be noted that in this expansion the non-episcopal Churches of America played a large part. The advance continued throughout the century and great names now stand upon the scroll of missionary pioneers.

Note should be taken of certain interdenominational organizations which were founded to assist the work of the missionary societies. In 1799 the Religious Tract Society was formed for the spread of the faith at home and abroad by means of the printed page, and in this both Anglican and Nonconformist joined. In 1804 came the formation of the British and Foreign Bible Society for the distribution of the Scriptures, translated into the languages of the peoples, an organization which was to become an invaluable aid for the work of evangelization through the missionary societies.

VII

Two significant evangelistic impulses emerged in the last quarter of the nineteenth century and these produced a distinct advance within the Nonconformist Churches in England.

In the years 1873-4 Dwight L. Moody, an American evangelist, visited Britain, accompanied by his friend Ira D. Sankey. Together they left the mark of their ministry over a wide area. Beginning the work in Scotland the movement spread southwards, and with restrained but definite spiritual appeal won many to the Christian faith who were outside the Churches, and also many, who though connected with the Churches, were lacking in decision or were of slender spiritual conviction. As an evangelist, Moody was

> singularly free from the weaknesses sometimes imputed to men of this class such as personal vanity and love of money. He seemed always to be sensible that he owed his opportunity to the labours of the regular ministry before him in the field, as well as that the perfecting of his work would depend on the sympathy and fidelity of the same labourers in the field after he had left. . . . At the time the prevailing impression was the sense of a movement directed from above, in which all the human agencies concerned were swallowed up and forgotten.[76]

It is not too much to assert that the results of this mission are still traceable.

Of more native growth was the rise of what came to be known as the 'Forward Movement' in Methodism, the great concern of which was the spread of the Gospel to the untouched masses of the

[76] 'Revivals of Religion', *E.R.E.*, X.755.

cities. Two names are associated with this enterprise. The Rev. Charles Garrett (1849-1900) was one of the principal founders of the Manchester and Salford Mission which afterwards, particularly under the dynamic ministry of Samuel F. Collier (1879-1921) developed into the great organization for evangelistic and social ministry which has made it outstanding. In Liverpool, Garrett continued work along similar lines. The other great pioneer of the 'Forward Movement' was Hugh Price Hughes (1847-1902) in London. This new development became the subject of supreme interest in Methodism. A zeal for the provision of halls and mission centres spread throughout the country until in most of the larger towns they were established. As centres of both evangelistic preaching and pastoral work, together with manifold philanthropic agencies, they soon began to have an impact upon the life of the towns in which they were placed.

Within Methodism alongside this work in the cities there was also a movement towards greater care for rural populations. There was the establishment of larger circuits consisting of country societies in the villages clustered around a fairly populous centre, such circuits having a staff of ministers and local preachers serving the churches. This secured greater cohesion and planned economy of administration and support. Though there was some loss in terms of concentration of service, as compared with those denominations whose churches were mainly single pastorates, this movement gave opportunity for expansion at many points and a sense of security to small societies.

In both these enterprises invaluable work was done by women of the Wesley Deaconess Order, a work which extended into other spheres both at home and overseas.[77]

Similarly associated with these evangelistic enterprises within Methodism, the need for the training of men in the work of evangelism was felt and it was in 1886 that the Rev. Thomas Champness (1832-1905) opened a home in Rochdale for such instruction to local preachers, Bible visitors, and lay missionaries. Permanence came to the enterprise in the establishment of Cliff College, at Calver, in Derbyshire. This institution accommodates

[77] This parallel ministry of women took shape about 1890 and at the beginning of the century under the leadership of Dr Stephenson, the Order became established at the Wesley Deaconess Institute at Ilkley. The strength of the Order of Wesley Deaconesses in 1961 was 423.

about a hundred men whose training is expressly designed to make them effective evangelists.

VIII

As we have seen this 'century of advance' in Christian missions is the period in which great growth in Nonconformity in England took place, and this is manifest whether for judgement of the situation we think in terms of statistics, or of the rise and growth of new organizations, or of influence upon the national life.

Although statistical evidence always needs to be cautiously accepted it is not without value. It has been reckoned that at the beginning of the nineteenth century there were 270 Presbyterian, 708 Baptist, and 1,024 Congregational congregations—a total of 2,002.[78] Assuming the average congregation numbered about 200—probably this number is too high—this would give a membership of about 400,000.[79] To this number should be added the 72,000 members and some 500,000 adherents in Methodism at the time of Wesley's death in 1791, for as yet Methodists were not reckoned as Dissenters.[80] Thus the total Nonconformist allegiance, amongst the four main denominations at the beginning of the century would be about a million. In 1851, under official Government direction, a religious census was taken, and it may be regarded as 'one of the landmarks in the ecclesiastical history of England and Wales'.[81] It was discovered that the various worshippers in Nonconformist Churches[82] numbered nearly as many as those attending the Church of England.[83] A further table gives figures of those 'most numerously attending service', and shows 1,939,896 for the Nonconformists as compared with 2,541,244 for

[78] Clark (*History of English Nonconformity*, II.315) follows Bogue and Bennett (*History of Dissenters*, 2nd edn, II.543-4). This shows a considerable advance on the calculation by Josiah Thompson, a Baptist minister, who stated in 1772 that the total number of Nonconformist congregations in 1760 was 1,252 (Bogue and Bennett, op. cit., II.256-7).

[79] H. Davies, *The English Free Churches*, p. 175.

[80] Townsend, Workman and Eayrs, *A New History of Methodism* (1909), I.369.

[81] The official Report has long been out of print but there is a summary in Skeats and Miall, pp. 521-8. Not the least important element in the enquiry was the fact that for the first time Dissenters were dealt with in a State Paper, and justice done to religious bodies outside the pale of the Establishment. The initiative was due to the Registrar-General at the time. There were some 40,000 enumerators. To quote the Report: 'For the first time there was given to the country a full picture of the state of its religion as exhibited by its religious institutions.'

[82] In this reckoning Roman Catholics were counted as 'Nonconformists'.

[83] The figures were: Church of England 3,773,474; other denominations (including Roman Catholics and minor sects), 3,487,558.

the Church of England. Making every allowance for the inadequacies of census returns, these figures indicate a remarkable Nonconformist advance.

Stepping just beyond the close of the century, statistics compiled in 1910 indicate that the Free Churches had 2,125,275 communicants, whilst the Anglican communicants numbered 2,231,735. These figures indicate that in Britain the Free Churches had raised themselves to a position of virtual numerical equality with the Anglican Church.[84] Yet 'if we compare them with those of previous years we find that they do not indicate a growth commensurate with the population, and that . . . the Free Churches are doing little more than mark time and holding the ground they have won'.[85]

[84] This figure includes Presbyterians, Independents, Baptists, Quakers, Wesleyans, Methodist New Connexion, Primitive Methodists, Bible Christian Methodist Association, Methodist Reformers, Calvinist Methodists, Countess of Huntingdon. It does *not* include Roman Catholics.

[85] W. B. Selbie, *Nonconformity*, pp. 233-4. It is also stated that international statistics show a greater numerical disparity. The four main Free Church denominations (Methodist, Baptist, Presbyterian, Congregational) covering the United Kingdom, British Colonies, United States of America, and India, show a total of 21,862,092 communicants as compared with 4,022,119 for the Church of England. This indicates something of the vitality of Nonconformist missionary enterprise. As H. Davies points out (*The English Free Churches*, p. 182), the difference is also due to the great resources of the non-episcopal communions in the United States of America, themselves being the outreaches of seventeenth-century Puritanism and eighteenth-century Methodism in England.

CHAPTER TEN

THE TWENTIETH CENTURY: TOWARDS UNITY

AT the opening of the new century English Nonconformity was exerting a considerable influence throughout the nation. As never before in its history it had come to possess both freedom and prosperity, out of which arose a sense of expectancy. But in the next half-century its witness and achievement were to be set upon the background of two world-convulsions and the aftermath which followed. It is not surprising, therefore, that these decades witnessed a decline.[1] The background became that of a growing materialization through the general forsaking of spiritual values throughout the country. If one travels through the streets of most industrial towns one sees abandoned and derelict chapels; they are now workshops, or garages or warehouses; once they were centres of piety for groups of English folk. Doubtless in some cases the shift of population is the reason for this, but in many, perhaps most, the reason lies deeper. These groups not merely ceased to grow, but began to diminish. Such decline was the mark of a change in the mind of the nation which affected both Church and Dissent. It was in part a change of belief with an intellectual explanation, but it was in large part caused by a change in habit; it was a change in the interests of people who did not even bother to change their beliefs.[2]

In our own time there is no serious indication that the situation has greatly altered. The tide has not yet turned.

Yet, as in all such situations, contrary forces have been at work, and the last sixty years reveal developments and tendencies in English Nonconformity which have had great significance not least for the future of religion in England. It is the record of these years that we have to trace in this chapter.

[1] D. W. Brogan, *The English People*, p. 21 (quoted by Payne): 'It is probable that Nonconformity reached its height of political power, was most representative of the temper of the English people, round the beginning of the century. . . . But in the generation that has passed since the great Liberal landslide of 1906, one of the greatest changes in the English religious and social landscape has been the decline of Nonconformity.'

[2] G. Kitson Clark, *The English Inheritance* (1950), p. 132: 'To believe in the very great importance of material things is common sense: materialism comes when you come to underrate the importance of what is spiritual.'

I

In the first place we must examine briefly the changes in theological thought which marked this period in the history of the Free Churches.[3]

As we have already observed, in the latter part of the nineteenth century the general ferment of ideas, particularly in scientific terms, had already made its impact upon Nonconformity. Old conceptions were giving way before new ones, in science, in comparative religion and biblical scholarship. The result was a reaction against systematic theology as 'the last phase of a reaction against the Calvinist orthodoxy that had dominated English Nonconformity until the middle of the nineteenth century'.[4] There was a transfer of interest from doctrine to apologetics and ethics, and the widespread repudiation of any kind of dogmatic theology. Those who accepted the critical view of the Scriptures were set down as 'liberals' or 'modernists'. The failure of the early twentieth-century liberalism lay in the fact that what was intended as a means to a clearer understanding of the Bible was taken as an end in itself, and so there was a failure to gain the true perspective of the critical position, as a foundation upon which to build and not the final edifice.[5] There was no synthesis between critical method and theological interpretation.

The outstanding example of the extreme view emerged in the first decade through the movement associated with R. J. Campbell (1867-1956) of the City Temple, London, and which was expressed in his book *The New Theology* (1907), in which the main emphasis was upon the immanence of God in nature and in man; further, it asserted that in this was involved a theological manifestation of socialism. The influence of the movement was shown in the preaching of this decade, which tended in not a few cases to be the proclamation of a merely social gospel, though such influence was only temporary.

[3] The terms 'Dissenter' and 'Nonconformity' were negative in character. It was towards the end of the nineteenth century that the term 'Free Churches' came into use, largely through the influence of Hugh Price Hughes, who placed the emphasis entirely upon the positive aspect of the movement.

[4] J. W. Grant, *Free Churchmanship in England, 1870-1940* (1956), p. 118.

[5] Cf. T. W. Manson, 'The Failure of Liberalism to interpret the Bible as the Word of God' in *The Interpretation of the Bible*, ed. C. W. Dugmore (1944), p. 101: 'The application of critical principles and critical methods to the Bible can only be set on one side by a sacrifice of intellectual integrity which would infallibly stultify any attempt at theological reconstruction!'

But there were other influences which proved an anchorage to the Reformed tradition. The work of John Oman (1860-1939) and Peter Taylor Forsyth (1848-1921), and, in matters of biblical interpretation, A. S. Peake's *The Bible: Its Origin, Significance and Abiding Worth* (1913), followed in 1919 by *Peake's Commentary*, had far reaching effect. It would be difficult to exaggerate the influence of the last-named work in setting forth a reasonable statement of the critical position. In the return to a closer association with the Reformed tradition an important external force emerged through the works of Karl Barth,[6] which became available for English readers in the thirties, though this neo-Calvinist system of thought had received attention before that time. Barth introduced into Nonconformity 'a theological leaven the effects of which are difficult to estimate', but the result of this Barthian influence was to send Nonconformists back to their own traditions.

Such theological tensions still persist, and they are not to be found only in the Free Churches. The scholarship of Nonconformity has given much to the world of thought and has come to be highly regarded by those outside its borders. On the other hand in these matters the Free Churches have growingly appreciated the contributions of Anglican scholars and have gained much thereby. Upon this wider intellectual background much depends for future development of mutual relations.

In the period under consideration, there are great names which may be listed. In the realm of biblical scholarship there are the following: J. Hope Moulton, W. H. Bennett, G. Buchanan Gray, John Skinner, A. S. Peake, H. Wheeler Robinson, J. Estlin Carpenter, W. F. Howard, and T. W. Manson. In the field of theology: A. M. Fairbairn, P. T. Forsyth, John Oman, A. E. Garvie, J. Scott Lidgett, and R. Mackintosh. In the field of Church history: J. Vernon Bartlett, P. Carnegie Simpson, F. J. Powicke, C. J. Cadoux, and H. McLachlan. Two outstanding laymen must also be mentioned; T. R. Glover and B. L. Manning.

It is fitting at this point to remember that this period in the life of the Free Churches was also marked by a galaxy of preachers,[7] and though it may seem invidious to select individuals,

[6] Barth's works were not translated into English until some years after they were first written. *The Word of God and the Word of Man* appeared in 1928; *Commentary on the Epistle to the Romans* in 1933, and *Credo* in 1936.

[7] See W. R. Nicoll, *Princes of the Church* (1921), and E. H. Jeffs, *Princes of the Modern Pulpit* (n.d.), for interesting appreciations.

mention should be made of R. F. Horton, of Lyndhurst Road, Hampstead; J. H. Jowett, of Carr's Lane, Birmingham; R. J. Campbell, of the City Temple;[8] G. Campbell Morgan, of Westminster Chapel, Buckingham Gate, and J. D. Jones, of Richmond Hill, Bournemouth, amongst the Congregationalists. R. C. Gillie, of Marylebone, and John Watson, of Sefton Park, Liverpool, amongst the Presbyterians. Dinsdale T. Young, of Westminster Central Hall, and William Edwin Sangster, his successor, among the Methodists. F. B. Meyer, of Leicester; John Clifford, of Westbourne Park, London, and Charles Brown of Ferme Park, London, amongst the Baptists. Standing in a unique position denominationally was Dr W. E. Orchard, of King's Weigh House, London, one of the pioneers of the Free Catholic movement, who in 1932 passed over to the Roman Catholic Church.[9]

A further outstanding feature of this period was the rise and development of a liturgical movement within the Free Churches. Although it has often been asserted that this represented a mere imitation of Anglican modes of worship, the origins of this movement lie much deeper. The simpler forms of worship, with a strong feature of extempore prayer, were by no means either lost or disregarded, but the recognition of the legacy of prayer through the ages was more and more regarded as an inheritance which could be incorporated in Free Church worship with spiritual profit. There was also a deeper recognition of the significance of the Christian Year, and the importance of sacramental worship alongside the ministry of preaching. The first impulse towards a liturgical interest among the more liberal Free Churchmen was supplied by Dr John Hunter (1849-1912), a Scot who became minister of the King's Weigh House, in London. His *Devotional Services*[10] provided a varied series of more formal Orders of Service. The English Presbyterians were early in the field with the *Directory of Public Worship*,[11] in 1921, which was succeeded in the same year by the Congregationalists with the publication of *A Book of Congregational Worship*, followed, in 1948, by *A Book of*

[8] R. J. Campbell, of the City Temple, went over to the Anglican Church in 1916.

[9] See W. E. Orchard, *From Faith to Faith: An Autobiography of Religious Development* (1933). Dr Orchard was remarkable for a combination of theological power, catholic outlook, and deep evangelical preaching. Two books from his pen have had a remarkable influence: *The Necessity of Christ* (1917) and *The Temple: A Book of Prayers* (1913). His last work was a further book of prayers under the title, *Sancta Sanctorum* (1955).

[10] The fourth edition was published in 1890.

[11] First published in 1898, revised in 1921.

Public Worship compiled for the use of Congregationalists. In 1929 *A Free Church Book of Common Prayer* was published. It bears close resemblance to the Revised Prayer Book of 1928, and is a valuable compilation, but it does not appear to have been widely adopted. In 1936 the Methodists produced *Divine Worship.*[12] Probably the Baptists were least affected by this new liturgical impulse, in which there was an attempt to secure a balance between the subjective and the objective aspects of Christian worship.

A more extreme example of this same movement within the Free Churches arose in the twenties as 'The Society of Free Catholics', the leaders of which were J. M. Lloyd Thomas, of the Unitarian Old Meeting, Birmingham, and Dr Orchard. Free Catholics rejected the Anglican conception of orders and credal subscription, but adopted its sacramentalist views. It was an attempt to combine Christian faith with freedom of thought, but had little permanent effect upon the life of the Free Churches.[13]

Allied with the developments which we have just considered was a growing recognition amongst the Free Churches of the place of music in divine worship. Also within this deepening realization of the aesthetic aspect there arose a new architectural impulse. Pseudo-Gothic structures had begun to arise towards the end of the nineteenth century as new chapels were built, though some edifices continued to be built in variant Roman or Greek styles. After 1920 the tendency was towards simplicity of design, with little tracery or ornament, 'preserving intact our Protestant and Puritan tradition'.[14]

II

We must now turn to the most outstanding feature in the experience of the English Free Churches during the last forty years —the development of Christian Unity. But for a moment we must retrace our steps.

We must note here two important movements for reunion within the Methodist communions. In 1907 the Methodist New Connexion, the United Methodist Free Churches, and the Bible

[12] To the present writer the late Dr F. W. Dwelly, Dean of Liverpool, one of the most eminent Anglican liturgiologists, stated that, in his mature judgement, *Divine Worship* was only surpassed by *The Book of Common Prayer.*

[13] For some account of the Free Catholics, see W. E. Orchard, *From Faith to Faith,* pp. 13ff.

[14] M. S. Briggs, *Puritan Architecture and its Future* (1945)—a useful survey of architectural development in Nonconformity.

Christians came together to form the United Methodist Church. This was followed, in 1932, by a union of the Wesleyan Methodists, the Primitive Methodists, and the United Methodists to form the Methodist Church. The membership of this united Methodist Church at the time of union, covering Great Britain, Ireland and its work overseas, reached almost a million and a quarter. This union represents the major impulse towards reunion amongst the Free Churches.

In the middle of the nineteenth century the various Free Churches in Britain began to create world-organizations linking them with their expanding work overseas. As early as 1877 the World Alliance of Reformed Churches holding the Presbyterian System was created.[15] In 1881 the first Methodist Ecumenical Conference was held in London, representing twenty-eight Methodist groups from twenty countries, since which time the Conference has met approximately once in ten years, the number of constituent churches being gradually reduced as Methodism developed unity within itself.[16] In 1891 came the first International Congregational Council, followed by similar meetings at approximate intervals of ten years.[17] In 1905 largely under the labours of J. H. Shakespeare, the Baptist World Alliance was formed with delegates from twenty-three nations.[18] Although possessing no ecclesiastical authority for the denominations concerned, these movements have resulted in greater denominational cohesion and the growth of an ecumenical consciousness.

In the closing years of the nineteenth century a further step forward in the development of unity took place in the creation of the National Free Church Council.[19] During the latter half of the previous century there had been sporadic impulses towards closer co-operation, but in 1891-2 informal conferences were held under the hospitality of Dr Henry S. Lunn, at Grindelwald, in Switzerland, at which both Anglicans and Free Churchmen met to talk in general terms about the problem of the reunion of the Churches.[20] Amongst those present were Hugh Price Hughes and

[15] G. Slosser, *Christian Unity: Its History and Challenge* (1929), pp. 162, 316; Rouse and Neill, *A History of the Ecumenical Movement* (1954), p. 266.

[16] Slosser, ibid. p. 169; Rouse and Neill, ibid. p. 267.

[17] Slosser, ibid. p. 315; Rouse and Neill, ibid. p. 267.

[18] Slosser, ibid. pp. 13-14; Rouse and Neill, ibid. pp. 267-8; Underwood, pp. 280-1.

[19] For detailed study, see E. K. H. Jordan, *Free Church Unity: History of the Free Church Council Movement, 1896-1941* (1956).

[20] An important influence was the publication of *The Review of the Churches* under the editorship of Dr Lunn. This journal continued until 1930.

Charles Berry, both of whom were to be prominent in advocating a closer *rapprochement* between the Free Churches, ultimately leading to the establishment of the Free Church Council. Its first Congress was held in Manchester in November 1892.

It is sometimes said that the origin of the movement was in the alarm caused by the changes in the English Church due to the influence of the Tractarian movement,[21] but there is only a small degree of truth behind this assertion. Certainly Free Churchmen were opposed to sacerdotal tendencies—and this was also the attitude of many within the English Church itself—but the main intention of the new Free Church Council was not negative but positive. It was concerned with common action between the Free Churches on the religious, moral and social issues of the time.

Membership of the Congress was personal and in no sense was delegational from the various denominations. Its main interest was theological and it was soon revealed that there was no essential difference of opinion on these matters. Much attention was focused on the practical problem of evangelism. The closing scene of the first Congress was a joint Communion Service conducted by Dr Alexander Maclaren.

Although warmly welcomed by most Free Churchmen there were some who held aloof: some fearing lest it might become involved in political issues;[22] others, desiring a more representative assembly, doubtful of its principle of membership. Steadily, however, the movement gained momentum, and a network of Local Councils[23] became built up throughout the country, largely through the energies of Hugh Price Hughes and Charles Berry. In 1899 a Free Church Catechism was issued in an attempt to express the fundamental theological unity of the Free Churches in England.

[21] C. S. Horne, *A Popular History of the Free Churches* (1905), p. 424. Cf. the following from the Address of Dr Charles Berry, as First Congress President in 1895 (quoted Jordan, pp. 49-50): 'This is not a nonconformist congress whose *raison d'être* lies in a negative and critical attitude towards the Established Church. This is a Free Church Congress based upon our common and positive adherence to the great verities of evangelical history.'

[22] It was on these points that R. W. Dale refused to ally himself with the new movement (*Life*, pp. 647ff). Nevertheless he strongly supported evangelical Free Church enterprise in Birmingham.

[23] By 1896 the number of Local Councils and Federations had reached 209; by 1899 the number was 500; by 1901 there were some 700 Councils and 36 District Federations. Jordan, p. 55.

Space will only allow for a brief enumeration of the enterprises and achievements of the Council in the succeeding years. From the earliest beginnings there was the conviction that the evangelization of England was its central mission, and this extensive evangelism was focused in the Great Simultaneous Mission of 1901, which began in London and spread to the large towns and cities, as well as to many villages, particularly in the North of England. This indicated something of the latent resources available in united effort as distinct from denominational enterprise. Local Councils engaged widely in this work, and in addition gave considerable attention and challenge to the various social problems of the time.[24]

Despite the utmost caution in approach to political issues, it soon became evident that such could not be altogether avoided. In 1901 there was divided opinion amongst Free Churchmen as to the manifesto on the South African War, issued by the Council on the basis of the six points originally suggested by Dr John Clifford.[25] Further, most Free Churchmen were Liberals, and not infrequently the position of Free Churchmen in regard to social and political problems was similar to that of the rising Liberalism—a position which has been frequently misunderstood. Whilst it may be that eventually the alliance between Free Churchmen and Liberalism went too far, yet the words of Dr Jordan are salutary:

> Some have supposed that there was an organic connection between the Liberal Party and the Council movement, and that the latter could justly be described as a committee-room of the political party. There is not a vestige of truth in such a supposition.[26]

The advent of the Liberal Government to power in 1906[27] seemed to Free Churchmen to provide a way particularly for the redress of grievances in the matter of education, to which the Commons sought to provide a remedy, though without success. The obstacle lay in the clerical opposition of the Upper House. Both in the Liberal ranks and in the Free Churches there was a

[24] A remarkable instance of this is the work of the Council in South Central London. Whole streets of disorderly houses and brothels were closed; in one week eighteen were disposed of and the owners proceeded against. Jordan, p. 57.

[25] Jordan, pp. 73-5.

[26] Jordan, p. 75.

[27] Payne, p. 124: 'The new Parliament contained more Nonconformists than had been there since the days of Cromwell.'

growing conviction that only a reformation of the constitutional situation could allow the will of the people to prevail. Hence the political issue of the reform of the House of Lords arose, to which Free Churchmen gave enthusiastic support[28] in defence of the rights of Parliament and of the people. Thus in view of a General Election ahead the Council decided to enter into the area of political strife. A manifesto was issued declaring that the interest of true progress as well as the Free Churches demanded the return of the Liberals. Dr Jordan is probably right in asserting that

> there is more than a residuum of truth in the claim that, by their support of the Liberals at this crucial moment in British history, Free Churchmen were serving the wider interests of that eternal kingdom where no forces of privilege or monopoly hold sway.[29]

The outbreak of war brought a situation far beyond the region of party politics. At first there was some reluctance upon the part of Free Churchmen, but the turning point in Free Church opinion came in November 1914, following a dynamic speech by Mr David Lloyd George. From this point onwards the Council set its machinery to work in the interests of widespread relief and welfare work. Three important issues were stimulated by the influence of the Council: the appointment of Free Church Chaplains to the Forces;[30] the right of any man in the Forces to state uninfluenced his religion; the reasonable treatment of conscientious objectors to military service.[31] It should be noted that the normal work of the Council in evangelistic enterprise still continued unabated.

In the General Election which took place after the war, the Council took no side, but issued a manifesto calling for the establishment of the League of Nations, and for social reform in many fields. One significant fact is worth recording. On 16th November 1918 a Solemn Service of Thanksgiving was held in the

[28] In December 1909 the Upper House committed a breach with parliamentary custom when they rejected the Budget, thus usurping the traditional right of the Lower House on matters of finance.

[29] Jordan, p. 120.

[30] Prior to this, only Anglican, Presbyterian and Wesleyan Chaplains existed. Lloyd George, despite the opposition of Lord Kitchener, insisted in the Cabinet on the appointment of Free Church Chaplains, largely due to the pressure of the Free Church Council.

[31] On this issue there was division of opinion in the Council, some being unwilling to agree that the Council should take action. But a conviction as to the inviolable sanctity of the human conscience triumphed. An important and influential document came forth from the pen of A. S. Peake, in 1918: *Prisoners of Hope*.

Albert Hall, London under the auspices of the Free Church Council. It was attended by King George V and Queen Mary—the first time a reigning monarch had attended a Free Church occasion. For Nonconformists things had changed greatly since the days of Charles II.[32]

When the League of Nations became established, the support of the Free Church Council was widely forthcoming.[33] In 1924 Viscount Cecil declared:

> The League of Nations owes much to the Free Churches in this country perhaps more than to any other Christian denomination. They have recognized the religious appeal of the League and have done their best to bring it home to the people.[34]

In the thirties there was considerable pacifist pressure upon the Council, but it was decisively rejected. Nevertheless, although the clouds were again darkening on the horizon in Europe, for a decade the Council maintained an unflinching support for the policy of disarmament. In this failure to realize the seriousness of the situation the Free Churches did not stand alone.

The rise of the Labour Movement and its separation from the Liberalism which had stood for many of its ideals must be considered for a moment in its connection with the Free Churches. As we have already observed, the close connection of its early pioneers with Nonconformity was important, most of all in relation to the development of Trades Unions. Yet the last thirty years show that the movement has very largely lost its religious inspiration. The Free Churches have been eager to bring the gospel to bear upon social questions and many Local Councils have developed various schemes for social welfare, but, although many Free Churchmen are politically associated with the Labour movement, there has yet been a definite decline in the influence of Nonconformity in the great industrial centres, and also a suspicion of the movement itself. There is more than one reason for this, but there is some truth in the following statement:

> It is difficult not to trace a connection between, on the one hand, the new social opportunities that came to Free Churchmen and the

[32] Jordan, p. 152.

[33] In 1922 over four hundred Free Church Councils staged demonstrations in support of the League; ibid. p. 180.

[34] In a Speech to the Council (quoted Jordan, p. 181).

increasing funds at their disposal, and on the other, a gradual alienation from the working-classes.[35]

It is also true, on the other side, that there has always been a section of the Labour Movement desirous of following the path of social reform without reference to or the stimulus of the religious motive. It still remains, however, that not a few leaders of the Free Churches have strongly supported the Movement.[36]

One important issue for the Free Churches, sometimes involving political implications, was the question of Education.[37] Mr Balfour's Education Act of 1902 was regarded with dissatisfaction by Free Churchmen generally despite the elements in it that were commendable. The main grounds of offence were that under its provisions public money could be spent on sectarian dogmatic teaching and that in many places teachers would be subject to ecclesiastical tests.[38] Opposition took the form of a policy of passive resistance by refusal to pay the Education Rate. The outstanding leader of this movement was Dr John Clifford. It should be understood quite clearly that the Free Church Council did not either organize or sponsor this Passive Resistance Movement: it was directed by a special National Passive Resistance Committee which was not associated with the Council although the latter stood firmly in opposition to the Bill. The Act came into force on 26th March 1903. Passive resistance continued to spread and some of the most cultured and respected citizens supported it. In some cases goods were distrained and many suffered imprisonment.[39] Lest it should be thought that the attitude of the Free Church Council was that of mere negative objection, it should be remembered that in 1904 the Council declared a policy for national education of which the main points were the following: There should be one type of elementary school controlled by a public education authority; denominational

[35] Payne, p. 128.

[36] In Methodism, for example, the following names are eloquent: Arthur Henderson, S. R. Keeble, Henry Carter, J. E. Rattenbury, and George Thomas.

[37] For a detailed account see Jordan, Chs. 5 and 14.

[38] Some Free Churchmen were prepared to support the Bill; e.g. at the Wesleyan Conference of 1903 there were three schools of thought—a minority supported a movement for passive resistance; a second group, mainly Tory and with Anglican sympathies, followed W. L. Watkinson and supported the Bill because their own voluntary schools would benefit; a third, friendly to Liberalism and Nonconformity were opposed to the Bill but not to the extent of agreeing with passive resistance (Maldwyn Edwards, *Methodism and England* [1943], p. 124).

[39] By October 1905 there had been over 230 imprisonments.

school buildings, if required for provided schools, should be rented on equitable terms; all schools maintained by public funds should be under the entire control of elected representatives; there should be no religious tests in the appointment and training of teachers; there should be no denominational teaching in elementary schools during school hours, but simple Bible-teaching subject to a conscience clause.[40]

It was perhaps inevitable that the Free Church Council would sooner or later be drawn into the arena of party politics on this issue. It was decided to show its disapproval by committing itself to work for a Liberal victory at the forthcoming General Election. It is certain that *one* of the factors in the downfall of Mr Balfour's government in December 1905 was the Nonconformist opposition to the Education Act, including the challenge of the Passive Resistance Movement. To the whole country, the Council issued a manifesto dealing with the four following points: the need for a completely national educational system under effective public control; the need for immediate temperance reform; the need for immediate action regarding Chinese indenture labour in South Africa; the need for attention to the urgent social problems.

It is not possible to estimate how far the Liberal victory of 1906 was due to the influence of the Council, but it is certain that the above manifesto had a wide influence, even beyond the ranks of Free Churchmen. The occasion certainly revealed the enormous strength of Nonconformity at this time of crisis.

It is indeed a vexed question as to how far this political alignment on the part of the Free Churches was justifiable. Certainly the position of the Free Church Council in the matter has not always been entirely understood, but the issues can now be seen in clearer perspective. It is plain that the attitude to the Act of 1902 failed to appreciate the definite improvements in educational policy which the Act provided. The religious teaching within the voluntary schools was but a fraction of the work of the schools, though admittedly an important one. Moreover, under the Act, Anglican rate-payers and those who were antagonistic to any religious teaching at all, would, for example, be supporting Methodist voluntary schools. It still remains, however, that for those who resisted, the religious issues involved a matter of conscience—and the question of freedom of conscience in religion

[40] Jordan, p. 92.

had been the fundamental issue throughout all the history of English Nonconformity. It was on that ground that there had been resistance to the Act of Uniformity in 1662. It was believed equally by those who supported passive resistance and by those who opposed the Bill apart from such action that the way to secure this freedom in regard to religion was by the constitutional instrument of the electoral polls, and that the Liberal party offered the way through. Beyond this nothing remains to be said.

One thing further must be remembered. Through all the upheaval the Free Church Council remained primarily a spiritual organization and its evangelizing activity did not diminish.

It is probably true to say that following the achievements of 1906, although the Council remained vigorous, it suffered change and perhaps loss of influence. Further, there was a growing desire for a more representative body, despite the fact that it had long been regarded as 'the free voice of Nonconformity'. To this development we must turn later.

The Fisher Education Bill of 1918 did not remove the grievances which had been challenged by the Passive Resistance Movement, but the Free Church Council welcomed it because it was a distinct advance towards greater efficiency in education.[41] In 1927 a Joint Education Committee, composed of representatives from both the Free Church Council and the Federal Council[42] was formed, and this exercised an important influence in discussions until 1939, in particular concerning the promotion of biblical and religious syllabuses as a basis of common religious instruction for all types of schools. There was also growing co-operation between the Free Churches and the Anglican Church, in which movement Dr J. Scott Lidgett was an outstanding leader.

In 1936 Mr Oliver Stanley introduced a Bill which was a further advance,[43] though the Free Church Council considered

[41] The Bill provided for improvement of salaries; the creation of State scholarships for universities; a single school certificate as a basic qualification for most professions; compulsory attendance between the ages of five and fourteen and continuation classes to the age of eighteen; and severe restriction upon the employment of children.

[42] The Federal Council was formed in 1919; see *infra*, pp. 179-80.

[43] The main provisions were the raising of the school-leaving age to fifteen; the authorization of Local Education Authorities to provide emergency grants (up to seventy-five per cent) for cost of building extension; permission to parents to ask for religious instruction from Agreed Syllabuses; a distinction between 'reserved teachers' (i.e. those appointed in consultation with the school managers and who would give religious instruction according to the trust-deeds) and 'unreserved teachers' appointed solely by the Local Education Authority, and who would give religious instruction according to the Agreed Syllabuses.

building grants of fifty per cent adequate, and then, not to be used for building new denominational schools, as this would mean an extension of the dual system. They also declared that Agreed Syllabuses[44] should be made compulsory. The Bill was, however, not 'an agreed measure' as is sometimes supposed.

In the late thirties many unofficial conversations took place between Free Churchmen and Anglicans, and again Dr Scott Lidgett was the chief figure on the Free Church side. This indicated a growing spirit of goodwill through mutual discussion, and by it the problems of the dual system were minimized.

The 1944 Education Act of Mr R. A. Butler[45] was an attempt at compromise on the religious issue, and was again an advance. One fact is interesting, namely that by this time more than four hundred Local Education Authorities were using the Agreed Syllabuses, which is a strong vindication of the Free Church policy as outlined in 1918.

Much unanimity had now been reached but the provisions of the Education Act of 1959[46] brought protests from Free Churchmen because it seemed to extend and perpetuate the dual system yet again, and because it altered the settlement of 1944 without proper negotiations between the parties to that settlement. Nevertheless the creation of a Joint Anglican and Free Church Committee reveals a growing desire for co-operation in promoting the cause of Christian education.

We have dealt with this question of education at length because there are those in the present generation who are tempted through vagueness of understanding to dismiss the struggle as a mere expression of party-strife; there are others who are entirely ignorant of the inheritance which has been procured by the firm stand of Free Churchmen in the matter of freedom in religion.

[44] It should be noted that opposition to the adoption of these was shown by some local Education Authorities.

[45] This Act gave to Church schools the choice either to become aided schools with he promise to meet half the cost of reconstruction of premises to the standard of the Ministry of Education, the managers to retain control of school and staff: or to become controlled schools entirely financed by the State but with Church representatives retained on the managing board. In all (except aided schools) religious instruction to be based on Agreed Syllabuses.

[46] The provisions of this Act gave the Church of England increased grants (up to seventy-five per cent) for their aided schools, for which they themselves had asked: it also gave Roman Catholics help, for which they also had asked, for the building of new schools.

III

We must now retrace our steps to note a development in the life of the Free Churches which was to have far-reaching significance.

As early as 1910 John Howard Shakespeare (1857-1928), Secretary of the Baptist Union, had put forth an impassioned plea for a United Free Church of England. There was also a widespread opinion that a more officially representative body than the existing Free Church Council, limited as to its authority by its very constitution, was needed. The way to federation must be opened. In 1916 Shakespeare in his presidential speech at Bradford, declared that the divisions between the Free Churches were wasteful and ineffective because the full strength of the Churches was without a point of focus. So he pleaded for a federation:

> The feeling is advancing, with the inevitableness of the dawn and the springtime, that the differences between the Evangelical Free Churches are not sufficient ground for separation. . . . Denominationalism is a decaying idea. Today I rear upon the battlefield the standard of the United Free Church of England.[47]

Shakespeare followed his declaration by visitation of Free Church assemblies and sought the approval of the various denominations and also appointment of representatives for preliminary discussion. Although there was widespread agreement, there was also hesitancy in the Wesleyan Conference of 1916, but approval was given with only twenty against. In September 1916 a conference was held at Mansfield College, Oxford, followed by a further meeting in Cambridge in March 1917 and later in London. The outcome was a proposal for actual federation. In 1918 Shakespeare elaborated his ideal in *The Churches at the Cross Roads: A Study in Church Unity*, a book which had a wide circulation, and caused some controversy. It was recognized that denominational autonomy was sacrosanct, despite the fact that the proposal in no way intended invasion of denominational rights. In April 1918 the proposals came before the Baptist Union and were agreed to with little dissent. It was a similar situation with the other Free Churches,[48] with one exception. At the Wesleyan Conference of

[47] *Free Church Year Book* (1916).

[48] The proposals were presented to the following denominations: Baptist, Congregational, Wesleyan, Primitive Methodist, Independent Methodist, United Methodist, Moravian, Wesleyan Reform Union, Presbyterian, and Countess of Huntingdon's Connexion.

1918 it was decided to defer the matter, but a year later the proposals were adopted.

In October 1919 the first meeting of the Federal Council of Evangelical Free Churches took place. A new authoritative Free Church instrument had now been created. From this time the National Free Church Council and the Federal Council were to run parallel to each other until, they were united, twenty years later, to form the present Free Church Federal Council.

As we have seen the new Council was on a representative basis, and gradually it became recognized as the official voice of Nonconformity. A statement of common faith and practice was drawn up covering the general doctrinal position of the Free Churches,[49] but this did not allow for the inclusion of the Unitarians.

Although it is now more than forty years since the Federal Council was established upon the basis of the ideals of unity expressed by J. H. Shakespeare, comparatively little progress has been made towards the creation of a United Free Church in England, though admittedly there has been a growth in mutual understanding and fellowship. In 1930, under the call of Dr Charles Brown, a committee was set up to explore the possibilities and in 1932 Dr Hugh Martin pressed the matter still farther in *The Unity of the Free Churches*. An impressive statistical survey of the distribution of the Free Churches was also presented to the Council by Professor Frank Tillyard.[50] A theological commission was appointed but little progress was made, not a little due to the somewhat intransigent position of the Baptists on the question of Baptism. The Methodists held aloof because they were preoccupied with the problems arising out of the achievement of Methodist Union in 1932. Later the question of union fell into the background because of attention being centred upon the proposals to unite the Federal Council and the National Free Church Council. The war and its aftermath resulted in further delays. In the late forties prolonged conversations took place between the

[49] For this statement see *The Churches at the Cross Roads*, Appendix I. Although Shakespeare had insisted that a federation of the Free Churches was the ideal for which he strove, it soon became clear that he envisaged the further possibility of a closer union between the Free Churches and the Church of England, and declared himself in favour of a modified episcopacy and, if necessary, some form of re-ordination (Ibid. Ch. 12).

[50] 'The Distribution of the Free Churches in England', *Sociological Review*, XXVII. (1935).1-18. The present writer recalls the deep impression made upon the meeting of the Council when this paper was read by Professor Tillyard.

Presbyterians and Congregationalists but without resulting in a union between the two denominations, though a sense of deepened fellowship and co-operation ensued.[51] Congregationalists and Baptists also sought for understanding upon the basis of their common principle of Independency.[52] Recently the issue of Free Church Union has been raised again, but 'in spite of good endeavours on all sides no progress has been made . . . and it is highly probable that it will have to go into cold storage again'.[53]

Nevertheless the issue remains a serious one, not least in the light of the growing ecumenical movement and the spiritual needs of our times. There still exists a great degree of unwillingness to surrender denominational sovereignty. It is probably true to say, as does Dr Jordan, that

> the necessary spiritual conditions for an actual union of the Free Churches do not, at the moment, exist in large enough measure. . . . Before actual union can become a real possibility, the Free Churches must be set on fire with a burning spiritual constraint in the matter.[54]

One thing, however, is certain, namely, for a great many in the Free Churches denominational barriers mean considerably less than they did to earlier generations.

Despite the failure of these impulses towards closer union, a greater cohesion was secured by the uniting of the two Councils in 1940.[55] The new constitution of the Free Church Federal Council preserves the executive power for the former Federal Council, and the Annual Congress provides the platform for more public expression of Free Church opinion and the machinery for its exercise. This union was an adventure in comprehension.[56]

[51] *Joint Conference Report* (1947).

[52] *A Plea for Unity* and *A Plan for Unity* were important documents in this discussion. See *Report of the special Committee appointed by the Baptist Union on the question of reunion between Baptists, Congregationalists, and Presbyterians* (1937). Between 1941 and 1952 the Baptist Union entered into conversations with the Churches of Christ (Disciples of Christ), but although there was a strengthening of relations, union was not found possible.

[53] *Report of the Methodist Church on the Free Church Federal Council* (1961), p. 1.

[54] Jordan, pp. 24-5.

[55] See *infra*, Appendix VII. The final act of union took place in the Baptist Church House on 16th September 1940.

[56] For a summary of efforts towards Free Church Union see *Free Church Union: The Present Position* (1961). (Published by the Free Church Federal Council, Tavistock Square, London, W.C.1.)

IV

We must now turn to the relation of the Free Churches in England to the problem of wider union since the rise of the ecumenical movement in 1920. The post-war years were marked by a new and more generous spirit in Church-relations in England. A deeper understanding of one another, a mutual recognition of scholarship in the various communions, a new pressure for greater missionary co-operation in other lands, and the new situation created by the war contributed to this closer relationship. It was in this setting that the Anglican bishops, in August 1920, issued from Lambeth the historic *Appeal to All Christian People*.[57]

The time has come, we believe, for all the separated groups of Christians to agree in forgetting the things which are behind and reaching out towards the goal of a reunited Catholic Church. . . . The vision which rises before us is that of a Church, genuinely Catholic, loyal to all Truth, and gathering into its fellowship all 'who profess and call themselves Christians', within whose visible unity all the treasures of faith and order, bequeathed as a heritage by the past to the present, shall be possessed in common, and made serviceable to the whole body of Christ.

The bishops asserted that a united Church could come into being upon a fourfold basis:[58] the acceptance of Holy Scripture, the Nicene Creed, the two Sacraments of Baptism and Holy Communion, and a Ministry possessing the call of the Spirit, and episcopal in form 'exercised in a constitutional manner'. The *Appeal* evoked a ready response from the Free Churches, some dissentients notwithstanding, and a provisional statement from the two Free Church Councils was issued on 28th September 1920. This declared the main principles in the light of which the Free Churches were prepared to enter into discussion. In March 1921 a statement, *The Free Churches and the Lambeth Appeal*, was issued. The various Free Church denominations eventually endorsed this statement, and in addition the several denominations made their own replies.

From the Free Church side there were three vital matters: the due recognition of the Free Churches; episcopal ordination as proposed in the scheme; the spiritual freedom of the Church.

[57] G. K. A. Bell, *D.C.U.* (1920-4).

[58] This was the famous 'Lambeth Quadrilateral' put forward when considering the question of Home Reunion at the Lambeth Conference of 1888.

Following this reply the Archbishop of Canterbury (Dr Randall Davidson) suggested that appointed representatives from both sides should begin fraternal conference on the whole question. So began a long and historic series of meetings, the like of which had not been seen since the Savoy Conference of 1661. Clearly the divided stream which had issued so disastrously from that assembly and the Act of Uniformity of 1662 which followed it had now begun to converge.

The Federal Council, as the officially representative body of the Free Churches, became responsible for the conduct of negotiations and the task which it discharged, and its wise defence of Free Church principles revealed the power of Free Church statesmanship. Its most outstanding and sagacious leader was Dr Carnegie Simpson.[59] Conversations proceeded during the next four years, and important issues were raised. A Preliminary Statement was issued in May 1922.[60] In July 1923 an important Memorandum of the status of the existing Free Church Ministry was put forth from the Anglican side.[61] It contained the following important affirmation.

> Such Free Church ministries we find it impossible to regard as 'invalid', that is, as null and void, or as effecting none of the purposes for which the ministry has been divinely ordained in the Church of Christ. Indeed we wish that the terms 'valid' and 'invalid' could be discontinued, involving as they seem to do a knowledge of the Divine Will and purpose and grace which we do not possess, and which it would be presumptuous to claim. . . . It seems to us to be in accordance with the Lambeth Appeal to say, as we are prepared to say, that the ministries which we have in view in this memorandum . . . are real ministries of Christ's Word and Sacraments in the Universal Church.

It is on record that on the occasion of the presentation of this memorandum Dr Simpson declared that if the Anglicans realized the full implications of the phrase—'real ministries of Christ's Word and Sacraments in the Universal Church'—it was 'the most notable thing which Lambeth had said to any non-episcopal

[59] H. Townsend, *The Claims of the Free Churches* (1949), p. 313, in which, though the writer expressed strong disapproval of reunion, states: 'Carnegie Simpson's leadership of Free Church discussions and negotiations with the Anglican leaders changed the religious atmosphere of the time.' To speak of Dr Carnegie Simpson's leadership is not to deny the valuable contributions of other members, amongst whom were Dr S. M. Berry, Dr A. E. Garvie, Dr J. Scott Lidgett, and Professor A. S. Peake.

[60] Bell, *D.C.U.*, pp. 143-5.

[61] Ibid. pp. 156-64.

Church since the time of, say, Bancroft or Laud'.[62] He further warned the Anglican representatives that this phrase would be much quoted by Free Churchmen in the future—as indeed has been the case. Dr Simpson suggested that they should reconsider the statement, and asked if they really meant it. The reply was in the affirmative, but there was a measure of reservation for the words immediately following in the memorandum were these: 'Yet ministries even so regarded may be in varying degrees irregular or defective.' It is not surprising that the declaration led to protests from Free Churchmen. The Memorandum further declared:

> The Anglican Church is bound to secure the authorization of its ministers for its own congregations, and no one could be authorized to exercise his ministry among them who had not been episcopally ordained.[63]

It was further stated that this rule 'embodied principles to which the Anglican Church has throughout its history adhered'; further, the setting aside of this would involve relations to other episcopal Churches in East and West.

These points were dealt with in the reply of the Federal Council on 18th September 1923. In particular the insistence upon episcopal ordination according to the 'Preface' attached to the Ordinal in 1661 (which had been quoted in the Memorandum) was an important issue. The passage in the Reply is of such crucial importance as to justify quoting it at length.

> This is but one indication that we are dealing today not with the Anglicans of the Restoration, which deliberately desired to exclude Nonconformists and which penalized them, but with the Anglicans of the Lambeth Appeal, which earnestly seeks reunion and which approaches Nonconformity with friendship. But we should do injustice to our Anglican brethren who presented this memorandum if we suggested that they grounded themselves merely on a clause from a preface inserted at a time more marked by controversy than by charity. They say that this preface 'embodied principles to which the Anglican Church has throughout its history adhered'. We submit that this is hardly accurate historically. It is well known that up to the time of this deliberately exclusive preface, there were ministering in the cures of

[62] P. Carnegie Simpson, *Recollections* (1943), p. 78; F. A. Iremonger, *William Temple* (1948), p. 457.

[63] Bell, *D.C.U.*, p. 160.

the Church of England 'many'—it is Bishop Cosin's reckoning—who had not received episcopal ordination, and whom the bishops did not ordain. We do not magnify these cases, which were, we admit, exceptional. But if the Church of England in the seventeenth century could receive ministers from certain reformed Churches without episcopal ordination and yet did not thereby lose its catholic identity, then it could and can—so far as principle goes—in the twentieth century admit, by some method other than ordination, those whom, despite their not having had episcopal hands laid upon them, it has just formally and fully recognized as being really in the ministry of Christ's Word and Sacraments in the Universal Church. It could do it so far as any 'principles to which the Anglican Church has throughout its history adhered' are concerned.

On receipt of this reply the Anglicans considered and proposed a modification[64] in terms of ordination *sub conditione*, that is, as ordination according to the Anglican Ordinal but prefaced and governed by a condition expressed in such words as: 'If thou art not already ordained. . . .' 'The persons thus conditionally ordained would simply be acknowledging as a fact the existence of a doubt in the mind of the ordaining authority without necessarily implying that he himself admitted its validity.'[65] Although this was a sincere attempt on the part of the Anglican bishops to bridge the gulf, it was quite unacceptable to the Federal Council;[66] but in reply the latter made the suggestion of conferment of 'an extended commission' mutually, and not from one side only, indicating 'unambiguously' that such was not ordination.[67]

For the time being conversations were suspended, some twenty meetings having been held, it seemed to many with little result. Yet there had been a fine manifestation of the Christian spirit, and the basis of goodwill had been secured. It was inevitable that the crucial question should be that of the ministry; but it should be noted that there was common agreement as to the importance of presbyteral and the congregational elements in the polity of any united Church. Furthermore it had become apparent that there

[64] *A Second Memorandum of the Status of the existing Free Church Ministry*, Bell (Second series, 1930), pp. 77-85.

[65] Ibid. p. 84.

[66] In an article on 'Progress in Reunion', *The Times* (25th September 1925) declared: 'The Free Church conclusions that this statement removed any necessity for the reordination of such ministers even *sub conditione* seems to the ordinary observer one that is obvious and natural and even irresistible' (quoted Jordan, p. 175).

[67] Bell, *D.C.U.*, II.86

were large areas of agreement on basic Christian verities. During 1926-7 the several denominations severally expressed their views.[68]

It should be remembered that these negotiations did not receive unanimous approval on either side. Amongst the Anglicans the Anglo-Catholics were in strong disagreement; on the Free Church side there were also serious misgivings, and the tension was keenest amongst the Baptists[69] and the Congregationalists.

We have dealt with these early stages of negotiations regarding reunion because they reveal questions of fundamental importance, which forty years later still remain unsolved.

The controversy which resulted in the rejection by Parliament of the Revised Prayer Book in 1928 caused considerable concern amongst Free Churchmen, not least because it occurred during this period of negotiations on reunion.[70] The greater portion of the Book was not open to question, but the provision for the Reservation of the Sacrament was the crux of controversy. To the Archbishop of Canterbury, Dr Davidson, this was cause for alarm, for he was aware that many clergy and congregations were insisting on the use of the Reserved Sacrament not only for purposes of communion for the sick, but also for purposes of devotion 'in a way which would have been not only surprising but repellant to Lancelot Andrewes, or William Laud, or E. B. Pusey, or John Keble'.[71] In 1926 the two Free Church Councils had expressed concern about Romanizing tendencies in the Church of England, but in the matter of the Revised Book they were prepared to proceed cautiously recognizing that so far at least it was a domestic matter within Anglicanism. The Federal Council, however, received an official request from the Parliamentary Ecclesiastical Sub-committee for an expression of opinion on the Revised Book. In reply the Council declared that the important

[68] Bell, *D.C.U.*, pp. 102-13.

[69] For Resolution of the Baptist Union Assembly of 1926, see Bell, *D.C.U.*, II.77-85. Dr T. R. Glover and Dr Henry Townsend were strong in opposition to the proposals. For the reply of the Congregational Union, see Ibid. pp. 113-16.

[70] For an account of the proceedings see Jordan, Ch. 13; G. K. A. Bell, *Randall Davidson* (1935), Ch. 82; J. G. Lockhart, *Cosmo Gordon Lang* (1948), Ch. 25. The Revised Book was presented to Parliament in December 1927 and rejected by the Commons by 238 to 205 votes. After revision it was presented again in June 1928 and was rejected by 266 to 220 votes. It was not intended to supersede the 1662 Prayer Book but to be for optional use.

[71] G. K. A. Bell, *Randall Davidson*, pp. 798ff.

question was 'the adequacy of the guarantees' against misuse. In March 1928 under the strong conviction that even in its final form no such effective measures were assured, the Federal Council urged that Parliament should withhold consent. Following the rejection the bishops proclaimed 'the inalienable right' of the Church to order its own worship and at the close of 1928 the Revised Prayer Book was published, but with clear statement that it must not be regarded as authorized. In July 1929 the bishops declared that they would not regard deviations within the limits of the Book as implying disloyalty. Later the Archbishop forbade Continuous Reservation, but the bishop of each diocese must be responsible for authorizing any change in worship.

This permissive use naturally brought disapproval from the Free Churches which may be expressed in the oft-quoted word of Dr Carnegie Simpson: 'An umpire . . . had given his decision but the decision was to be ignored. Really, this was hardly cricket.'[72] It will be seen at once that the decision of the bishops to grant permissive use was a departure from the terms of the Act of Uniformity, and this step was taken in face of the decree of Parliament.

Basically the attitude of the Free Churches in this question is expressed in the words of Dr Jordan:

> The Free Churches had a certain right to act as a trustee of Evangelical Protestantism. They could not stand by in silence and indifference while a new Prayer Book was brought forward which seemed to them to threaten certain aspects of Reformation doctrine.[73]

In addition, despite the Anglican approach in the Lambeth Appeal, this innovation raised new problems as to any possibility of reunion. Nevertheless the Free Church attitude was wise and cautious. Again in the words of Dr Jordan:

> It would have been hard to forgive the Free Churches if they had endeavoured to make capital out of the unfortunate situation. To their credit they did not.[74]

Returning now to the question of reunion, there was considerable disappointment amongst the Free Churches that at the

[72] P. Carnegie Simpson, *Recollections* (1943), p. 91.
[73] *Free Church Unity*, p. 202.
[74] Ibid. p. 203. It is worth noting that the issue of Prayer-Book revision is now (1962) being raised by Dr Ramsay, Archbishop of Canterbury, as one which cannot be long postponed.

Lambeth Conference of 1930[75] only scanty reference was made to the negotiations with the Free Churches. In the following year, however, at the invitation of Archbishop Lang, conversations were resumed. The Federal Council, in its acceptance of such proposal, urged that in the light of the previous discussions some attempt at practical expression of unity should be made. Already occasional authorization had been given to non-episcopal ministers to preach in Anglican churches,[76] and early in 1932 there came the further suggestion that Free Churchmen might be admitted to the Sacrament of Holy Communion if they were unable to partake in their own churches through distance or other circumstance; or if present at united gatherings particularly in connection with reunion. These suggestions were not regarded favourably by some Free Churchmen, but others regarded the offer as a step forward, and one which only a short while before would have never occurred.

In taking up the new conversations there was an early realization that something must be done to inform opinion and allay suspicions amongst both Anglicans and Free Churchmen generally. The result was a document bearing the title of *A Sketch of a United Church*,[77] in which there was an attempt to portray a United Church in action, and as one in which the essential principles in the constituent elements would be preserved. The document presented 'a picture of a united Church in which the Episcopal, Presbyteral and Congregational systems all find harmonious expression'. It was concerned with 'agreement in action', so that the Churches concerned might consider its possibilities. The system of government was the representative or conciliar type, in a gradation of courts—the Congregational Council, the Diocesan Synod, and the General Assembly, in all of which both laity and clergy would be represented. The Bishop would take his place along with the presbyters and representatives of the laity and though 'naturally' he would preside,

[75] *The Report of the Lambeth Conference* (1930), p. 118. See also J. G. Lockhart, *Cosmo Gordon Lang* (1949), pp. 347-8, 367, and F. W. Iremonger, *William Temple* (1948), pp. 459-60.

[76] In one instance acute controversy arose when Dr L. P. Jacks, a leading Free Churchman and Unitarian, preached at a non-statutory service in Liverpool Cathedral in 1933. The traditions of this Cathedral as 'a University of the Spirit' were broad, and Dr Dwelly (Dean) and Canon Raven made a dignified *apologia* of their action when they were censured by the Convocation of York. See *Two Letters . . . concerning the Action . . . against Liverpool Cathedral* (1934).

[77] Published in 1935.

this would not be of necessity, and in any case he 'would not have any final authority in legislation or administration apart from the concurrence of presbyters and laity'.[78] The Congregational Council would be responsible not only for finance and property but also 'over the practice of the congregation in worship'. Diocesan Synod would have responsibility for administration, together with some legislative authority within its area, and the General Assembly would be the supreme conciliar authority with legislative powers.[79] 'The united Church would be a Church *with* bishops but not *under* bishops.'[80]

As to the ministry, recognizing that in previous discussion the Free Church representatives had agreed that the episcopal element in ordination was to be preserved,[81] it is important to notice the accompaniments of this retention of this episcopal element. Presbyters are to be associated with the bishop in the act of ordination; it was also declared that the constitution of the United Church 'must leave room for and recognize as permissible various theories of the origin and nature of the episcopate'. Thus whilst some would say that the principle of the ordination is that of an apostolic succession through the episcopate, such would legitimately be an individual opinion, but *not* a principle of the united Church. Non-episcopal Churches could not reasonably condition episcopacy in ordination, in usage and in principle beyond this. Two other important matters are contained in this document. There is the recognition that the people 'should have a full effective voice in the selection of the minister of the congregation',[82] and also there is unqualified assertion of the spiritual liberty of the Church, the action and decision of which 'in respect of faith, worship, morals, discipline and government must be free from the control of or reversal by any secular authority'.[83]

Surveying this document, the influence of the principles of the Free Churches is apparent and may be summed up in the words of Dr Simpson, which still have penetrating influence.

[78] Ibid. p. 10.

[79] Ibid. p. 9.

[80] P. Carnegie Simpson, in *British Weekly* (17th January 1935). The present writer recalls the universal acceptance of this summary phrase when used by Dr Simpson in a session of the Federal Council.

[81] 'It is hopeless and useless to discuss unity at all with our Anglican brethren—even the more liberal among them—on the idea that episcopal ordination is to be ended' (Ibid.).

[82] *A Sketch of a United Church*, p. 9.

[83] Ibid. p. 11.

If we of the Free Churches hand down to the future, as agreed positions indispensable in any proposals for union with Anglicanism, such bases about government, about episcopacy, about the rights of the people and about spiritual freedom, . . . then we shall not have failed in our contribution.[84]

The document reveals an enormous change in the relations between Anglicans and Nonconformists, especially when the position in the seventeenth century is remembered.[85] Such a document would have delighted the soul of Richard Baxter, who throughout his life was the apostle of Christian Unity, and who attempted again and again to secure a framework for the union of the divided Church in England. The separating streams, which even in the time of Baxter were becoming wider apart, had now drawn closer than ever before in a declaration which embodied some of his own proposals made two-and-a-half centuries earlier. It seemed to respond to Baxter's own entreaty:

Will God never put it into the hearts of rulers to call together some of the most godly, learned, moderate and peaceable of all opinions, to agree upon a way of union and accommodation and not to cease till they have brought it to this issue? To come as near together as they can possibly in their principles, and where they cannot, yet to unite as far as may be in their practice though on different principles: and when that cannot be, yet to agree on the most loving, peaceable course in the way of carrying out our different practices: that so we may have unity in things necessary, liberty in things unnecessary and charity in all.[86]

In January 1938 a further document was issued, which incorporated the substance of *A Sketch of a United Church*, but indicated more fully the pattern of a United Church in England. It bore the title: *An Outline of a Reunion Scheme*.[87] In 1941 the Federal Council presented a reply gathering together the findings of the various denominations following a consideration of this *Outline*.[88]

The preoccupation of the Free Church Council and the

[84] *British Weekly* (17th January 1935).

[85] Two other explanatory documents were issued alongside the above: *The Practice of Intercommunion and The Doctrine of the Church* and *1662 and Today*.

[86] *Saints' Everlasting Rest* (1650).

[87] Bell, *D.C.U.*, III.71-102. In 1933 'Friends of Reunion' was formed as a group for detailed study and research, and with the purpose of spreading information and fostering the spirit of unity generally. It produced *Friends of Reunion Bulletin* from 1934 onwards.

[88] Bell, Ibid. pp. 102-19.

Federal Council with arrangements for uniting the two bodies, together with the outbreak of war and the unavoidable postponement of the Lambeth Conference which should have been held in 1940, brought a cessation of conversations on reunion, though it was agreed that eventually the work should be resumed.

A notable development in inter-Church relations was the formation in September 1942 of the British Council of Churches with Archbishop Temple as its first President. The Church of England, and the Free Churches together with the Church in Scotland, Wales and Ireland, are represented in this Council.

On 3rd November 1946, Dr Fisher, Archbishop of Canterbury, in a now famous sermon preached before the University of Cambridge[89] raised again the whole question of reunion and the possibility of further conversations. It represented a new line of approach. Dr Fisher suggested that the 'constitutional method' involving 'schemes of union' was really 'the most difficult of all ways to reunion'. Further, he suggested 'a process of assimilation, of growing alike' . . . 'a movement towards a free and unfettered exchange of life in worship and sacrament'. Starting from the earlier agreement that both episcopal, presbyteral and congregational elements 'must all have an appropriate place in the order of life of a reunited Church',[90] Dr Fisher proposed that, accepting the fact of episcopacy—yet apprehensive concerning it 'for reasons obvious enough in Church history'—the non-episcopal Churches might 'try it out on their own ground first'.

> They [i.e. non-episcopal Churches] accept the fact of it. If they do so for a reunited Church, why not also and earlier for the process of assimilation, as a step towards full communion? It may be said that in a reunited Church they could guard themselves in the constitution against the abuses of episcopacy. But they could do so far more effectively by taking it into their own system.[91]

Towards the close of his Cambridge sermon the Archbishop spoke the following challenging words:

[89] The sermon is printed in *Church Relations in England* (1950), pp. 5-12, under the title, 'A step forward in Church Relations'.

[90] So far every proposed constitution had proceeded on the assumption which had been unequivocally declared at Lausanne Conference (1927)—*Faith and Order: Proceedings of the World Conference, Lausanne 1927*, p. 469.

[91] It is unfortunate that this last phrase about 'taking episcopacy' into the systems of the Free Churches has been so often taken out of its context, thereby giving the impression of a suggested imposition of episcopacy upon these Churches, whereas the context is that of 'growing together' by a process of 'assimilation'.

It is, I think, not possible yet nor desirable that any Church should merge its identity in a newly constituted union. What I desire is that I should be able freely to enter their Churches and they mine in the Sacrament of the Lord and in the full fellowship of worship, that His life may freely circulate between us. Cannot we grow to full communion with each other before we start to write a constitution? . . . Have we the wisdom, the humility, the love and spirit of Christ sufficient for such a venture as I have suggested? If there were agreement on it, I would thankfully receive at the hands of others their commission in their accustomed form and in the same way confer our own: that is the mutual exchange of love and enrichment to which Lambeth, 1920, called us.[92]

Never before had the Primate of All England spoken thus to the non-episcopal Churches of this country. As we have already said his utterance was the opening of a new door. The suggestions made by the Archbishop aroused widespread interest and later, in November 1946, the Free Church Federal Council appointed representatives to explore the implications of the Cambridge sermon. Early in 1947 these representatives met the Archbishop, and it was proposed that if formal discussions were to take place it would be wise that they should be between the Church of England and individual Free Churches and not between the Church of England and the Federal Council, though the latter would naturally be associated. A definite invitation to resume conversations was given. A Joint Conference met at Lambeth on 23rd May 1947.[93] An *Interim Report* was published in March 1949 under the title *Church Relations in England*. It was suggested by Dr Fisher that on both sides an interval of at least a year should be allowed for full discussion before a judgement upon it should be given.

This document was not concerned with an attempt to draw up any scheme for reunion or intercommunion, but was rather an explication of the suggestions contained in the Cambridge sermon. Its main issue concerned the experimentation of episcopacy upon the part of the Free Churches, in such a way as to make intercommunion possible. It was recognized that temporarily at least this would involve the extension of parallel episcopates exercising jurisdiction in denominational Churches, with arrangements for

[92] *Church Relations in England*, p. 12.

[93] There were two chairmen of the Committee, The Bishop of Derby and Dr Nathaniel Micklem—and the Report was issued under both signatures.

intercommunion and interchange of ministers based upon a series of concordats between the Churches concerned. The following indicates the purpose and spirit of the document.

The question before our Church is whether, for the sake of greater visible unity, for the sake of a swifter and surer growing together of the separated Christian traditions, and for the sake of eucharistic fellowship, which is at present impossible, the link with the historic succession of bishops, which is preserved in the Church of England, should be accepted by the Free Churches; whether this can be done without the abandonment on either side of vital principles; whether even if some ambiguities still remain, the spiritual advantage for all would manifestly outweigh the difficulties which would have to be faced and overcome.[94]

As we have already observed it had previously been decided that if further conversations were resumed these should be between the Church of England and individual Free Churches. In due course observations upon the document, *Church Relations in England*, were forthcoming, and these show differences of emphasis. The Baptists found the main difficulty in the view that intercommunion should be made dependent upon episcopacy, even though liberty of interpretation by the Free Churches should be allowed as already obtained in the Church of England itself. Though convinced that the Report did not indicate 'the right step forward', the Baptists still hoped that conversations would continue. The Methodist Church, welcoming the Report, recognized the practical difficulties which would be created by parallel episcopates, but also declared that *within* Methodism there exists no obstacle to the immediate establishment of intercommunion with the Church of England. 'The door is already open.' Given the assurances of liberty of interpretation and the preservation of relations and intercommunion with other non-episcopal Churches as now enjoyed, the Methodist Church would be prepared

[94] Op. cit. p. 38. It should be noted further that the Lambeth Conference of 1948 gave detailed consideration to the question of unity not only with regard to the non-episcopal Churches in England but also far afield. Whilst declaring that 'there has come to us a new sense of the divine imperative', there is an unambiguous assertion that 'the acceptance of episcopacy as the rule of the Church is a pre-requisite for the formation of a United Church with Anglican participation, or for the establishment of rules of intercommunion' (*Lambeth Conference Report* [1948], p. 50). There is a useful *excursus* on 'Supplemental Ordination' which 'without denying the reality of a previous ordination by Christ in part of his Body, shall confer all that *may* be lacking of grace and authority through the failure of the whole Body to associate itself with the previous ordination' (Ibid. pp. 64-6).

'to proceed to a further stage'. The Congregationalists do not seem to have made an official reply, but one aspect of thought amongst them is represented by Dr Nathaniel Micklem's *Congregationalism and Episcopacy*, in which he urges sympathetic understanding and, if possible some experiment.

In 1957 an important document, *Relations between Anglican and Presbyterian Churches*, appeared. It dealt not so much with the relation between the Church of England and the Church of Scotland, but with 'the more fundamental subject of the relation between the Episcopalian and the Presbyterian systems of Church order'. As the Presbyterian Church of England was represented in the conversations we are justified in giving a brief account of this movement. It was in fact the result of the third of a series of conversations between Presbyterians and Anglicans in Scotland and England.[95] The report indicates a much closer approximation to the suggestions of the Cambridge sermon. On the Presbyterian side there is willingness to consider the functions of a bishop, as recognized by Anglicans, so long as the office is duly integrated with the presbytery and the whole Church. Hence the concept of 'a presiding Bishop-in-Presbytery', exercising functions in regard to ordination and pastoral oversight with authority given by consecration at the hands of bishops as well as with the authority of the collective presbytery. Over against the possibility of the acceptance of the 'historic episcopate' by the Presbyterian Churches there was set the possibility of the acceptance of a greater measure of 'corporate episcopacy' by the Anglican churches.[96] The report shows the impact of the affirmations made at Lausanne in 1927. On its appearance the *Church Times* observed:

> By far the most significant thing . . . is that it should have been produced at all. . . . The iron curtain of separation between brethren in Christ has been well and truly pierced, at least at one point, by this unprecedented unanimity.[97]

The Report represented 'a new approach to unity through mutual adaptation'. Whilst considerable discussion was aroused within

[95] The first series was in 1932-4; the second 1949-51 on the question of intercommunion. This produced two documents: *Things Believed in Common* and *Things that Might be Undertaken in Common*.

[96] *Relations between Anglican and Presbyterian Churches*, p. 12.

[97] 3rd May 1957.

the Presbyterian Churches in England, in Scotland unfortunately a storm of controversy developed. Despite the clear statement in the Report that the proposals 'do not envisage one single Church of Great Britain . . . but *a fullness of sacramental communion* between these two Churches, involving fully authorized interchange of communicants and mutual recognition of ministries',[98] it was taken by many 'as though it were an actual blue-print of a prospective union'.[99] In May 1959 the General Assembly of the Church of Scotland rejected the proposals by a vote of 300 to 266. Remembering the acrimonious debate concerning the term 'bishops' the margin of difference of opinion might have been considerably greater.

In 1953 the Faith and Order Committee of the Methodist Church proposed that steps should be taken 'in promotion of intercommunion with the Church of England' and in 1955 both Churches agreed upon conversations. In 1958 the findings were issued in a report: *Conversations between the Church of England and the Methodist Church: An Interim Statement.* No specific recommendations are contained in the Report, but it was felt advisable to inform the Churches of the progress of the consultations. By emphasizing visible, organic unity as the ultimate goal and by the suggestion of an interim stage of 'parallelism in unity' involving *the unification of both ministries at the start,*[100] it takes a step even beyond the Anglican-Presbyterian report which we have just considered. The statement indicates the common ground already existing between the two Churches, and this is followed by an outline of 'the special situation of the Methodist Church in relation to the Church of England' and the circumstances of the separation which occurred two centuries ago.[101] In the light of the specific 'marks' of Methodism, the attitude of Methodism to episcopacy is considered and plainly stated.

Whilst it is undoubtedly true that a ministry in the apostolic succession as commonly understood is authentic and valid, it is certainly not true that ministries which God has raised up outside the succession cannot be authentic and valid ministries of the Church. Methodism could never accept either the contentions that without episcopacy there is no Church or any theory of the transmission of grace and authority

[98] Op. cit. p. 13.
[99] *The Ecumenical Review*, XII.247.
[100] Op. cit. p. 41.
[101] This chapter is the work of Dr Norman Sykes and Dr E. Gordon Rupp.

which would deny her a place in the Catholic Church and reduce her ministry and sacraments to spurious imitations. . . .

Methodism has never opposed episcopacy as a method of Church government. . . . Episcopal functions in British Methodism are distributed among various offices, most notably the President, the Chairmen of Districts, particularly in their pastoral care of the ministry, and the administration of their Districts, and superintendent ministers. But they act as representatives of the Conference, the governing body of the Church which itself exercises other episcopal functions such as the authorization of ordination. Methodism must consider whether it would not be making a substantial contribution to the reunion of Christendom and to the development of her own inheritance if these necessary functions now dispersed were brought together in the office of a consecrated person, called of God, authorized by the Church, and representative of the continuity and solidarity of the Church.

The bishop here conceived is not the prelate of the Middle Ages, nor the powerful, autocratic, political figure of more recent times,[102] but the humble man of God, the father of Christ's flock, the *pastor pastorum* who builds up the life of the Churches, maintains faith and order, and represents the unity and universality of the Church. Thus freed from the secular forces which have deflected it from its true character, episcopacy could be restored to its original spiritual purpose. Such an episcopacy would not be 'monarchical' but 'constitutional', providing for the due co-operation of the presbyterate and the 'congregation of Christ's faithful people', and would ensure their rightful place in the government of the Church.

As already emphasized, this Report is only *an interim statement*, and should be so regarded;[103] it is not a final verdict.

This survey of the relations between the Church of England and the Free Churches reveals the enormous change which has taken place within the comparatively short space of fifty years. The old animosities have disappeared and a new spirit prevails despite the continuance of differences in opinion maintained with conscientious conviction upon each side. 1662 and today form great contrasts. Though the divided streams still exist, these years have shown a great convergence, only to be accounted for ultimately by the work of the Spirit of God in the hearts and minds of sincere Christians.

[102] Cf. *Church Relations in England*, p. 39: 'The Anglican episcopate has been steadily shedding autocratic pretensions.'

[103] *Anglicans and Methodists Talk Together*, by the Bishop of Oxford and Dr Harold Roberts, is a popular exposition of the conversations, intended for study in the parishes and circuits.

It is also quite clear that the two focal points of difficulty still remain. The problems of episcopacy and intercommunion—deeply related to each other—are still unsolved, but possible solution is nearer than ever before. It is also important to remember that thought upon these matters within Anglicanism is not homogeneous. This is revealed by the recent declaration upon the part of a distinguished group of Anglicans concerning Intercommunion.[104] Whilst affirming the historic episcopate as 'an important expression of the continuity of the Church in time and the unity of its fellowship across space', the signatories further assert that 'it is our Lord who calls and commissions his ministers and that He is not tied to any one form of ministry'. On the nature of non-episcopal ministries the Letter continues:

We believe that our Lord conveys through these ministries the same grace of the Word and Sacraments as He bestows through the historic ministry of bishops, priests and deacons, and that He does this, not as an act of uncovenanted mercy, but because they are real and efficacious ministries within the Body of His Church.

We understand this to mean that inasmuch as non-episcopally ordained ministers, in these communions whose essential orthodoxy our Church has repeatedly recognized, are regularly commissioned by prayer and the laying-on of hands to proclaim God's Word and administer His Sacraments, they exercise a ministry that is both priestly and prophetic, no less than do their brethren who have been episcopally ordained to the office of a priest in the Church of God. . . . We have no doubt that every faithful minister of the non-episcopal communions who has been duly called and commissioned to act as such exercises the one priestly ministry of Christ no less than do his Anglican brethren. . . .

We believe that, as far as the doctrine of the Ministry is concerned, there is no barrier to intercommunion between members of such Christian bodies as are corporately seeking full and organic unity with one another.

We believe that the Holy Communion is not only the goal of unity but also an efficacious means of the grace of unity, as of all grace.

Such a declaration stands forth as a hopeful sign of our times in the midst of a divided Church of England. There is also an expression of dissent from the statement of the Lambeth Committee on 'Church Unity and the Church Universal'[105] that 'Anglicans

[104] *Intercommunion: An Open Letter to the Archbishop of Canterbury and the Archbishop of York* (1961).
[105] *Lambeth Conference*, 1958, p. 245.

conscientiously hold that the celebrant of the Eucharist should have been ordained by a bishop standing in the historic succession and generally believe it to be their duty to bear witness to this principle by receiving Holy Communion only from those who have been thus ordained'. The Letter continues:

We do not acknowledge such a duty and we know that our conviction is shared by many other Anglicans. Moreover we hold that our view is in full accord with the teaching of our Church and its traditions as both Catholic and Reformed.[106]

V

One further question demands brief consideration, namely the relation between Church and State as considered by the Free Churches.[107]

From the very beginnings of English Nonconformity the Church has been regarded as essentially 'a gathered church', that is, a company of Christian believers gathered 'out of the world' by the divine Spirit, for worship and service. Such a conception is in entire contrast to the Anglican conception, long held but latterly widely denied within the Church of England itself, that the nation looked at from the secular aspect is the State and from the religious side is the Church.[108] It was this difference as to the true nature of the Church which lay behind the Separatists of the sixteenth century and the Nonconformists of the seventeenth. One of the fundamental principles of this Nonconformity was the decided objection to any alliance of ecclesiastical systems with the civil power in terms of established control of the latter. To use an honoured phrase, 'the crown rights of the Redeemer' are supreme.

This is not to imply that the State is to be regarded as merely a secular authority. For Free Churchmen,

[106] It was natural that the 'Open Letter' should provoke adverse comment from other schools of Anglican thought, e.g. the correspondence in *The Church Times* (10th November, *et seq.*), much of which is legalist in approach to the problem. An expression of Free Church opinion is seen in a letter to *The Guardian* (13th November) from twenty theological tutors in Methodist Colleges.

[107] For detailed study the following are important documents: (1) *The Report of the Archbishops' Committee on Church and State* (1916); (2) *The Archbishops' Commission on the Relations between Church and State* (1935); (3) *Church and State: The Report of a Commission appointed by the Church Assembly* (1952); (4) C. Garbett, Archbishop of York, *Church and State in England* (1950) and *The Claims of the Church of England* (1947); (5) *The Free Churches and the State: The Report of the Commission of Church and State* (1953); (6) B. L. Manning, *The Protestant Dissenting Deputies* (1952), Ch. 4: (7) H. Townsend, *The Claims of the Free Churches* (1949).

[108] The establishment of the Parochial Roll is so far a recognition that the Church is not the nation, nor yet the baptized citizens.

Church and State are two 'orders' set up by God for the good of men. If it is not the business of the State to urge them to love God, it is certainly concerned with the love of one's neighbour, the ethical expression of religion. . . . But the State must not make transcendent claims: it has no absolute and ultimate authority. The State exists under God to promote the good life of its citizens: its citizens do not exist for the sake of the State. Both Church and State stand under His authority and their service of Him should be complementary and not antithetical.[109]

In view of the existence, on the one hand, of the Church of England so definitely 'established' by the Act of Uniformity in 1662 with the consequent privileges, and, on the other, the prolonged disabilities of Nonconformists, it is not surprising that from time to time organized impulses to secure the 'disestablishment' of the Church of England should arise, for illustration of which we need not go farther into the past than the nineteenth century.

The most powerful challenge is associated with Edward Miall (1809-81)[110] who made the advocacy of disestablishment his life's work, and the main issue in the *Nonconformist*, the newspaper which he founded in 1841. In 1844 'The British Anti-State Church Associations' was formed, later to change its name to the 'Society for the Liberation of Religion from State Patronage and Control', now commonly known as 'The Liberation Society'. In the 1830 also the Dissenting Deputies manifested a growing concern for Church reform in the light of existing grievances for Dissenters, though their approach was cautious.[111] In the 1870's an open campaign began and intense agitation for disestablishment continued until about 1886, prompted mainly by the Educacation Act of 1870. In the campaigns of 1875-6 R. W. Dale was the main protagonist.[112] A further impetus arose from the ritual troubles which caused considerable uneasiness within the Church of England. In the following decade concentration was given to Welsh Disestablishment, and it was also hoped that it would prove possible for Scotland—in each case the Established Church forming only a minority of the population. In 1902 the Education

[109] *The Free Churches and the State* (1953), p. 55.

[110] See *supra*, p. 145. For earlier examples see Skeats and Miall, *History of the Free Church of England, 1688-1891*, pp. 471-3.

[111] There was also growing uneasiness as to the rightness of the *regium donum*, the State benefaction for Dissenters, and it was under Dissenting pressure that it was withdrawn in 1851; see *supra*, p. 113.

[112] A. W. W. Dale, *Life of R. W. Dale of Birmingham*, pp. 377-97.

Act and a Royal Commission on Ecclesiastical Disorders provided a further impulse.

Before the 1930's a decline in enthusiasm for disestablishment is noticeable in the Free Churches. In 1929 the Dissenting Deputies themselves expressed the opinion that it might be left to develop from within the Anglican Church itself.[113] The situation had changed radically. Many of the grievances of Dissenters had been removed, and thus establishment meant something much different and less antagonistic than at the beginning of the nineteenth century. Moreover, many Anglicans were as ready to assert the necessity of spiritual freedom of the Church as were Free Churchmen.[114] The rejection of the Revised Prayer Book in 1927 and 1928 raised the question acutely for the Anglicans. The Anglican Report on *Church and State* clearly presented a dilemma—the spiritual freedom of the Church and the preservation of the existing establishment; but there was no indication of a definite move in the direction of disestablishment.

This is also the situation at the present time amongst the Free Churches though this should not be regarded as any diminution of the conviction regarding State-control. There is, however, a firm opinion that some *State-recognition* is not only possible but desirable. Already a valuable co-operation between Church and State exists, for in the recent years the Free Churches have approved and accepted both recognition and, for educational and social work, financial aid. This is true of chaplaincy posts for Free Church ministers.[115]

In the light of the modern situation, therefore, it would appear unwise to pursue a demand for disestablishment. The position is well summarized in a resolution of the Free Church Federal Council in 1941:

> We should welcome a thorough examination of the forms in which such State recognition of the Church may be accepted without impairing in any way the independence of the Church in the discharge of its proper functions. We recognize that the increasing complexity of the structure of modern society involves an expansion of the function of the State to

[113] Manning, *The Protestant Dissenting Deputies*, p. 402.

[114] Cf. Archbishop Garbett in *Church and State in England*, p. 314.

[115] In an excellent booklet, *The Free Churches and the State*, Dr E. A. Payne indicates the position: 'There is of course a good deal of difference between the endowment or settlement by the State of one particular Church and the payment to several groups of Christians of money for service rendered of a social and educational character' (p. 14).

preserve and promote culture and morals, and that in order to protect these higher values against secularization, a close co-operation of the activities of the Church and of the State in those spheres it is necessary and should be encouraged so long as the distinction between these two organs of the thought and life of the nation is preserved.[116]

[116] Bell, *D.C.U.*, III.111-2.

CHAPTER ELEVEN

CONCLUSION

IN the foregoing pages we have attempted an outline of the development of English Nonconformity during the last three hundred years. Following this survey it is perhaps necessary to gather up some of the basic implications which are involved in this movement in the religious life of England.

I

We must pause briefly to note the present range and distribution of the English Free Churches. In the decline of religious allegiance which has characterized the national life for more than a generation, these Churches have suffered severely. In this they do not stand alone. Nevertheless, despite these inroads of secularism, the Free Churches remain an important factor in English religious life.

The Free Churches show great variety of distribution.[1] In the industrial areas and large centres of population in the Midlands and the North of England the Free Churches are numerous, whereas in the South of England they are less frequently found. In the rural areas of Cornwall and Lincolnshire there are chapels in almost every parish, largely because of the success of Methodism in these regions, a fact which explains the presence of Free Churches in industrial centres. The Baptist and Congregational Churches are found in urban centres, but in East Anglia and the south-west where Puritan influences were strong in the seventeenth century the number is considerable.[2] The Presbyterians are found mostly in the North and in Liverpool. The most recent statistics show more than a million and a half members.

Of the 9,786 ministers in England and Wales about one half are Methodist. In lay preachers the number reached over thirty

[1] See F. Tillyard, 'The Distribution of the Free Churches in England', *Sociological Review*, XXVII.(1935).1-18; Payne, pp. 140-1.

[2] Some three hundred Free Churches, mainly in London, the Eastern Counties, and the South-west, have a continuous history reaching back to 1662 and in some cases earlier still.

thousand, of which some twenty-two thousand are in the Methodist Church.[3]

It must also be remembered that the English Free Churches are the mother-churches of world-communities, and these show a remarkable extension of work overseas. It has been calculated that the world-communicant membership of the main groups of Free Churches is now more than thirty-nine and a half millions.[4] This reveals that the development of non-episcopal Churches is firmly planted and widespread.

II

It is sometimes asserted that the main responsibility for the present divided state of the Church in England rests upon those who for more than three centuries have been counted Nonconformists. Such an assertion betrays an entire misunderstanding of Church relations in England since the middle of the sixteenth century. A deeper understanding of the situation reveals a far wiser judgement. The story of these centuries shows with unmistakable clearness that on the one hand the desire to impose uniformity led to the sacrifice of unity; on the other, it is equally plain that those who became or were forced to become Nonformist did so out of no mere petulance but because they had conscientious convictions in regard to certain principles which not seldom had scant consideration from those who were in authority. This is the plain evidence which arises out of the record set down in the foregoing pages of this book. The fact is that many who ultimately became Nonconformists, remained for a long time within the national Church, hoping to influence its polity and development. Finally, when their hopes of so doing vanished, they considered separation to be the only alternative and accordingly organized their own Churches. The truth is that Presbyterians, Congregationalists, and Baptists, broke away from, or were excluded from, the Church of England because they stood firmly for certain positive principles. 'It was not merely dissidence which led to Dissent.' The Presbyterians stood for a certain parity of the ministry as opposed to a hierarchical system, and did so

[3] See Appendix VIII (*infra*, p. 252). The figures do not include statistics of the Society of Friends or those of Unitarian and Free Christian Churches.

[4] *The Catholicity of Protestantism*, ed. R. Newton Flew and R. E. Davies (1950), pp. 17ff. The figures stated are: Presbyterian 11,586,393, Baptist 13,500,000, Congregational 2,000,000, Methodist 12,496,000. The Anglican world-communicant membership is given as 9,000,000.

upon New Testament grounds. Clearly for those Presbyterians who were in incumbencies in 1662 the Act of Uniformity raised the whole issue of reordination. Other scruples were similarly involved for those already episcopally ordained, and for which they suffered ejection. Baptists and Congregationalists, by their separation in the sixteenth century, held strong convictions as to the autonomy of each separate congregation under the guidance of the Holy Spirit. At the end of the eighteenth century Methodists separated from the Church of England because they found no acceptance or opportunity for the exercise of their evangelistic endeavours.

In fairness it must be stated that a survey of the Nonconformity of these centuries reveals the fact that not only was there a firm and intransigent attitude against the Church of England, but also sometimes between Nonconformist groups themselves. There was antagonism between Presbyterians and Independents in the seventeenth century and between the Methodist groups in the first half of the nineteenth. The spirit of charity was sometimes lacking and out of it sprang divisive influences. Richard Baxter believed that if the right spirit in terms of Christian love had been manifest upon both sides of the conflict, the main divisions of the Church could have been healed; writing in 1656:

> The most that keeps us at odds is but about the right form and order of Church-government. Is the distance so great that Presbyterian, Episcopal and Independent might not be well agreed? Were they but heartily willing and forward for peace, they might—I know they might . . . If we could not in every point agree, we might easily find out and narrow our differences and hold Communion upon our agreement in the main . . . But is this much done? It is not done. To the shame of all our faces be it spoken, it is not done. Let each party flatter themselves now as they please, it will be recorded to the shame of the ministry of England, while the gospel shall abide in the Christian world.[5]

One thing is outstandingly clear. It was on the ground of conscience that these separations occurred. Men chose what they deemed to be right in scorn of consequence. What is to be admired is not so much their beliefs—many of which we have outgrown—but their fidelity to the beliefs they held, and their loyalty to what they took to be the voice of God, and for which

[5] *The Reformed Pastor* (1656), p. 187.

loyalty they were prepared to suffer. We may also observe that it was the same loyalty to conscience in not a few among the sequestered clergy under the Commonwealth, because they were unable to accept the Presbyterian system with its repudiation of the Book of Common Prayer. The voice of conscience, wherever it is found is 'the categorical imperative'.

The whole setting of the Restoration made the witness of the ejected the more significant. In the words of F. J. Powicke:

> The highest interests of England . . . lay in the unconscious keeping of the two thousand. We know the reactions to the licentiousness of every sort which came in with the King. . . . England's vital need was a break-water against the surrounding flood of iniquity, and this, to a greater extent than by anything else, was reared by the men whose lives bore witness to the holy Will of God which they had striven to obey, and by the multitudes whom they influenced.[6]

III

From our survey of English Nonconformity two basic principles emerge.

The first is the insistence upon the reality of individual experience of religion. The acceptance of the divine offer of salvation through Christ is regarded as of prime importance. 'We are not born Christians, nor can we be made Christians by others, not even by the Church.'[7] The requirement is personal faith. The nature of man is such that there is open to him 'the competence of the soul in matters of religion'.[8] Hence 'the dignity and value of the individual soul have been asserted and defended in opposition to those who would place the groups or the Church in a position of authority'.[9] We may recall a sentence of Isaac Watts:

> The great God who gave us all reason and conscience never appointed the conscience, nor the reason, nor the will of man absolutely to appoint the religious duties of another.[10]

The Nonconformist stood firmly by the Reformation principle of 'the direct access of the soul to God'. This is the fundamental principle behind the Quaker doctrine of 'The Inner Light'; it is seen in the 'covenants' which formed the basis of many Congregational churches, and in the case of the Baptists, the insistence

[6] *The British Congregationalist* (April 1912).
[7] Payne, p. 144.
[8] Quoted by Payne, p. 144.
[9] Ibid.
[10] *A New Essay on Civil Power*. *Works*, II.20

on the baptism of believers. It is seen in the recoil of the ejected ministers from the indiscriminate giving of the sacraments, from medieval excesses of ceremonial, and in the case of the Presbyterians, from the implicit denial of their call to the ministry when reordination was demanded. It is seen later on in the Methodist revival in its insistence upon 'conversion' as a fundamental requirement for admission into the membership of the Church at a time when spiritual religion was at an exceedingly low ebb.

The second principle which emerges from our study is the insistence upon the supremacy of life over organization. H. W. Clark discerns in this principle 'the crucial dividing-line' between the spirit of Nonconformity and that of Conformity.

The Nonconformist spirit is in succinct summary, the spirit which exalts life above organization. More than that, it is the spirit which holds that life should *make* organization, and that organization is at least greatly reduced in value (sometimes even valueless, sometimes even actually harmful) unless it be thus the direct product of life. . . . With one school of thought—the Conformist—the more distinctly ecclesiastical . . . the organization is looked upon as the power house, the manufactory in which the forces which make the life reside and out of which they issue; so that the primary duty of the religious man is to conform himself to the organization, in order that he may obtain the needed action upon life. Life is the ultimate aim, certainly; but in the actual construction of things, organization comes first. . . . With the other school of thought—the Nonconformist—the starting-point is different. The Nonconformist spirit begins not with the construction of an organization which, on theoretical or argumentative considerations is held to be the one necessary for the production of life, but farther down and farther back. Whatever organization comes into existence . . . must be the natural and automatic, producing, by the existing life, a system which that existing life finds necessary. . . . So the primary duty of the religious man, on this view, is not to conform to whatever religious organization he finds already occupying the field, but to secure for himself the presence and energizing power of a religious life and thereafter to let that work itself out into an organization, which shall be at the same time the life's product and the life's new inspiration.[11]

Whilst the record of Nonconformity shows that it has by no means always fulfilled this ideal at the highest level it still remains a fact that throughout its history it has insisted on 'the primacy

[11] Clark, pp. 3-4.

of the gospel over all matters of Church policy and organization', and in practice this has developed an elasticity rarely found in insistent Conformist organization. It has afforded a heritage of freedom, only limited by its members' loyalty to Christ.

Out of this twofold insistence just considered, Nonconformity has stood for two affirmations.

The first is its conception of the nature of the Church. In the seventeenth century Anglicans thought of the Church of England as coterminous with the nation. This view was still held even when membership of the Church meant little or nothing to numbers of English folk who had been baptized into it. Against this view Nonconformity insisted that 'the true Church must consist of believers gathered out of the world, and was a spiritual not a geographical reality'. This conception of the 'gathered Church' is of prime importance. The ideal is expressed in the following passage from *The Protestation Protested* (1641), published anonymously by Henry Burton (d. 1648):

Christs voyce must first bee heard, to call forth his sheepe, and to gather them into their flockes, and folds. For *'Εκκλησία* the Church is properly a Congregation of Beleevers, called out from the rest of the world. . . . Surely Gods people must be separatists from the world and from false churches, to become a pure and holy people unto the Lord.[12]

We may compare a sentence from Richard Baxter, who was but 'a meer Nonconformist':

The Church's separation from the unbelieving world is a necessary duty; for what is a Church but a society dedicated or sanctified to God, by separation from the rest of the world.[13]

In such a community 'the crown rights of the Redeemer' are paramount as the source of authority; the community lays itself open to the promptings of the Spirit of God in all its decisions and determinations.

Out of this insistence arises the second affirmation, namely an understanding of the responsibility that rests implicitly upon the individual Christian. There is a responsibility regarding his own spiritual condition. Holiness of life becomes a prime demand:

[12] Op. cit. f.B.3. For this quotation I am indebted to G. F. Nuttall's exposition of 'the Congregational Way' in *Visible Saints* (1957), pp. 52-3.

[13] *A Christian Directory* (1673), III.53.

the acceptance of 'the principle of Fitness'.[14] To quote Henry Burton again:

A particular Church or Congregation rightly collected and constituted consists of none, but such as are living Members of Christ the head, and visible Saints under him, the one and onely living King of Saints.[15]

The same truth finds expression in John Wesley's *A Plain Account of Christian Perfection* (1777). As Wesley declared in a letter to Joseph Benson: 'Holiness is the love of God and man, or the mind which was in Christ.'[16] In the exultant words of Charles Wesley:

Thy nature be my law,
Thy spotless sanctity,
And sweetly every moment draw
My happy soul to Thee.

Soul of my soul remain!
Who didst for all fulfil,
In me, O Lord, fulfil again,
Thy heavenly Father's will![17]

The quality of such holiness is positive. Such was the affirmation regarding the nature of spiritual life within the Church. In the words of Dr Bett:

There can be no real divorce between the life and the work . . . either of the individual believer or of the whole fellowship of believers that we call the Church. The work and witness of the Church is always both energized and authorized by the hidden life of faithful souls. There is always a proportion between the holiness of the members of the Church and the success of the work of the Church.[18]

Arising from this is the service of the individual Christian in the world. Nonconformity has always reaffirmed the Reformation principle of 'the priesthood of all believers'. The late Bishop of Oxford, Dr Kirk, acclaimed this as 'the decisive formula of all non-episcopal Christendom'.[19] The phrase is not always

[14] G. F. Nuttall, *Visible Saints*, Ch. 4.
[15] Op. cit. f.B.3; quoted by G. F. Nuttall, ibid. p. 132.
[16] Dated 5th October 1770; *Letters*, V.203.
[17] *MHB* 547.
[18] H. Bett, *The Spirit of Methodism* (1937), p. 157.
[19] *The Apostolic Ministry*, ed. Kirk (1946), p. 48.

completely understood, but the words of the late T. W. Manson form an adequate definition:[20]

The priesthood of believers means that they are permitted and enabled to share in the continuing high-priestly work of Christ by offering themselves in love and obedience to God and in love and service of men.

So in Nonconformity there has developed the apostolate of the laity; further, this principle lies behind the widespread concern for social issues and the challenge to social evils; it also accounts for the widespread missionary enterprise. The Nonconformist movements from the time of their origin were sealed to self-commitment for Christ's sake.

Their roots were in the faith of the individual, their scene of action the experience of the individual, their sanction the responsibility of the individual.[21]

In the light of the above the attitude to hierarchical authority on the one hand and to the secular authority on the other became inevitable.

The impulse of Nonconformity which was the result of the Act of Uniformity was fundamentally a repudiation of hierarchical demands. It is a mistake to say that their action was determined by stubborn adherence to a few trifling scruples. The majority of the ejected ministers felt no fanatical objection to kneeling at the Lord's Supper, or wearing the surplice, or to the cross in baptism, or to a liturgy, or in some cases even to episcopacy as such. What brought them to refusal was the oath demanding that they should agree to everything in a Prayer Book made 'more grievous than before'. As Baxter said: 'A weight more grievous than a

[20] T. W. Manson, *Ministry and Priesthood: Christ's and Ours* (1958), pp. 38-9, 70. Manson points out that some of the functions implied in the concept of *sacerdos* had been taken over by a new ministerial order in the non-episcopal communions. Under the Presbyterian system the administration of the sacrament is reserved to ministers (Westminster Confession, XXVII.4); ordination can be given only by those already in the order of ministry. In contrast, thoroughgoing Independency (Congregational and Baptist) maintains the inalienable right of the congregation to choose and ordain their own minister, at the same time asserting that he has no function or status which cannot be claimed in principle by any other member. Methodists, whose Church-government is presbyterian in pattern, take a middle course as to those administering the Sacrament. Though normally administered by ordained ministers, authority is given by the Conference to laymen to administer in cases where frequent and regular communion in wide circuits is not possible otherwise.

[21] E. Kitson Clark, *The English Inheritance* (1950), p. 137.

thousand ceremonies was added to the old conformity with a grievous penalty.'

It was the same principle at work in the attitude of those who were in the Passive Resistance Movement—to take an extreme example—of the twentieth century in the matter of religious education. There was a repudiation of the interference of secular authority in spiritual concerns. Nonconformity has always emphatically affirmed the necessity of liberty for the Church in spiritual affairs. The whole attitude of English Nonconformity may be summed up in the following sentence: 'Theirs is the true *via media* between an ultra-montanism which claims too much power for the Church, and an Erastianism which claims too much power for the State.'[22]

In this attempt to express the underlying principles of English Nonconformity we have outlined the ideal. It would be wrong to assume that during the three centuries of Nonconformist witness this ideal has always been maintained at times even approximately. But this does not invalidate the ideal itself.

Further it would also be wrong to ignore the great changes that have occurred in the Anglican communion during, say, the last fifty years. The temper and spirit of Conformists and Nonconformists have altered since the seventeenth century, and have drawn both sides to take up positions closer to one another. Ever since 1662 Anglicans and Nonconformists have not only seen the truth in both sides of the controversy, but, in fact, have mutually influenced one another.

Anglicans have come to admit among themselves claims which they once rejected when urged by Nonconformists; and Free Churchmen also have come to see that in the stress of pressing some claims they have underestimated the force of others.[23]

In particular, the Church of England, whilst retaining its relation to the State as a National Church, no longer thinks of the Church of England as coterminous with the nation. There is much concern, for the danger of indiscriminate baptism and confirmation rests upon the basis of spiritual decision. Bishops in the Church of England 'not only of necessity but of choice' have long ceased to lord it over their flocks and act with increasing regard to the mind of the Church as a whole. In the matter of worship few,

[22] H. Davies, *The English Free Churches* (1952), p. 199. [23] *1662 and Today*, p. 8.

if any, will be found to favour the universal imposition of one form of worship. It is interesting to reflect that some of the very proposals made by the Nonconformist divines and rejected by the bishops at the Savoy Conference in 1661 were themselves proposed by the bishops in 1927.

If the Church of England had been as comprehensive in belief and ritual in 1662 as it is today, the great ejection of many of its best and most devoted sons might not have been necessary. . . . Many walls that seemed insurmountable to our forefathers have crumpled.[24]

IV

Surveying the Free Churches of today—the inheritors and representatives of that English Nonconformity which in the foregoing pages we have sought to recount—we should be closing our eyes to the facts of the situation if we did not recognize a certain spirit of frustration and sometimes even a sense of defeat. There has been a heavy diminution in congregations—a mark of our generation which unhappily is also shared by the Anglican communion. From the beginnings many Nonconformist congregations have been small, and in this century have been further reduced.

Remembering the principles which are fundamental to the Nonconformist witness, however, it would be wrong to underestimate their importance. In this matter the following words are both exceedingly wise and deeply encouraging in our time:

The Divine Presence is promised to those who come together with one accord, of one heart and of one soul, and who know one another with a depth of intimacy which permits this. . . . Today such small communities of those closely bound in Christian discipleship and in a mutual surrender of Christian love are needed more urgently than ever. In the impersonal conditions which obtain so widely in modern life their contribution to the health of the Church Catholic and indeed more widely is beyond dispute.[25]

So the Free Churches of England must face the future. They must do so with a renewed faith in the Gospel as for ever the ground of man's salvation. They must do so with a firm faith that the remaining walls of partition will eventually be broken down through the working of Christ's Spirit among all those who profess and call themselves Christian. Until that day comes those

[24] Ibid, pp. 11-2. [25] G. F. Nuttall, *Visible Saints*, p. 164.

P

who belong to the Churches which claim to be both evangelical and free must affirm the truths for which they stand and for which their forefathers have suffered, always bearing in mind the words of Rupertus Meldenius—so often quoted by Richard Baxter, that apostle of Christian unity, that they are frequently taken to be his own: *Sit in necessariis Unitas, in non necessariis Libertas, in omnibus Charitas*—'Let there be Unity in things necessary, in things unnecessary Liberty, in all things Charity'.[26]

[26] The quotation is from a German treatise, *Paraenesis votive pro pace ecclesiae* (1626), by Peter Meiderlin (1582-1651), a Lutheran theologian. Rupertus Meldenius is an anagram for the latinized form of his name. It is not without significance for our time that Pope John XXIII quoted the saying in his encyclical, *Ad Petri cathedram,* on reunion. (E.Tr., *Truth, Unity and Peace* [1959].)

APPENDIX I

THE DECLARATION OF BREDA, 1660

CHARLES, by the grace of God, King of England, Scotland, France, and Ireland, defender of the faith, &c. To all our loving subjects of what degree or quality soever, greeting. If the general distraction and confusion which is spread over the whole kingdom doth not awaken all men to a desire and longing that those wounds which have so many years together been kept bleeding may be bound up, all we can say will be to no purpose. However, after this long silence, we have thought it our duty to declare how much we desire to contribute thereunto; and that, as we can never give over the hope in good time to obtain the possession of that right which God and nature hath made our due, so we do make it our daily suit to the divine Providence, that he will, in compassion to us and our subjects, after so long misery and sufferings, remit, and put us into a quiet and peaceable possession of that our right, with as little blood and damage to our people as is possible: nor do we desire more to enjoy what is ours, than that all our subjects may enjoy what by law is theirs, by a full and entire administration of justice throughout the land, and by extending our mercy where it is wanted and deserved.

And to the end that the fear of punishment may not engage any conscious to themselves of what is past to a perseverance in guilt for the future, by opposing the quiet and happiness of their country in the restoration both of king, peers, and people to their just, ancient, and fundamental rights, we do by these presents declare, that we do grant a free and general pardon, which we are ready upon demand, to pass under our great seal of England, to all our subjects, of what degree or quality soever, who within forty days after the publishing hereof shall lay hold upon this our grace and favour, and shall by any public act declare their doing so, and that they return to the loyalty and obedience of good subjects; excepting only such persons as shall hereafter be excepted by Parliament. Those only excepted, let all our subjects, how faulty soever, rely upon the word of a king, solemnly given by this present Declaration, that no crime whatsoever committed against us or our royal father, before the publication of this, shall ever rise in judgement, or be brought in question, against any of them to the least endamagement of them, either in their lives, liberties, or estates, or (as far forth as lies in our power) so much as to the prejudice of their reputations, by any reproach, or term of distinction from the rest of our best subjects; we desiring and ordaining, that henceforward all notes of discord, separation, and difference of parties, be utterly abolished among all our subjects; whom we invite and conjure to a perfect union among themselves, under our protection, for the resettlement of our just rights and theirs, in a free parliament; by which, upon the word of a king, we will be advised.

And because the passion and uncharitableness of the times have produced several opinions in religion, by which men are engaged in parties and animosities against each other; which, when they shall hereafter unite in a freedom of conversation will be composed, or better understood; we do declare a liberty to tender consciences; and that no man shall be disquieted, or called in question, for differences of opinion in matters of religion which do not disturb the peace of the kingdom; and that we shall be ready to consent to such an act of parliament, as, upon mature deliberation, shall be offered to us, for the full granting that indulgence.

And because in the continued distractions of so many years, and so many and great revolutions, many grants and purchases of estates have been made to and by many officers, soldiers, and others, who are now possessed of the same, and who may be liable to actions at law, upon several titles; we are likewise willing that all such differences, and all things relating to such grants, sales, and purchases, shall be determined in parliament; which can best provide for the just satisfaction of all men who are concerned.

And we do farther declare, that we will be ready to consent to any act or acts of parliament to the purposes aforesaid, and for the full satisfaction of all arrears due to the officers and soldiers of the army under the command of General Monk; and that they shall be received into our service upon as good pay and conditions as they now enjoy.

Given under our sign manual, and privy signet, at our court at Breda, the 4/14th day of April 1660, in the twelfth year of our reign.

APPENDIX II

THE ACT OF UNIFORMITY, 1662

AN Act for the Uniformity of Public Prayers and Administration of Sacraments and other Rites and Ceremonies: and for establishing the form of making, ordaining, and consecrating Bishops, Priests, and Deacons, in the Church of England.

WHEREAS, in the first year of the late Queen Elizabeth, there was one uniform order of common service and prayer, and of the administration of sacraments, rites, and ceremonies of the Church of England (agreeable to the Word of God, and usage of the primitive church) compiled by the reverend bishops and clergy, set forth in one book, entitled 'The Book of Common Prayer, and Administration of the Sacraments, and other Rites and Ceremonies of the Church of England', and enjoined to be used by Act of Parliament, holden in the said first year of the said late queen, entitled An Act for Uniformity of Common Prayer and service in the Church and administration of the sacraments, very comfortable to all good people desirous to live in Christian conversation, and most profitable to the estate of this realm, upon the which the mercy, favour, and blessing of Almighty God is in no wise so readily and plentifully poured as by common prayers, due using of the sacraments, and often preaching of the gospel, with devotion of the hearers. And yet this, notwithstanding, a great number of people in divers parts of this realm, following their own sensuality, and living without knowledge, and due fear of God, do wilfully and schismatically abstain and refuse to come to their parish churches, and other public places where common prayer, administration of the sacraments, and preaching of the Word of God is used upon the Sundays and other days ordained and appointed to be kept and observed as holy days: And whereas, by the great and scandalous neglect of the ministers in using the said order or liturgy so set forth and enjoined as aforesaid, great mischiefs and inconveniences, during the time of the late unhappy troubles, have arisen and grown, and many people have been led into factions and schisms, to the great decay and scandal of the reformed religion of the Church of England, and to the hazard of many souls. For prevention whereof in time to come, for settling the peace of the church, and for allaying the present distempers which the indisposition of the time hath contracted, the king's majesty (according to his declaration of the five-and-twentieth of October, one thousand six hundred and sixty,) granted his commission, under the great seal of England, to several bishops and other divines, to review the Book of Common Prayer, and to prepare such alterations and additions as they thought fit to offer. And afterwards the convocations of both the provinces of Canterbury and York, being by his majesty called and assembled, (and now sitting) his majesty hath been pleased to authorize and require the presidents of the said convocation, and other the bishops and clergy of the same, to review the said Book of Common Prayer, and the book of the form and manner of the making and consecrating of bishops, priests, and deacons: and that, after mature consideration, they should make such additions and alterations in the said books respectively, as to them should seem meet and convenient; and should exhibit and present the same to his majesty in writing, for his further allowance or confirmation; since which time, upon full and mature deliberation, they the said presidents, bishops, and clergy of both provinces, have accordingly reviewed the said books, and have made some alterations which they think fit to be inserted to the same; and some additional prayers to the said Book of Common Prayer, to be used upon proper and emergent occasions; and have exhibited and presented the same unto his majesty in writing, in one book, entitled 'The Book of Common Prayer, and Administration of the Sacraments, and other Rites and Ceremonies of the Church, according to the use of the Church of England, together with the Psalter or Psalms of David, pointed as they are to be sung or said in churches; and the form and manner of making, ordaining, and consecrating of bishops, priests, and deacons'. All which his majesty having duly considered, hath fully approved and allowed the same, and recommended to this present parliament, that the said Book of Common Prayer, and of the form of ordination and consecration of bishops, priests, and deacons, with the alterations and additions which have been so made and presented to his majesty by the said convocations, be the book which shall be appointed to be used by all the officiate in all cathedral and collegiate churches and chapels, and in all chapels of colleges, and halls in both the Universities, and colleges of Eton and Winchester, and in all parish churches and chapels within the kingdom of England, dominion of Wales, and town of Berwick-upon-Tweed, and by all that make or consecrate bishops, priests, or deacons, in any of the said places, under such sanctions and penalties as the Houses of Parliament shall think fit.

II. Now in regard that nothing conduceth more to the settling of the peace of this nation (which is desired of all good men) nor to the honour of our religion, and the propagation thereof, than a universal agreement in the public worship of Almighty God, and to the intent that every person within this realm, may certainly know the rule to which he is to conform in public worship, and administration of sacraments, and other rites and ceremonies of the church of England, and the manner how, and by whom bishops, priests, and deacons are, and ought to be made, ordained, and consecrated. Be it enacted by the king's most excellent majesty, by the advice and with the consent of the lords spiritual and temporal, and of the commons in this present parliament assembled, and by the authority of the same, that all and singular ministers in any cathedral, collegiate, or parish church or chapel, or other place of public worship within this realm of England, dominion of Wales, and town of Berwick-upon-Tweed, shall be bound to say and use the morning prayer, evening prayer, celebration and administration of both the sacraments, and all other the public and common prayer, in such order and form as is mentioned in the said book annexed, and joined to this present Act, and entitled, 'The Book of Common Prayer, and Administration of the Sacraments, and other Rites and Ceremonies of the Church, according to the use of the Church of England, together with the Psalter or Psalms of David: pointed as they are to be sung or said in churches: and form or manner of making, ordaining, and consecrating of bishops, priests, and deacons': and that the morning and evening prayers therein contained, shall, upon every Lord's day, and upon all other days and occasions, and at the times therein appointed, be openly and solemnly read by all and every minister or curate in every church, chapel, or other place of public worship, within this realm of England, and places aforesaid.

III. And to the end that uniformity in the public worship of

God (which is so much desired may be speedily effected,) Be it further enacted by the authority aforesaid, that every parson, vicar, or other minister whatsoever, who now hath and enjoyeth any ecclesiastical benefice or promotion within this realm of England, or places aforesaid, shall in the church, chapel, or place of public worship belonging to his said benefice or promotion, upon some Lord's day before the feast of St Bartholomew, which shall be in the year of our Lord God, one thousand six hundred and sixty-two, openly, publicly, and solemnly read the morning and evening prayer appointed to be read by and according to the said Book of Common Prayer, at the times thereby appointed; and after such reading thereof, shall openly and publicly, before the congregation there assembled, declare his unfeigned assent and consent to the use of all things in the said book contained and prescribed in these words and no other.

IV. I, A.B., do here declare my unfeigned assent and consent to all and everything contained and prescribed in and by the book intituled, 'The Book of Common Prayer, and Administration of the Sacraments, and other Rites and Ceremonies of the Church, according to the use of the Church of England, together with the Psalter or Psalms of David, pointed as they are to be sung or said in churches: and the form or manner of making, ordaining and consecrating of bishops, priests, and deacons.'

V. And that all and every such person who shall (without some lawful impediment, to be allowed and approved of by the ordinary of the place) neglect or refuse to do the same within the time aforesaid (or in case of such impediment), within one month after such impediment removed shall, *ipso facto*, be deprived of all his spiritual promotions. And that from thenceforth it shall be lawful to, and for all patrons and donors of all and singular the said spiritual promotions, or of any of them, according to their respective rights and titles, to present or collate to the same, as though the person or persons so offending or neglecting were dead.

VI. And be it further enacted by the authority aforesaid, that every person who shall hereafter be presented or collated, or put into any ecclesiastical benefice or promotion within this realm of England, and places aforesaid, shall, in the church, chapel, or place of public worship belonging to his said benefice or promotion, within two months next after that he shall be in the actual possession of the said ecclesiastical benefice or promotion, upon some Lord's day, openly, publicly, and solemnly, read the morning and evening prayers appointed to be read by and according to the said Book of Common Prayer, at the times thereby appointed, or to be appointed, and after such reading thereof, shall openly and publicly, before the congregation there assembled, declare his unfeigned assent and consent to the use of all things therein contained and prescribed, according to the form before appointed. And that all and every such person, who shall (without some lawful impediment, to be allowed and approved by the ordinary of the place) neglect or refuse to do the same within the time aforesaid, (or in the case of such impediment, within one month after such impediment removed,) shall, *ipso facto*, be deprived of all his said ecclesiastical benefices and promotions. And that from thenceforth it shall and may be lawful to and for all patrons and donors of all and singular the said ecclesiastical benefices and promotions, or any of them, according to their respective rights and titles, to present or collate to the same, as though the person or persons so offending or neglecting were dead.

VII. And be it further enacted, by the authority aforesaid, that in all places where the proper incumbent of any parsonage, or vicarage, or benefice with cure, doth reside on his living and keep a curate, and incumbent himself in person (not having some lawful impediment, to be allowed by the ordinary of the place), shall once (at the least) in every month, openly and publicly, read the common prayers and service, in and by the said book prescribed, and (if there be occasion) administer each of the sacraments, and other rites of the church, in the parish church or chapel of, or belonging to the same parsonage, vicarage, or benefice, in such order, manner, and form, as in and by the said book is appointed: upon pain to forefeit the sum of five pounds to the use of the poor of the parish, for every offence, upon conviction by confession, or proof of two credible witnesses upon oath, before two justices of the peace of the county, city, or town corporate where the offence shall be committed (which oath the said justices are hereby empowered to administer), and in default of payment within ten days, to be levied by distress and sale of the goods and chattels of the offender by the warrant of the said justices, by the church-wardens, or overseers of the poor of the said parish, rendering the surplusage to the party.

VIII. And be it further enacted by the authority aforesaid, that every dean, canon and prebendary of every cathedral or collegiate church, and all masters, and other heads, fellows, chaplains, and tutors of or in any college, hall, house of learning, or hospital, and every public professor and reader in either of the universities, and in every college elsewhere, and every parson, vicar, curate, lecturer, and every other person in holy orders, and every schoolmaster keeping any public or private school, and every person instructing or teaching any youth in any house or private family as a tutor or schoolmaster, who upon the first day of May which shall be in the year of our Lord God one thousand six hundred and sixty-two, or at any time thereafter shall be incumbent or have possession of any deanery, canonry, prebend, mastership, headship, fellowship, professor's place, or reader's place, parsonage, vicarage, or any other Ecclesiastical dignity or promotion, or any curate's place, lecture or school; or shall instruct or teach any youth as tutor or schoolmaster, shall before the feast day of St Bartholomew which shall be in the year of our Lord one thousand six hundred and sixty-two, or at or before his or their respective admission to be incumbent or have possession aforesaid, subscribe the declaration or acknowledgement following:—*scilicet.*

IX. I, A.B., do declare, that it is not lawful, upon any pretence whatsoever, to take arms against the king: and that I do abhor that traitorous position of taking arms by his authority against his person, or against those that are commissioned by him: and that I will conform to the liturgy of the church of England as it is now by law established: and I do declare, that I do hold there lie no obligation upon me, or any other person, from the oath commonly called, The Solemn League and Covenant, to endeavour any change or alteration of government either in church or state; and that the same was in itself an unlawful oath, and imposed upon the subjects of this realm against the known laws and liberties of this kingdom.

X. Which said declaration and acknowledgement shall be subscribed by every of the said masters, and other heads, fellows, chaplains, and tutors of, or in any college, hall, or house of learning, and by every public professor and reader in either of the universities, before the vice chancellor of the respective universities, for the time being, or his deputy; and the said declaration or acknowledgement shall be subscribed before the respective archbishop, bishop, or ordinary of the diocese, by every other person hereby enjoined to subscribe the same; upon pain that all and every of the persons aforesaid failing in such subscription, shall lose and forfeit such respective deanery, canonry, prebend, mastership, headship, fellowship, professor's place, reader's place, parsonage, vicarage, ecclesiastical dignity or promotion, curate's place, lecture, and school, and shall be utterly disabled, and *ipso facto* deprived of the same: and that every such respective deanery, canonry, prebend, mastership, headship, fellowship, professor's place, reader's place, parsonage, vicarage, ecclesiastical dignity or promotion, curate's place, lecture and school shall be void, as if such person so failing were naturally dead.

XI. And if any schoolmaster or other person instructing or teaching youth in any private house or family as a tutor or schoolmaster shall instruct or teach any youth as a tutor or schoolmaster, before license obtained from his respective archbishop, bishop, or ordinary of the diocese, according to the laws and statutes of this realm, (for which he shall pay twelvepence only,) and before such subscription or acknowledgement made as aforesaid: then every such schoolmaster, and other instructing and teaching as aforesaid shall, for the first offence, suffer three months' imprisonment, without bail or mainprize; and for every second and other such offence shall suffer three months' imprisonment, without bail or mainprize, and also forfeit to his majesty the sum of five pounds: and after such subscription made, every such parson, vicar, curate, and lecturer, shall procure a certificate, under the hand and seal of the respective archbishop, bishop, or ordinary of the diocese, (who are hereby enjoined and required upon demand to make and deliver the same,) and shall publicly and openly read the same, together with the declaration or acknowledgement aforesaid, upon some Lord's day within three months then next following in his parish church where he is to officiate, in the presence of the congregation there assembled in the time of divine service; upon pain that every person failing therein shall lose such parsonage, vicarage, or benefice, curate's place or lecturer's place respectively, and shall be utterly disabled and *ipso facto* deprived of the same; and that the said parsonage, vicarage, or benefice, curate's place or lecturer's place, shall be void as if he was naturally dead.

XII. Provided always, that from and after the twenty-fifth day of March, which shall be in the year of our Lord God one thousand six hundred and sixty-two, there shall be omitted in the said declaration or acknowledgement so to be subscribed and read, these words following, *scilicet*:

And I do declare, that I do hold there lies no obligation on me or any other person, from the oath commonly called The Solemn League and Covenant, to endeavour any change or alteration of government either in church or state, and that the same was in itself an unlawful oath, and imposed upon the subjects of this realm, against the known laws and liberties of this kingdom.

So as none of the persons aforesaid shall from thenceforth be at all obliged to subscribe or read that part of the said declaration or acknowledgement.

XIII. Provided always and be it enacted, that from and after the feast of St Bartholomew which shall be in the year of our Lord one thousand six hundred and sixty-two, no person who now is incumbent and in possession of any parsonage, vicarage, or benefice, and who is not already in holy orders by episcopal ordination, of shall not before the said feast-day of St Bartholomew be ordained priest or deacon according to the form of episcopal ordination, shall have, hold, or enjoy the said parsonage, vicarage, benefice, with cure or other ecclesiastical promotion within this kingdom of England, or the dominion of Wales, or town of Berwick-upon-Tweed, but shall be utterly disabled and *ipso facto* deprived of the same, and all his ecclesiastical promotions shall be void as if he was naturally dead.

XIV. And be it further enacted by the authority aforesaid, that no person whatsoever shall thenceforth be capable to be admitted to any parsonage, vicarage, benefice, or other ecclesiastical promotion or dignity whatsoever, nor shall presume to consecrate and administer the holy sacrament of the Lord's supper before such time as he shall be ordained priest according to the form and manner in and by the said book prescribed, unless he have formerly been made priest by episcopal ordination; upon pain to forfeit for every offence the sum of one hundred pounds, one moiety thereof to the king's majesty the other moiety thereof to be equally divided between the poor of the parish where the offence shall be committed; and such person or persons as shall sue for the same by action of debt, bill, plaint, or information in any of his majesty's courts of record, wherein no essoin, protection, or wager of law shall be allowed, and to be disabled from taking or being admitted into the order of priest by the space of one whole year then next following.

XV. Provided, that the penalties in this act shall not extend to the foreigners or aliens of the foreign reformed churches, allowed or to be allowed by the king's majesty, his heirs and successors, in England.

XVI. Provided always, that no title to confer or present by lapse, shall accrue by any avoidance or deprivation *ipso facto* by virtue of this statute, and after six months after notice of such avoidance or deprivation given by the ordinary to the patron, or such sentence of deprivation openly and publicly read in the parish church of the benefice, parsonage, or vicarage becoming void, or whereof the incumbent shall be deprived by virtue of this act.

XVII. And be it further enacted by the authority aforesaid, that no form or order of common prayers, administration of sacraments, rites or ceremonies, shall be openly used in any church, chapel or other public place, of, or in any college or hall in either of the universities, the colleges of Westminster, Winchester, or Eton, or any of them, other than what is prescribed and appointed to be used in and by the said book; and that the present governor or head of every college and hall in the said universities, and of the said colleges of Westminster, Winchester, and Eton, within one month after the feast of St Bartholomew which shall be in the year of our Lord one thousand six hundred and sixty-two; and every governor or head of any of the said colleges or halls hereafter to be elected or appointed, within one month next after his election or collation and admission into the same government or headship, shall openly and publicly in the church, chapel, or other public place of the same college or hall, and in the presence of the fellows and scholars of the same, or the greater part of them then resident, subscribe unto the Nine-and-Thirty Articles of religion mentioned in the statute made in the thirteenth year of the reign of the late queen Elizabeth, and unto the said book, and declare his unfeigned assent and consent unto and approbation of the said articles, and of the same book, and to the use of all the prayers, rites, and ceremonies, forms and orders, in the said book prescribed and contained, according to the form aforesaid; and that all such governors or heads of the said colleges and halls, or any of them, as are, or shall be, in holy orders, shall once (at least) in every quarter of the year (not having a lawful impediment) openly and publicly read the morning prayer and service in and by the said book appointed to be read in the church, chapel, or other public place of the same college or hall; upon pain to lose and be suspended of and from all the benefits and profits belonging to the same government or headship, by the space of six months, by the visitor or visitors of the same college or hall; and if any governor or head of any college or hall, suspended for not subscribing unto the said articles and book, or for not reading of the morning prayer and service as aforesaid, shall not, at or before the end of six months next after such suspension, subscribe unto the said articles and book, and declare his consent thereunto as aforesaid, or read the morning prayer and service as aforesaid, then such government or headship shall be *ipso facto* void.

XVIII. Provided always, that it shall and may be lawful to use the morning and evening prayer, and all other prayers and service prescribed in and by the said book, in the chapels or other public places of the respective colleges and halls in both the universities, in the colleges of Westminster, Winchester, and Eton, and in the convocations of the clergies of either province, in Latin; anything in this Act to the contrary notwithstanding.

XIX. And be it further enacted, by the authority aforesaid, that no person shall be, or be received as a lecturer, or permitted, suffered, or allowed to preach as a lecturer, or to preach or read any sermon, or lecture in any church, chapel or other place of public worship, within this realm of England, or the dominion of Wales, and town of Berwick-upon-Tweed, unless he be first approved, and thereunto licensed by the archbishop of the province, or bishop of the diocese, or (in case the see be void) by the guardian of the spiritualities, under his seal, and shall, in the presence of the same archbishop, or bishop, or guardian, read the Nine-and-Thirty Articles of religion mentioned in the statute of the thirteenth year of the late queen Elizabeth, with declaration of his unfeigned assent to the same; and that every person and persons who now is, or hereafter shall be licensed, assigned, and appointed, or received as a lecturer, to preach upon any day of the week, in any church, chapel, or place of public worship within this realm of England, or places aforesaid, the first time he preacheth (before his sermon) shall openly, publicly, and solemnly read the common prayers and service in and by the said book appointed to be read for that time of the day, and then and there publicly and openly declare his assent unto the approbation of the said book, and to the use of all the prayers, rites and ceremonies, forms and orders therein contained and prescribed, according to the form before appointed in this Act; and also shall, upon the first lecture day of every month afterwards, so long as he continues lecturer or preacher there, at the place appointed for his said lecture or sermon, before his said lecture or sermon, openly, publicly, and solemnly read the common prayers and service in and by the said book appointed to be read for that time of the day at which the said lecture or sermon is to be preached, and after such reading thereof, shall, openly and publicly, before the congregation there assembled, declare his unfeigned assent and consent unto and approbation of the said book and to the use of all the prayers, rites and ceremonies, forms and orders, therein contained and prescribed according to the form aforesaid; and that all and every such person and persons who shall neglect or refuse to do the same, shall from thenceforth be disabled to preach the said or any other lecture or sermon in the said or any other church, chapel, or place of public worship, until such time as he and they shall openly, publicly, and solemnly read the common prayers and service appointed by the said book, and conform in all points to the things therein appointed and prescribed, according to the purpose, true intent, and meaning of this Act.

XX. Provided always, that if the said sermon or lecture be to be preached or read in any cathedral or collegiate church or chapel it shall be sufficient for the said lecturer, openly at the time aforesaid, to declare his assent and consent to all things contained in the said book, according to the form aforesaid.

XXI. And be it further enacted, by the authority aforesaid, that if any person who is by this Act disabled to preach any lecture or sermon, shall during the time that he shall continue and remain so disabled, preach any sermon or lecture; that then, for every such offence, the person and persons so offending shall suffer three months' imprisonment in the common gaol, without bail or mainprize; and that any two justices of the peace of any county of this kingdom and places aforesaid, and the mayor or other chief magistrate of any city or town corporate within the same, upon certificate from the ordinary of the place made to him or them, of the offence committed, shall, and are hereby required to commit the person or persons so offending, to the gaol of the same county, city, or town corporate accordingly.

XXII. Provided always, and be it further enacted, by the authority aforesaid, that at all and every time and times when any sermon or lecture is to be preached, the common prayers and service in and by the said book appointed to be read for that time of the day, shall be openly, publicly, and solemnly read by some priest or deacon, in the church, chapel, or place of public worship where the said sermon or lecture be preached; and that the lecturer then to preach shall be present at the reading thereof.

XXIII. Provided nevertheless, that this Act shall not extend to the university churches in the universities of this realm or either of them, when or at such times as any sermon or lecture is preached or read in the said churches, or any of them, for or as the public university sermon or lecture; but that the same sermons and lectures may be preached or read in such sort and manner as the same have been heretofore preached or read, this Act or anything herein contained to the contrary thereof in any wise notwithstanding.

XXIV. And be it further enacted, by the authority aforesaid, that the several good laws and statutes of this realm, which have been formerly made, and are now in force for the uniformity of prayer, and administration of the sacraments within this realm of England, and places aforesaid, shall stand in full force and strength to all intents and purposes whatsoever, for the establishing and confirming of the said book, entitled 'The Book of Common Prayer, and Administration of the Sacraments and other Rites and Ceremonies of the Church according to the use of the Church of England, together with the Psalter or Psalms of David, pointed as they are to be said or sung in churches, and the form or manner of making, ordaining, and consecrating of bishops, priests, and deacons', herein before mentioned, to be joined and annexed to this Act. And shall be applied, practised, and put in use for the punishing of all offences contrary to the said laws, with relation to the book aforesaid, and no other.

XXV. Provided always, and be it further enacted, by the authority aforesaid, that in all those prayers, litanies, and collects which do any way relate to the king, queen, or royal progeny, the names be altered and changed from time to time, and fitted to the present occasion according to the direction of lawful authority.

XXVI. Provided also, and be it enacted by the authority aforesaid, that a true printed copy of the said book, entitled 'The Book of Common Prayer, and Administration of the Sacraments, and other Rites and Ceremonies of the Church, according to the use of the Church of England, together with the Psalter or Psalms of David, pointed as they are to be sung or said in churches, and the form and manner of making, ordaining, and consecrating of bishops, priests, and deacons' shall at the costs and charges of the parishioners of every parish church and chapel, cathedral, church, college, and hall, be attained and gotten before the feast day of St Bartholomew, in the year of our Lord, one thousand six hundred and sixty and two, upon pain of forfeiture of three pounds, by the month, for so long time as they shall then-after be unprovided thereof, by every parish or chapelry, cathedral, church, college, and hall making default therein.

XXVII. Provided always, and be it enacted by the authority aforesaid, that the Bishops of Hereford, St David's, Asaph, Bangor, and Landaff, and their successors, shall take such order among themselves, for the souls' health of the flock committed to their charge, within Wales, that the book hereunto annexed be truly and exactly translated into the British or Welsh tongue; and that the same so translated, and being by them, or any three of them at the least, viewed, perused, and allowed, be imprinted to such number at least, so that one of the said books, so translated and imprinted, may be had for every cathedral, collegiate and parish church, and chapel of ease, in the said respective dioceses and places in Wales, where the Welsh is commonly spoken or used, before the first day of May, one thousand six hundred and sixty-five: and that from and after the imprinting and publishing of the said book so translated, the whole divine service shall be used and said by the ministers and curates throughout all Wales, within the said dioceses where the Welsh tongue is commonly used, in the British or Welsh tongue, in such manner and form as is prescribed according to the book hereunto annexed to be used in the English tongue, differing nothing in any order or form from the said English book, for which book, so translated and imprinted, the churchwardens of every the said parishes shall pay out of the parish money in their hands for the use of the respective churches, and be allowed the same on their account; and that the said bishops and their successors, or any three of them at the least, shall set and appoint the price for which the said book shall be sold. And one other Book of Common Prayer, in the English tongue, shall be bought and had in every church throughout Wales, in which the Book of Common Prayer in Welsh is to be had by force of this Act, before the first day of May, one thousand six hundred and sixty-four; and the same books to remain in such convenient places within the said churches, that such as understand them may resort at all convenient times to read and peruse the same; and also such as do not understand the said language, may, by conferring both tongues together, the sooner attain to the knowledge of the English tongue, anything in this Act to the contrary notwithstanding. And until printed copies of the said book so to be translated, may be had and provided, the form of Common Prayer established by parliament before the making of this Act, shall be used as formerly in such parts of Wales where the English tongue is not commonly understood.

XXVIII. And to the end that the true and perfect copies of this Act and the said book hereunto annexed may be safely kept and perpetually preserved, and for the avoiding of all disputes for the time to come, be it therefore enacted by the authority aforesaid, that the respective deans and chapters of every cathedral or collegiate church within England and Wales shall, at their proper costs and charges, before the twenty-fifth day of December, one thousand six hundred and sixty-two, obtain under the great seal of England, a true and perfect printed copy of this Act, and of the said book annexed hereunto, to be by the said deans and chapters and their successors, kept and preserved in safety for ever, and to be also produced and shewed forth in any court of record as often as they shall be thereunto lawfully required; and also there shall be delivered true and perfect copies of this Act, and of the same book into the respective courts at Westminster, and into the tower of London, to be kept and preserved for ever among the records of the said courts, and the records of the tower, to be also produced and shewed forth in any court as need shall require; which said books, so to be exemplified under the great seal of England, shall be examined by such persons as the king's majesty shall appoint under the great seal of England for that purpose, and shall be compared with the original book hereunto annexed, and shall have power to correct and amend in writing any error committed by the printer in the printing of the same book, or of anything therein contained, and shall certify in writing, under their hands and seals, or the hands and seals of any three of them, at the end of the same book, that they have examined and compared the same book, and find it to be true and perfect copy, which said books, and every one of them so exemplified under the great seal of England, as aforesaid, shall be deemed, taken, adjudged, and expounded to be good and available in the law to all intents and purposes whatsoever, and shall be accounted as good records as this book itself hereunto annexed; any law or custom to the contrary in any wise notwithstanding.

XXIX. Provided also, that this Act, or anything therein contained, shall not be prejudicial or hurtful unto the king's professor of the law within the University of Oxford, for or concerning the prebend of Shipton, within the cathedral church of Sarum, united and annexed unto the place of the same king's professor for the time being by the late king James of blessed memory.

XXX. Provided always, that whereas the Six-and-Thirtieth Articles of the Nine-and-Thirty Articles, agreed upon by the archbishops and bishops of both provinces, and the whole clergy in the convocation holden at London, in the year of our Lord, one thousand five hundred and sixty-two, for the avoiding of diversities of opinions, and for establishing of consent touching true religion, is in these words following, viz.:

'That the book of consecration of archbishops and bishops, and ordaining of priests and deacons, lately set forth in the time of king Edward VI, and confirmed at the same time by authority of parliament, doth contain all things necessary to such consecration and ordaining. Neither hath it anything that of itself is superstitious or ungodly: and therefore whoever are consecrated and or ordered according to the rites of that book, since the second year of the aforenamed king Edward, unto this time or hereafter shall be consecrated or ordered according to the same rites. We decree all such to be rightly, orderly, and lawfully consecrated and ordered.'

XXXI. It be enacted, and be it therefore enacted by the authority aforesaid, that all subscriptions hereafter to be had or made unto the said Articles, by any deacon, priest, or ecclesiastical person, or other person whatsoever, who by this Act, or any other law now in force, is required to subscribe unto the said Articles, shall be construed and taken to extend and shall be applied (for and touching the said Six-and-Thirtieth Article) unto the book containing the form and manner of making, ordaining, and consecrating of bishops, priests, and deacons in this Act mentioned, in such sort and manner as the same did heretofore extend unto the book set forth in the time of king Edward VI, mentioned in the said Article, or in any statute, act, or canon heretofore had or made to be contrary thereof in any wise notwithstanding.

XXXII. Provided also, that 'The Book of Common Prayer, and Administration of the Sacraments, and other Rites and Ceremonies of the Church of England, together with the form and Manner of Ordaining and Consecrating of Bishops, Priests, and Deacons' heretofore in use, and respectively established by Act of Parliament, in the first and eighth years of queen Elizabeth shall be still used and observed in the church of England until the feast of St Bartholomew, which shall be in the year of our Lord God, one thousand six hundred and sixty and two.

APPENDIX III

EDMUND CALAMY AND HIS *ACCOUNT*

ST BARTHOLOMEW'S Day, 24th August 1662, was afterwards regarded quite naturally by many generations of Nonconformists as the symbol of great injustice done to their forefathers. They spoke of it as 'Black Bartholomew', and on their printed pages it was set in bold capital lettering. Gradually the story of the ejection assumed a certain completeness, and this was largely due to the influence of Edmund Calamy's *Abridgement of Mr Baxter's History of his Life and Times,* which became a standard work for any Nonconformist library. The circumstances of its publication were briefly as follows.

Baxter died in 1691. To Matthew Sylvester (1636?-1708), as his literary executor, he entrusted a large mass of papers for publication. Out of profound reverence for Baxter, in 1696 Sylvester published these papers in a large folio volume of some eight hundred pages, under the title *Reliquiæ Baxterianæ, or Mr Richard Baxter's Narrative of the Most Memorable Passages of his Life and Times,* a work which suffered greatly from the lack of any attempt on Sylvester's part to edit or rearrange the material left in his hands. In his task Sylvester accepted help from Edmund Calamy (1671-1732), his young, though unordained, assistant at Blackfriars. Recognizing the fault of Sylvester's work, Calamy determined to rewrite the original work in the form of a history of Nonconformity, with Baxter as the central figure, and with particular emphasis on an account of the ejected ministers. The first edition of Calamy's production, the *Abridgement,* appeared in May 1702.

The ninth chapter, which occupied nearly half the work, gave a detailed account of the ejected ministers. Calamy states that one reason for this was that there were some who had 'taken a liberty strangely to diminish' the number of the ejected; others 'have taken much pleasure in bespattering these worthy men . . . none more . . . than Mr Anthony Wood, the Oxford historiographer'.

Calamy declares that the *Abridgement* is 'a convenient mixture of history and argument', and it is not surprising that controversy rose out of it. Any criticism of the Restoration Church settlement of 1662 naturally impinged on the Church of 1702. In the 'preface' to the second edition (1713) he wrote:

I have indeed had my share of reproach. . . For some years there was scarce a pamphlet came out on the Church side in which I had not the honour of being referred to in the invective part of it.

The heaviest onslaught came a year later, in 1714, by the publication of a large work from the pen of Dr John Walker, a High Church clergyman, of Exeter, who had given ten years of labour to the production. In the controversy it was frequently asserted as a counter-claim to the sufferings of the ejected ministers, that severe measures had been taken against the episcopalians in the years before—between 1640 and 1660. Walker determined to settle the issue once for all by his challenge to Calamy's work.

Calamy's second edition appeared eleven years after the first, the length of the interval being explained probably by the fact that he expected Walker's volume to appear, in which case a reply would be forthcoming. The second edition was much larger than the first, and formed two volumes of which the first gave the narrative of Baxter's life and time as before, but with 'Historical Additions' down to 1711. The second volume was an expansion of the ninth chapter and really formed a separate work under the title: *An Account of the Ministers, Lecturers, Masters and Fellows of Colleges and Schoolmasters who were ejected or silenced after the Restoration in 1660.* It would appear that Calamy deliberately anticipated the challenge of Walker's work, for in his 'Preface' he writes:

I must own myself well pleas'd instead of being at all disturb'd or griev'd at the attempt to transmit to Posterity former sufferings on the other side. I desire, instead of fearing the publication of that History that has been so long talked of, of the Hardships endur'd by the Episcopal Party between 1640 and 1660. I am glad if I have been the occasion of its Publication. . . . At the same time, I must acknowledge I should have been glad if this work which has been so long expected had seen the light before the Publication of this my Second Edition.[1]

Calamy formally requests that those 'lovers of Nonconformity or Enemies of Persecution', who were to read Walker's book when it appeared, would send any contrary evidence so that he might insert it in his 'design'd appendix' which he intended to print.[2]

[1] Pages xxvii-xxviii. [2] Ibid. p. xxviii.

Fourteen years later, in 1727, Calamy published this 'design'd appendix' in two volumes, under the title: *A Continuation of the Account.* This forms a supplement to the earlier work and indicates corrections and additions.

Since the beginning of the nineteenth century Calamy's volumes have been more widely known in an abridged form published by Samuel Palmer (1741-1813), entitled *The Nonconformist's Memorial,*[3] a work intended to give 'a concise view' of the ejected ministers. Although useful in its alphabetical arrangement it is secondary to Calamy's original work.

In 1934 Mr A. G. Matthews published his *Calamy Revised,* 'designed as a supplement to the original rather than a substitute for it'. This eminent Congregational scholar has brought together information scattered in many publications bearing upon the material in Calamy. In his 'Preface' Mr Matthews writes:

> Directly and indirectly, here a little and there more, Calamy has been in course of getting revised for a great number of years. Not only the histories of local nonconformity and the transactions of the different denominational historical societies, but also the journals of country antiquarian societies; the publications of parish register societies, country and parish histories, and more general works of reference such as the calendars of state papers, and the *alumni* of Oxford; and Cambridge have all made their contribution. From this standpoint revision was never as possible as at the present.

It is this wide scope of Mr Matthew's research which has made this work indispensable for every serious student of this subject.[4]

[3] 1st edn, 1775 (1777, 1778), 2 vols; 2nd edn (1802), 3 vols.
[4] A. Gordon, *Transactions of the Congregational Historical Society,* VI.246-7, 'Calamy as Biographer'.

APPENDIX IV

THE NUMBER OF THE EJECTED

THE first printed record of ejected ministers appeared anonymously in 1663, entitled: *An Exact Catalogue of the Names of several ministers Lately ejected out of their Livings in several counties of England, because they could not conform for conscience sake.* It records ejections in London, Essex, Surrey, Hertfordshire, Wiltshire, Devon, Durham, Northumberland, Lancashire, Westmorland, and Cumberland, and lists 519 names of those ejected either in 1660 or 1662.

Edmund Calamy derived the material for his roll of the ejected from four sources. In his *Account* he writes: 'I sought out everywhere for Assistance, and after some time obtain'd Four written Catalogues'. One was from William Taylor, an ejected minister of Newbury, who 'while Chaplain to the late Lord Wharton, had a correspondence in most parts of England in pursuit of this Design'. Two other lists he received from another ejected minister, Roger Morrice, who 'had taken a great deal of pains in order to the compleating of such a Design'. The fourth was 'receiv'd from another Hand'.[2] Calamy 'collated them together, and drew one List out of all of them, omitting none where they were all agreed: and when they differed I sometimes follow one Copy, and sometimes another: . . . according to the Information and Advice of such I consulted in Person and by Letter, for the Places with which they were best acquainted'.[3]

The first mention of the number of the ejected is by Richard Baxter. 'When Bartholomew Day came, about One thousand eight hundred or Two Thousand Ministers were silenced and cast out.' Later, in his book *The True History of Councils* (1682) (p. 231) he writes:

I never medled with gathering the number. Mr Calamy did, and shewed us a list of 1800, which I long mentioned no more, and seldom saw

[1] These lists are among the Morrice MSS. in Dr Williams's Library, London.

[2] Probably from the papers of Henry Sampson, of Framlingham, Suffolk. *C.R.*, p. xxxv, p. 425.

[3] Calamy, *Account*, p. v. *C.R.*, pp. xxxv-xxxvii, notes three other lists of ejected ministers: (1) Sir Edward Harley, of Brampton Bryan, Herefordshire, in Welbeck Abbey MSS.; (2) Bodleian Library, Rawl. MS., D.144. (3) Bodl., Tanner MS., 152.48.

him afterwards: But Mr Ennis,[4] who was more with him, assuring me that they had after an account of at least 200 more, who were omitted, I some time to speak the least mention the 1800, and sometime say about 2000 and by his last account that was the least.

Turning now to Calamy's *Abridgement* (1st edn, 1702) we find in Chapter 9 (pp. 183-497) there are listed 2,435 names. These Mr. A. G. Matthews has classified as follows: 1,875 as ejected in English dioceses; 185 silenced, without fixed, or known, charge; 175 afterwards conforming; 97 as ejected at Oxford and Cambridge; 31 as ejected at Eton and other schools; 74 as silenced or ejected in Welsh dioceses.[5] In Calamy's second edition of his *Abridgement* (1713)—*An Account*—the number given is 2,523, similarly classified as follows: 1,897 as ejected from English dioceses; 153 silenced without fixed, or known, charge; 244 as afterwards conforming; 97 as ejected at Oxford and Cambridge; 45 ejected at Eton and other schools; 87 as ejected or silenced in Welsh dioceses. Calamy was prepared to admit that there might be errors in his lists, and that further information might bring modifications.[6] Only a slight change of numbers occurs in his *Continuation*.

Palmer's *The Nonconformist's Memorial* (1775; 2nd edn, 1802) gives 2,480 names including only 230 after-conformists, but adding some new entries, making the number 2,250 as those loyal to their Nonconformity. An earlier calculation made by William Raistrick (1650-1752), of Lynn, in Norfolk, gives 2,257; this index was given to Calamy (after 1727) and was used by Palmer.[7]

It was inevitable that sooner or later a critical examination would be given to Calamy's calculations on a more scientific basis and in the light of new information. In 1911 one writer calculated a total of 2,447 names including 254 who afterwards conformed, but this was based on Palmer's first edition, not on his later and better edition.[8] In 1912 Mr T. G. Crippen compiled a complete list, totalling 2,492 names, in addition to which there were sixty doubtful cases. Of this number not less than 1,938

[4] I.e. James Innes, of St Breock, Cornwall; *C.R.*, p. 289.
[5] *C.R.*, p. xxvi.
[6] *Account*, p. 359.
[7] Op. cit. (1st edn), p. xiii. The title of the MS. is: *Index Eorum Theologorum Aliorumque No* 2257 *Qui propter Legem Uniformitatis Aug. 24 Anno 1662, ab Ecclesia Anglicana secesserunt*. A copy of the MS Index, 'a curious and valuable manuscript dated 1734 drawn up with great Labour', is in the Public Library, Lynn.
[8] *T.C.H.S.*, V.296-7.

were ejected or disabled by the Act of Uniformity; of these about 70 were *twice* ejected, first by the Act of 1660 and afterwards in August 1662; 254 or 257 afterwards conformed.[9]

The publication of the scholarly work by Mr A. G. Matthews, *Calamy Revised* (1934), has made available figures which are unlikely to be challenged in the future. By vast research and the most detailed analysis a calculation has been reached which is as accurate as it is possible to achieve. For the English counties the total number of ejections from benefices is 1,760, classified as follows: 695 ejected in 1660; 936 ejected in 1662; 129 ejected at uncertain date. The number who afterwards conformed is 171. To this number of ejections must be added academic and scholastic ejections, totalling 149 names, classified as follows: Oxford 66, Cambridge 47, Eton 7, and 29 other schoolmasters. Of these 6 afterwards conformed. Thus the total number of ejections recorded by Mr Matthews is 1,909. This figure is as accurate as it is possible to achieve. (It should be noted that the figure does *not* include the Welsh Counties.)

It is interesting to observe that only just over one-tenth of those ejected afterwards conformed. It is not possible to ascertain how many of those who were ejected were really Bartholomeans; there were some who had no opportunity of retaining their benefices by conformity; many had no option in the matter, namely those occupants of sequestered benefices of which the former incumbents claimed re-establishment and those preachers and lecturers who had been 'intruded' into cathedrals after the abolition of the old order. It is certain, therefore, that of the actual Bartholomeans 'considerably less than one-tenth proved recreant to their principle'; those who did, appear to have been rather severely censured by their more steadfast brethren, according to the pamphlets concerning 'The New Conformists'.[11]

[9] *T.C.H.S.*, III.293ff; V.386-98; *Christian World* (29th August 1912).
[10] *C.R.*, pp. xii-xiv. [11] *T.C.H.S.*, VI.265-6.

APPENDIX V

ARCHBISHOP USSHER'S MODEL OF CHURCH GOVERNMENT: 1641[1]

The Reduction of Episcopacy unto the Form of Synodical Government received in the Ancient Church, proposed in the Year 1691[1]

ON 12th March 1641 the House of Lords appointed a Committee to report on the innovations recently introduced into the Church. To a sub-committee they entrusted the task of devising a scheme of Church-government that might reconcile as far as possible the conflicting principles held by Presbyterians and Episcopalians respectively. Archbishop Ussher drew up the following scheme.

The Archbishop begins by claiming for Presbyterians their rightful place in the organization of the Church. Their duty, he asserts, is not only 'to minister the doctrines and sacraments', but also 'to rule the congregation of God'. At Ephesus, he points out, there were many Elders who ruled in common, under the headship of a President—'the Angel of the Church of Ephesus'—and he quotes other precedents from primitive usage to sustain his contention. He admits that in the Church of England 'this kind of presbyterian government hath long been disused, yet . . . the restraint of the exercise of that right proceedeth only from the custom now received in this realm'. It would be easy, however, 'by the united suffrages of the clergy' for this to be revived again; 'with little show of alteration the synodical conventions of the pastors of every parish might be accorded, with the presidency of the bishops of each diocese and province'.

He proceeds to suggest the following methods of accommodation for the two systems.

I

In every parish the rector or the incumbent pastor, together with the churchwardens and sidesmen, may every week take notice of

[1] *Rel. Bax.*, I.II.238-40; Gould, pp. 22-4. It is interesting to observe the close approximation of Ussher's scheme to that given in *A Sketch of a United Church* (1935). See *supra*, pp. 188-91.

such as live scandalously in that congregation, who are to receive such several admonitions and reproofs as the quality of their offence shall deserve; and if by this means they cannot be reclaimed, they may be presented unto the next monthly synod, and in the meantime be debarred by the pastor from access unto the Lord's Table.

II

Whereas by a statute in the twenty-sixth year of King Henry VII (revived in the first year of Queen Elizabeth) suffragans are appointed to be erected in twenty-six several places of this kingdom, the number of them might very well be conformed unto the number of the several rural deaneries into which every diocese is sub-divided, which being done, the suffragans . . . might every month assemble a synod of all the rectors, or incumbent pastors within the precinct, and according to the major part of their voices conclude all matters that should be brought into debate before them.

To this synod the rector and churchwardens might present such impenitent persons, as by admonition and suspension from the sacrament, would not be reformed; who if they should still remain contumacious and incorrigible, the sentence of excommunication might be decreed against them by the synod, and accordingly be executed in the parish where they lived. Hitherto also all things that concerned the parochial ministers might be referred, whether they did touch their doctrine or their conversation:—as also the censure of all new opinions, heresies, and schisms which did arise within that circuit, with liberty of appeal if need so required unto the diocesan synod.

III

The diocesan synod might be held once or twice in the year as it should be thought most convenient; therein all the suffragans and the rest of the rectors or incumbent pastors (or a select number out of every deanery in that diocese) might meet: with whose consent, or the major part of them, all things might be concluded by the bishop or superintendent (call him whether you will) or in his absence by one of the suffragans, whom he should depute in his stead to be moderator of that assembly. Here all matters of greater moment might be taken into consideration, and the orders of the monthly synods revised and (if need be) reformed. And if here also any matter of difficulty could not receive a full determination, it might be referred to the next provincial or national synod.

IV

The provincial synod might consist of all the bishops and suffragans, and such of the clergy as should be elected out of every diocese within the province. The primate of either province might be the moderator of this meeting (or in his room some one of the bishops appointed by him) and all matters be ordered therein by common consent as in the former assemblies. This synod might be held every third year, and if the parliament do then sit (according to the act for a triennial parliament) both the primates and provincial synods of the land might join together, and make up a national council; wherein all appeals from inferior synods might be received, all their acts examined, and all ecclesiastical constitutions which concern the state of the Church of the whole nation established.

We are of judgement, that the form of government proposed is not in any point repugnant to the Scripture, and that the suffragans mentioned in the second proposition may lawfully use the power both of jurisdiction and ordination, according to the Word of God, and the practice of the ancient Church.

APPENDIX VI

THE EJECTION OF THE EPISCOPALIANS, 1640-60

IN the years following the Ejection of 1662 much controversy arose on the question as to whether this expulsion was greater or less than the expulsion of the Anglican clergy under the Commonwealth. Ecclesiastical partisanship still allows this to be a debated question. It is asserted that in the period from 1646 to 1660, during which Presbyterians under the Commonwealth were in the ascendancy, there was a religious tyranny of the worst type. This notion has been considerably strengthened by the folio volume of nearly 450 pages from the pen of Dr John Walker, a clergyman of Exeter, bearing the title: *An Attempt towards recovering an Account of the Numbers and Sufferings of the Clergy of the Church of England, Heads of Colleges, Fellows, Scholars &c. who were sequestered, harrassed &c. in the late Time of the Grand Rebellion.* Published in 1714 it was a reply to Calamy's *Abridgement*, in particular to the ninth chapter of that work. An immense and laborious production, it is marked by bitterness and sarcasm—'a monumental piece of hate and patience'.[1] Walker's position may be illustrated by his description of many Bartholomeans as 'mechanicks and fellows bred to the meanest occupations, . . . troopers and others who had served in the rebel armies. . . . Even those of the first Rank among them had Plunder'd away, and eaten the Bread of the starving Royalists and their miserable Families, for Fourteen, Eighteen and some near Twenty Years together'.[2]

As to their being cast out that 'was done by the Course of a Regular and Unquestion'd Law; whilst neither their Goods, their Persons, nor their Temporal Estates, were Touch'd; and that their Friends were then in the full Enjoyment of their Rights and Possessions, and as Able as Willing to Support them'.

As to the characters of these ejected ministers, Walker declared that allowing for some exceptions, it could be discovered that there are 'other instances beside that of Mr Baxter, by which it appears that these Meek Men in the Depth of their Humility,

[1] *C.R.*, p. xxii. [2] Ibid., Preface, p. xiv.

have thought their examples of Importance enough to instruct the World; and for that End have either wrote their own Lives, or left Materials behind for that Purpose . . .'.

In 1719 Calamy published his rejoinder entitled: *The Church and Dissenters compared as to Persecution.* Later in 1727 when he published his *Continuation*, Calamy frequently took the opportunity of correcting Walker's errors, though, through lack of knowledge of Walker's side of the problem, he was hardly an effective critic. Walker made no reply. Because it is important to have as clear a judgement as possible upon the issues of this controversy, we must examine the matter in some detail.

The question of the number of Episcopalian clergy deprived of their livings by the Parliamentary Committee during the period of the Civil War and the Commonwealth is likely to remain unsolved. Wild calculations were made; there was a traditional belief that some 10,000 expulsions had occurred. The High Church Party regarded these ejections as practically universal.[3] Walker gives 3,334 cases of ejected clergy and schoolmasters, of which number John Withers, a Nonconformist minister of Exeter, who challenged the work, estimated that 2,399 were clergymen.[4] This was certainly an underestimate, and probably 3,500 would be nearer the truth. This can only be approximate because the Minutes of the Committee for Plundered Ministers are incomplete.[5] A. G. Matthews, in *Walker Revised* (1947), estimates that of the 8,600 livings existing at the time about 2,425 were sequestered.[6] Those ejected from cathedrals and collegiate churches and colleges numbered about 650; those from the Universities 829. About 400 others were 'harassed but not expelled from their livings, together with curates, perpetual and assistant, and schoolmasters'. Allowing for duplication through pluralities—'about three-quarters of the cathedral clergy held benefices, and about a quarter of the seniors deprived in the Universities' and 'a proportion of the ejected parish priests were double-beneficed men'—the grand total would be about 3,600. These calculations are not likely to be challenged. This total number probably represented the bulk of the Laudian clergy. As

[3] G. B. Tatham, *Dr John Walker and 'The Sufferings of the Clergy'* (1911), p. 227.

[4] J. Withers, *Remarks on Dr Walker's late Preface to the Attempt* (1717).

[5] G. B. Tatham, *Dr John Walker and 'The Sufferings of the Clergy'*, p. 132; Cf. G. B. Tatham, *The Puritans in Power* (1913), pp. 88-92.

[6] *W.R.*, pp. xiiiff.

Dr Bosher suggests,[7] in the light of the above figures, the larger proportion of parishes seems not to have been affected, though it would be wrong to assume that this indicates the extent of Puritan opinions. It is more likely that 'the figure indicates that many of the poorer and more remote benefices escaped the attentions of the sequestration committee, and that numbers of moderate men whose Anglicanism was rather a matter of preference than conviction accepted the new order'.

The charges that were brought against the sequestered clergy may be classified into three categories. There were charges of 'delinquency': the incumbents in some cases having deserted their parishes or gone over to the King's side; of 'scandalousness': the holders of benefices who were not only incompetent and ignorant but sometimes dissolute and even immoral; and of 'malignancy': those who were violently opposed to the governing authority and fostering rebellion.[8] As we have noted there was also the important question of pluralism, regarded by the Long Parliament as an offence and as one of the crying scandals of the time, and which was assailed by the Committee for Plundered Ministers concerned as it was to secure a more effective ministry and a greater care of the parishes.[9]

So far as political charges against the clergy were concerned it is not surprising that expulsion from their benefices took place and that serious consequences were involved for the incumbent. For any such person the pulpit was a natural opportunity for proclamation in support of the King's cause, but 'to leave this sounding-board in the possession of an enemy . . . was more than could be expected of any party in any civil war'.[10] The number of such cases was considerable.

Of cases where inefficiency and scandal were involved there is clear evidence. There is some truth in the assertion that 'it was then . . . common form to assume that a man whose opinions were wrong must be a man of bad character', and also that 'nothing points to the supposition that the standard of clerical conduct was lower at that date than it had been or was to be',[11] but the fact

[7] *The Making of the Restoration Settlement*, p. 5.

[8] B. Nightingale, *The Ejected of 1662 in Cumberland and Westmorland* (1911), p. 47.

[9] *W.R.*, p. xxiv.

[10] Ibid. p. xxv.

[11] Some 800 petitions were referred to the Committee for Scandalous Ministers within the first few months of its nomination in December 1640; W. Shaw, *A History of the English Church, 1640-60* (1900), p. 177. Tatham, *The Puritans in Power*, pp. 65-71.

remains that there were cases of serious delinquency, information concerning which came not seldom by complaint. The first public report of the Committee appointed to deal with such cases was published on 22nd November 1643, under the title, *First Century of Scandalous Malignant Priests.* It was published under the name of John White, chairman of the Committee. In his prefatory 'Epistle' he declared: 'The following centuries will make a full discovery of the wickednesses that are among us.' An analysis of the hundred cases recorded by White yields the following results.[12] They come from twelve counties and of the total, fifty-two are charged with drunkenness and profanity; twenty-four with breaches of morality; twelve cases, including six for drunkenness and three more grossly immoral, were reinstated at the Restoration. Walker's comments in regard to these cases reported by White are significant. In forty-one he openly or tacitly admits the charge; in twenty he likewise admits the charge but makes light of it; in eight cases the charge is doubted or denied; in thirteen he suggests that the charges of drunkenness are imputed merely to discredit those who were loyal to Church and King; eighteen are justified and commended for their conduct and these include teachers not only of Royalism but of doctrine verging on Romanism. Even if allowance be made for prejudice and exaggeration the record is illuminating.

The fortunes of those expelled from their livings varied considerably. Some stayed in their parishes; others went abroad;[13] only a small number went over to the Church of Rome.[14] In some cases the sequestered incumbent received financial help from Royalist gentry, or small legacies.[15] In many places, despite the proscription, services according to the Prayer Book continued surreptitiously, or with the connivance of the authorities; some sought 'by an underground movement'[16] to secure the restoration of the monarchy. Some continued to make their contribution to scholarship; in particular Bryan Walton, who completed his Polyglot Bible in 1657; fifteen out of twenty of his assistants were among the number of those sequestered.[17]

It still remains that there were many cases of real hardship amongst these sequestered clergy. Opportunities for other employments were few; chaplaincies and tutorships were forbidden

[12] *T.C.H.S.*, VI.57-68. [13] *W.R.*, p. xxv. [14] Ibid. p. xxvi. [15] Ibid. [16] Ibid. p. xxvii.
[17] *W.R.*, p. xxvii. Cf. *D.N.B.* art.: 'Walton, . . . an honourable monument of the vitality of the Church of England at a period of extreme depression.'

in 1665; similarly the keeping of school and the exercise of preaching were prohibited by Cromwell, who probably was more tolerant and liberal-minded than most, though some latitude appears to have existed;[18] a few took up medicine and some manual labour.

There were also cases of severe suffering. In the earlier part of Puritan ascendancy a large number of clergy were not only deprived of their benefices, but were committed to prison because of their enmity to the Parliamentary cause. At first prisoners were put into the ordinary jails in London, but as the number grew special provision was made in bishops' houses and other places.[19] Lambeth Palace, Ely House and St James's Palace were used for this purpose. This arrangement presented a change for the better for the prisoners, though they were compelled to pay in money for the privilege. 'The confinement was made as easy as was compatible with the privation of liberty.'[20] The next measure for prisoners was much more serious. In 1643, as a matter of public policy, a number of prisoners were transferred to ships lying in the Thames, the reason being that of the danger of a Royalist attack on the City of London; the risk of recapture or injury to the Parliamentary cause had to be avoided.[21] The experiment lasted only three weeks. The danger of advance on London had subsided. There is no doubt that, although the period was brief, the sufferings were severe.[22] There were also cases of prisoners being sent, as prisoners of war, to serve in the Virginia plantations as bound servants, but in Massachusetts they were allowed to cultivate their own land and redeem their freedom.

[18] 'But Cromwell seems to have meant this rather *in terrorem* than for serious use.' H. M. Gwatkin, *Cambridge Modern History* (1907), V.326.

[19] *C.J.*, II.894, 941.

[20] S. R. Gardiner, *Commonwealth and Protectorate* (1903), III.312.

[21] *C.J.*, III.209.

[22] See Letter from Richard Sterne, formerly Master of Jesus College, Cambridge, 9th October. He suffered fourteen months confinement including ten days on ship. 'We lay (the first night) without anything under or over us but the bare decks and the cloathes on our Backs; and after we had some of us got beds, were not able (when it rained) to ly dry in them, and when it was fair weather, were sweltered with heat and stifled with our own Breaths: there being of us in that one small Ipswich Coal Ship (so low built too, that we coud not walk, nor stand upright in it) within one or two of Threescore; whereof Six Knights, and 8 Doctors in Divinity and divers Gentlemen of very good worth, that woud have been sorry to have seen their Servants (nay, their Dogs) no better accomodated. Yet among all that Company I do not remember that I saw one Sad, or dejected Countenance all the while; so strong is God when we are weakest.' Tatham, *Dr John Walker and 'The Sufferings of the Clergy'*, pp. 244-6.

It is important to observe that when sequestration was proposed the convenience of the incumbent was taken into consideration.[23] Further, on 17th August 1643 Parliament declared that one-fifth of a sequestered living should be given over to the wife of the sequestered minister for the maintenance of herself and her family.[24] There is abundant evidence that a serious attempt was made to fulfil this ordinance. In some cases payments were made proportional to the clergyman's income. There were difficulties of administration but despite this, in August 1645 it was ordered by the Committee that 'whosoever shall neglect to pay the fifth part of the profits of such living as he enjoyeth by sequestration, contrary to any order in their behalf, and shall not upon summons show good cause for his nonpayment thereof, shall be sequestered'.[25] The Committee for Plundered Ministers, assisted by local committees, spent much time in deciding upon these cases. The general impression left by the records of the Committee is that, once granted the major injustice of the ejections, in matters comparatively minor they did their best to get the injured what justice remained to them.[26]

It is difficult not to feel that the conduct of the Commonwealth sequestrations stands in pleasant contrast to that of Clarendon, Sheldon and others who framed and administered the Act of Uniformity of 1662.

In his *Calamy Revised*, A. G. Matthews goes so far as to state that 'no doubt Walker was right in his contention that the sufferings of the Episcopalian loyalists during the Interregnum were greater than those of the Nonconformists'.[27] If the latter reference is limited to those who suffered ejectment in 1662 we should agree; if, however, the sufferings of Nonconformists as a whole is intended, we should affirm a reverse judgement, of which the story of the Quakers alone would be conclusive evidence. The penal Acts in enforcement of the demands of the Act of Uniformity intensified the initial sufferings immediately consequent upon ejectment.

[23] B. Nightingale, *The Ejected of 1662 in Cumberland and Westmorland* (1911), p. 47. For an example of the patience of the Committee see the case of Bernard Robinson of Tarpenhow (ibid. pp. 574-9).

[24] Ibid. p. 48.

[25] B.Mus., Add. MSS. 15,669, fol. 239, quoted Tatham, *The Puritans in Power*, p. 202. For detailed discussion of the whole question see Ibid. pp. 198-213. Cf. Shaw, *A History of the English Church, 1640-60*, II.191-2.

[26] *W.R.*, p. xxvi.

[27] *C.R.*, p. ix.

In any case there are some further facts which are important to remember. Whilst the Presbyterian attempt in 1644 to compel universal acceptance of the Solemn League and Covenant, including the extirpation of episcopacy, was not really excusable and resulted in the ejectment of many conscientious episcopalians for whom such acceptance was impossible, the background was that of civil war. It was a Conformist who, writing in 1681, emphasized the difference between the two periods of ejections.

Who can answer for the violence and injustice of actions in a civil war? Those sufferings were in a time of general calamity, but these were ejected not only in a time of Peace, but a time of joy to all the land after the Act of Oblivion, when all prepared to be reconciled and made friendly, and to those common rejoicings these suffering ministers had contributed their earnest prayers and great endeavours.[28]

Calamy asserts the same viewpoint, with some impartiality:

I must own that in my judgement, both sides have been excessively to blame; yet that the severities us'd by the Church to the Dissenters are the less excusable than those us'd by the Dissenters to the Church My reason is that the former were us'd in time of peace and a settled government; whereas the latter were inflicted in a Time of Tumult and confusion. So that the plundering and ravaging endured by the Church Ministers were owing (many of them at least) to the rudeness of the soldiers and the chances of war. They were plundered not because they were Conformists but Cavaliers of the King's Party. . . . The Parliament dealt severely with many of the clergy but they did it not so much because they were Episcopalians in their judgement, as because they oppos'd them in their practice and assisted their bitter enemies.[29]

Moreover, although the ejectments of the Interregnum were upon the background of what was regarded as military necessity, the movement began in the interests of public morality and spiritual ministration, and without any thought of reprisals for the past. It would be entirely wrong not to assert that many of the sequestered episcopal clergy were men of high moral character and spiritual integrity. But when Dr Walker accused Calamy of concealing the ill-character of some of the ejected of 1662, the latter was fain to reply in all honesty:

I cannot upon the strictest recollection say that I have heard anything scandalous of any one of the silenced ministers, that I have not taken

[28] [E. Pearse], *The Conformist's Plea for the Nonconformists* (1681), pp. 12-13.
[29] *The Church and the Dissenters compar'd as to Persecution* (1719), pp. 24, 58.

notice of. . . . 'Tis not to be supposed I should be able to deliver so many characters to posterity upon my own personal knowledge: I must be assisted by others. . . . As far as I can judge by the report of others, the characters given are very just; and I have in that respect endeavoured all along to use candour and stand upon my guard.[30]

Finally, it is not without significance that Richard Baxter, who had a wide acquaintance with those who were ejected in 1662, at the end of a long life, should write as follows:

There is not one of all these that was put out for any scandal . . . nor one of them that I ever heard any person charge or suspect of wantoness, idleness, surfeiting, drunkenness or any scandalous sin.[31]

[30] Ibid. pp. 91-2. [31] *Rel. Bax.*, III. § 209. Baxter's circle was a wide one.

APPENDIX VII

DOCTRINAL STATEMENT OF THE FREE CHURCH FEDERAL COUNCIL

I

THERE is One Living and True God, who is revealed to us as Father, Son and Holy Spirit, Him alone we worship and adore.

II

We believe that God so loved the world as to give His Son to be the Revealer of the Father and the Redeemer of mankind; that the Son of God, for us men and for our salvation, became man in Jesus Christ, who, having lived on earth a perfect human life, died for our sins, rose again from the dead, and is now exalted Lord over all; and that the Holy Spirit, who witnesses to us of Christ, makes the salvation which is in Him to be effective in our hearts and lives.

III

We acknowledge that all men are sinful, and unable to deliver themselves from either guilt or power of their sin; but we have received and rejoice in the Gospel of the grace of the Holy God, wherein all who truly turn from sin are freely forgiven through faith in our Lord Jesus Christ, and are called and enabled, through the Spirit dwelling and working within them to live in fellowship with God, and for His service; and in this new life, which is to be nurtured by the right use of the means of grace, we are to grow, daily dying unto sin and living unto Him who in His mercy has redeemed us.

IV

We believe that the Catholic or Universal Church is the whole company of the redeemed in heaven and on earth, and we recognize as belonging to this holy fellowship all who are united to God through faith in Christ.

The Church on earth—which is One through the Apostolic Gospel and through the living union of all its true members with its one Head, even Christ, and which is Holy though the indwelling Holy Spirit who sanctified the Body and its members—is ordained to be the visible Body of Christ to worship God through Him, to promote the fellowship of His people and the ends of His Kingdom, and to go into all the world and proclaim His Gospel for the salvation of men and the brotherhood of all mankind. Of this visible Church, and every branch thereof, the only Head is the Lord Jesus Christ; and in its faith, order, discipline and duty, it must be free to obey Him alone as it interprets His Holy will.

V

We receive, as given by the Lord to His Church on earth, the Holy Scriptures, the Sacraments of the Gospel, and the Christian Ministry.

The Scriptures delivered through men moved by the Holy Ghost, record and interpret the revelation of redemption, and contain the sure Word of God concerning our salvation and all things necessary thereto. Of this we are convinced by the witness of the Holy Spirit in the hearts of men to and with the World, and this Spirit, thus speaking from the Scriptures to believers and to the Church, is the supreme Authority by which all opinions in religion are finally to be judged.

The Sacraments—Baptism and the Lord's Supper—are instituted by Christ who is Himself certainly and really present in His own ordinances (though not bodily in the elements thereof) and are signs and seals of His Gospel not to be separated therefrom. They confirm the promises and gifts of salvation, and, when rightly used by believers with faith and prayer, are, through the operation of the Holy Spirit, true means of grace.

The Ministry is an office within the Church—not a sacerdotal order—instituted for the preaching of the Word, the ministration of the Sacraments and the care of souls. It is a vocation from God, upon which therefore no one is qualified to enter save through the call of the Holy Spirit in the heart; and this inward call is to be authenticated by the call of the Church, which is followed by ordination to the work of the Ministry in the name of the Church. While thus maintaining the Ministry as an office, we do not limit the ministries of the New Testament to those who are thus ordained, but affirm the priesthood of all believers and the obligation resting upon them to fulfil their vocation according to the gift bestowed upon them by the Holy Spirit.

VI

We affirm the sovereign authority of our Lord Jesus Christ over every department of human life, and we hold that individuals and peoples are responsible to Him in their several spheres and are bound to render Him obedience and seek always the furtherance of His Kingdom upon earth, not, however, in any way constraining belief, imposing religious disabilities or denying the rights of conscience.

VII

In the assurance, given us in the Gospel, of the love of God our Father to each of us and to all men, and in the faith that Jesus Christ, who died, overcame death and passed into the heavens, the first-fruits of them that slept, we are made confident of the hope of Immortality, and trust to God our souls and the souls of the departed. We believe that the whole world must stand before the final Judgement of the Lord Jesus Christ. And, with glad and solemn hearts, we look for the consummation and bliss of the life everlasting, wherein the people of God, freed for ever from sorrow and sin, shall serve Him and see His face in the perfected communion of all saints in the Church triumphant.

These things, as all else in our Christian faith, we hold in reverent submission to the guidance and teaching of the Holy Spirit who is Truth, and we shall ever seek of Him enlightenment and grace both to unlearn our errors, and also more fully to learn the mind and will of God, whom to know is life eternal and to serve is perfect freedom.

And being thus called of God unto the purpose of His redeeming love wherein He is delivering the world from sin and misery and is reconciling all things to Himself in Christ Jesus, and being animated with faith in the final triumph of our Lord, we set before us as our end and aim to carry the Gospel to every creature and to serve and stablish, in our land and throughout the earth, His reign of righteousness, joy and peace.

Grace be with all those that love our Lord Jesus Christ in sincerity. And to God be glory in the Church by Christ Jesus, throughout all ages, world without end. Amen.

APPENDIX VIII

FREE CHURCH STATISTICS, 1961[1]

Denomination	*Members*	*Ministers*	*Local and Lay Preachers*
Methodist Church	728,589	4,551	22,304
Independent Methodist Churches	8,415	294	—
Wesleyan Reform Union	5,964	20	280
Baptist Union of Great Britain and Ireland[2]	286,093	1,930	4,164
Congregational Union of England and Wales	211,329	1,838	3,504
Union of Welsh Independents	111,254	250	90
Presbyterian Church of England	71,329	283	52
Presbyterian Church of Wales	136,713	487	—
The Moravian Church	3,269	34	14
Churches of Christ	7,617	34	245
The Free Church of England	5,074	47	35
Total Nos.	1,575,646	9,768	30,688

Sunday-school Teachers	194,409
Sunday-school Scholars and Bible-Class Members	1,150,268

The returns for the Countess of Huntingdon's Connexion, a member of the Council, are not available.

The above figures do *not* include numerical returns for the Society of Friends, the Salvation Army, or the Unitarian and Free Christian Churches, as these are not members of the Council.

[1] *Free Church Federal Council: Annual Report and Directory* (1961), p. 27.
[2] These figures apply only to England and Wales.

SELECT BIBLIOGRAPHY

I. PRIMARY WORKS

An Abstract of the Sufferings of the People called Quakers, 3 vols (1738)

An Accompt of all the Proceedings of the Commissioners of both Persuasions for the Review of the Book of Common Prayer (1661)

Barclay, R., *An Apology for the True Christian Divinity* (1775)

Baxter, R., *The Judgement of the Nonconformists* (1676)

—— *The Nonconformist's Plea for Peace* (1679)

—— *The Second Part of the Nonconformist's Plea for Peace* (1680)

—— *The Defence of the Nonconformist's Plea for Peace* (1681)

—— *An Apology for the Nonconformist Ministry* (1681)

—— *A Second True Defence of the Meer Nonconformist* (1681)

—— *R.B.'s Sense of the Subscribed Articles of Religion* (1689)

—— *Cain and Abel Malignity* (1689)

—— *The English Nonconformity as under King Charles II and King James II truly stated and argued* (1689)

—— *Reliquiae Baxterianae* (1696)

Besse, J., *A Collection of the Sufferings of the People called Quakers*, 2 vols (1753)

Bold, S., *A Sermon against Persecution* (1682)

Bunyan, J., *Works*, ed. Offer, 3 vols (1862)

—— *A Relation of the Imprisonment of Mr John Bunyan* (usually printed with *Grace Abounding*)

Burnet, G., *Exhortation to Peace and Unity* (1681)

—— *History of my own Time*, ed. Airy, 2 vols (1879)

Calamy, E., *A Defence of Moderate Nonconformity* (1703-5)

—— *Comfort and Council to Protestant Dissenters* (1712)

—— *An Account of the Ministers . . . who were ejected after the Restoration* (1713)

—— *An Abridgement of Mr Baxter's History of his Life and Times* (1702), 2nd edn, 2 vols (1713)

—— *The Principles and Practice of Moderate Nonconformists with respect to Ordination* (1717)

—— *The Church and the Dissenters Compared as to Persecution* (1719)

—— *A Continuation of the Account . . .*, 2 vols (1727)

—— *A Historical Account of my Own Life*, 2 vols (1829)

Clarendon, *Life and Continuation* (edn 1843)

—— *History of the Great Rebellion* (edn 1843)

Corbet, J., *An Account given of the Principles and Practice of Several Nonconformists* (1682)

—— *The Nonconformist Plea for Lay Communion with the Church of England* (1683)

[Croft, H.], *The Naked Truth, or the True State of the Primitive Church* (1675)

Defoe, D., *The Present State of the Parties* (1712)

—— *The Shortest Way with Dissenters* (1702)

—— *An Enquiry into the Occasional Conformity of Dissenters* . . . (1697)

Ellwood, T., *The History of the Life of Thomas Ellwood*, ed. C. G. Crump (1900)

Evelyn, J., *Diary*, ed. Bray (1818)

An Exact Catalogue of the Names of Several Ministers lately ejected . . . in Several Counties (1663)

Farewel Sermons, A Collection of (1662)

Farewel Sermons, A Compleat Collection of (1663)

Fox, G., *Journal*, 3rd edn (1785)

—— *Journal*, ed. N. Penney (1911)

—— *Journal*, ed. J. L. Nickalls (1952)

The Grand Debate between the most Reverend the Bishops and the Presbyterian Divines (1661)

Henry, Matthew, *The Life of the Revd. Philip Henry*, ed. J. B. Williams (1839)

Henry, Philip, *Diaries and Letters of Philip Henry, M.A.*, ed. M. H. Lee (1882)

Heywood, Oliver, *His Autobiography, Diaries*, . . . ed. J. H. Turner, 4 vols (1882-5)

Howe, J., *The Whole Works of the Revd. John Howe*, 7 vols (1813)

—— *The Case of the Protestant Dissenters Represented and Argued* (1689)

—— *Some Considerations . . . concerning the Occasional Conformity of Dissenters* (1701)

Josselin, R., *The Diary of the Revd. Ralph Josselin, 1626-83* (Camden Society, 1908)

Kennett, White, *A Register and Chronicle, Ecclesiastical and Civil* (1728)

A Letter from a Gentleman in the City to a Friend in the Country about the Odiousness of Persecution (1675)

Martindale, Adam, *The Life of Adam Martindale* (Chetham Society, 1845)
Matthews, A. G., *Calamy Revised* (1934)
—— *Walker Revised* (1948)
The Mystery and Iniquity of Nonconformity (1664)
Neal, D., *History of the Puritans*, 5 vols (1822), Abridged edn, 2 vols (1811)
Newcome, H., *The Diary of the Revd. Henry Newcome* (Chatham Society, 1849)
Owen, John, *Works*, ed. Gould, 16 vols (1850-3)
—— *Present Distresses on Nonconformists examined* (1670)
—— *A Peace Offering or Plea for Indulgence* (1667)
—— *Indulgence and Toleration considered* (1667)
—— *Indulgence and Liberty of Conscience* (1668)
—— *A Brief Vindication of the Nonconformists from the Charge of Schism* (1680)
Parliamentary History of England, vols XXI-XXII (1760)
Palmer, S., *A Defence of the Dissenters' Education in their Private Academies* (1703)
—— *A Vindication . . . of the Dissenters. . . . in Answer to Mr Wesley's Defence . . .* (1705)
—— *The Nonconformists' Memorial*, 2 vols (1775); 3 vols (1802)
[Pearse, E.], *The Conformist's Plea for the Nonconformists* (1681)
—— *The Conformist's Second Plea for the Nonconformists* (1682)
—— *The Conformist's Third Plea for the Nonconformists* (1682)
—— *The Conformist's Fourth Plea for the Nonconformists*, (1683)
Penn, W., *The Great Case of Liberty of Conscience once more briefly debated* (1670)
—— *A Persuasion to Moderate Church Dissenters* (1686)
—— *The Reasonableness of Toleration* (1687)
Pennington, I., *Concerning Persecution* (1661)
Pepys, S., *Diary* Everyman Ed.
Pierce, J., *A Vindication of the Dissenters*, 2nd edn (1718)
Price, J., *The Mystery and Method of His Majesty's Happy Restoration* (1680)
A Proposition concerning Kneeling in the very act of Receiving (1660)
Record of the Sufferings of Quakers in Cornwall, 1655-1688, ed. N. Penney, in *Journal of Friends' Historical Society.*
A Short Treatise of the Cross in Baptism . . . (1660)

Sion's Groans for her Distressed (1661) Printed in *Tracts on Liberty of Conscience 1614-1661* (1846)
Sturgion, J., *A Plea for Toleration. . . .* (1661)
Terril, E., *The Records of a Church of Christ meeting in Broadmead, Bristol, A.D. 1640 to A.D. 1686*, ed. N. Haycroft (1865)
Troughton, J., *An Apology for the Nonconformists* (1681)
Turner, G. Lyon, *Original Records of Early Nonconformity*, 3 vols (1911-14)
Wesley, S., *A Letter from a Country Divine . . . concerning the Education of Dissenters in their Private Academies* (1703)
—— *A Defence of a Letter. . . .* (1704)
—— *A Reply to Mr Palmer's Vindication. . . .* (1707)

II. COLLECTIONS OF DOCUMENTS

Bell, G. K. A., ed., *Documents on Christian Unity* (1924); Second Series (1930); Third Series (1948); Fourth Series (1958)
Bettenson, H., *Documents of the Christian Church* (1943)
Calendar of State Papers, Domestic, in loc.
Cardwell, E., *A History of Conferences. . . .* (1849)
Dictionary of National Biography, in loc.
Gee and Hardy, *Documents illustrative of Church History* (1914)
Gould, *Documents relating to the Settlement of the Church of England by the Act of Uniformity of 1662* (1862)
Journals of the House of Commons
Journals of the House of Lords
Robertson, C. G., *Statutes, Cases and Documents* (1904)
Wilkins, D., *Concilia Magnae Brittaniae*, 4 vols (1737)

III. REPORTS

Church Relations in England (1950)
Church and State (1952)
Conversations between the Church of England and the Methodist Church: An Interim Statement (1958)
The Free Churches and the State (1953)
Free Church Federal Council Annual Reports
Intercommunion; An Open Letter to the Archbishop of Canterbury and the Archbishop of York (1961)
Joint Conference Report (Congregational-Presbyterian) (1947)
Lambeth Conference Reports (1930, 1948, 1958)

A Plan for Unity between Baptists, Congregationalists and Presbyterians in England (1937)
Relations between Anglicans and Presbyterian Churches (1947)
Sketch of a United Church (1934)

IV. SECONDARY WORKS

Abbey and Overton, *The English Church in the Eighteenth Century*, 2 vols (1878-1881)
St Bartholomew Bi-Centenary Papers, Two Series (1862)
Bate, F., *The Declaration of Indulgence, 1672* (1908)
Bebb, E. D., *Nonconformity and Social and Economic Life, 1660-1800* (1935)
Beckerlegge, O. A., *The United Methodist Free Churches* (1957)
Bett, H., *The Spirit of Methodism* (1937)
Bonet-Maury, G., *Early Sources of English Unitarian History* (1884)
Bogue and Bennet, *History of English Dissenters*, 2nd edn
Bosher, R. S., *The Making of the Restoration Settlement* (1951)
Bourne, F. W., *The Bible Christians; Their Origin and History* (1905)
Braithwaite, W. G., *The Second Period of Quakerism* (edn 1961)
Bready, J. W., *England before and after Wesley* (1938)
Brockett, A., *Nonconformity in Essex 1650-1875* (1962)
Carter, Henry, *The English Temperance Movement, 1830-99* (1932)
—— *The Methodist Heritage* (1951)
Cocks, H. Lovell, *The Nonconformist Conscience* (1943)
Clark, H. W., *History of English Nonconformity*, 2 vols (1911)
Colligan, J. G., *The Arian Movement in England* (1915)
—— *Eighteenth-Century Nonconformity* (1915)
Cragg, G. R., *Puritanism in the Period of the Great Persecution, 1660-1685* (1957)
—— *From Puritanism to the Age of Reason* (1950)
Dale, B., *Yorkshire Puritanism and Early Nonconformity* (1910)
Dale, R. W., *Manual of Congregational Principles* (1884)
—— *A History of English Congregationalism* (1907)
Davies, Horton, *The English Free Churches* (1953)
Drysdale, A. H., *History of Presbyterianism in England* (1889)
Edwards, M. L., *After Wesley* (1935)
—— *Methodism and England* (1943)
Elliott-Binns, L. E., *Religion in Victorian England* (1930)
—— *The Early Evangelicals* (1953)
Essays Congregational and Catholic, ed. A. Peel (1931)

Garbett, C., *The Claims of the Church of England* (1947)
—— *Church and State in England* (1950)
Glover, W. B., *Evangelical Nonconformists and Higher Criticism in the Nineteenth Century* (1954)
Gordon, Alex., *Freedom after Ejection* (1917)
—— *Addresses Biographical and Historical* (1922)
Grant, J. W., *Free Churchmanship in England, 1870-1940* (1954)
Green, V. H. G., *The Young Mr Wesley* (1961)
Halley, Robert, *Lancashire: Its Puritanism and Nonconformity*, 2nd edn (1872)
Harrison, A. W., *The Separation of Methodism from the Church of England* (1945)
—— *The Evangelical Revival and Christian Reunion* (1942)
Henson, H. H., *Studies in English Religion in the Seventeenth Century* (1903)
—— *Puritanism in England* (1912)
Holt, R. V., *The Unitarian Contribution to Social Progress in England* (1938)
Horne, C. S., *Popular History of the Free Churches* (1903)
—— *Nonconformity in the Nineteenth Century* (1905)
Jordan, E. K. H., *Free Church Unity: History of the Free Church Council Movement, 1896-1940* (1956)
Jones, R. M., *The Later Periods of Quakerism*, 2 vols (1921)
Jones, R. T., *Congregationalism in England. 1662-1962.* (1962)
Journal of the Friends' Historical Society
Kendall, H. B., *History of the Primitive Methodist Church*, 2 vols (1905)
Lewis, H. E., *The Ejectment of 1662 and the Free Churches* (1912)
Lincoln, A., *Some Political and Social Ideas of English Dissent* (1938)
McLachlan, H., *The Methodist Unitarian Movement* (1919)
—— *English Education under the Test Acts* (1931)
—— *The Unitarian Movement in the Religious Life of England: Its Contribution to Thought and Learning 1700-1900* (1934)
McLachlan, H. J., *Socinianism in Seventeenth Century England* (1950)
Manning, B. L., *Essays in Orthodox Dissent* (1939)
—— *The Protestant Dissenting Deputies* (1952)
Micklem, N., *Congregationalism and Episcopacy* (1948)
Moorman, J. R. H., *A History of the Church in England* (1953)
Morgan, I., *The Nonconformity of Richard Baxter* (1946)
Nightingale, B., *Lancashire Nonconformity*, 6 vols (1890-3)
—— *The Ejected of 1662 in Cumberland and Westmorland*, 2 vols (1911)

Nuttall, G. F., *The General Body of the Three Denominations: A Historical Survey* (1955)
—— *Visible Saints: The Congregational Way, 1640-1660* (1957)
Packer, J., *The Centenary of the Methodist New Connexion* (1897)
Parker, I., *Dissenting Academies in England* (1914)
Payne, E. A., *The Free Church Tradition in the Life of England* (1944)
—— *The Free Churches and the State* (1952)
—— *The Free Churches and Episcopacy* (1952)
—— *The Baptist Union: A Short History* (1959)
Peel, A., *These Hundred Years: A History of the Congregational Union of England and Wales* (1931)
Pickering, W. S. F., ed., *Anglican-Methodist Relations: Some Institutional Factors* (1961)
Powicke, F. J., *A Life of Richard Baxter* (1924)
—— *Richard Baxter Under the Cross* (1927)
—— 'Apology for the Nonconformist Arians of the Eighteenth Century' in *Transactions of Unitarian Historical Society* (1918)
Proctor, F. and Frere, W. H., *A New History of the Book of Common Prayer*. Ed. 1955
Rees, T., *History of Protestant Nonconformity in Wales* (1861)
Routley, E., *English Religious Dissent* (1960)
Seaton, A. A., *The Theory of Toleration under the Later Stuarts* (1911)
Selbie, W. B., *Nonconformity: Its Origin and Progress* (1912)
Life and Times of Selina, Countess of Huntingdon (1840)
Shakespeare, J. H., *The Churches at the Cross Roads* (1918)
Shillito, E., *The Hope and Mission of the Free Churches* (1912)
Skeats, H. S., and Miall, E., *History of the Free Churches of England 1688-1891* (1891)
Smith, H. F. F., *The Theory of Religious Liberty in the Reign of Charles II and James II* (1911)
Stephens, W. R. W., and Hunt, W., eds., *A History of the English Church*, 9 vols (1901-1910, Vols. VI-IX)
Stoughton, J., *History of Religion in England*, 8 vols (1901) vols IV-VIII
Swainson, W., *The Parliamentary History of the Act of Uniformity* (1875)
Sykes, N., *Church and State in England in the Eighteenth Century* (1934)
—— *Old Priest and New Presbyter* (1956)
Tanner, J. R., *English Constitutional Conflicts of the Seventeenth Century 1603-1689* (1947)

Tatham, G. B., Dr John Walker and '*The Sufferings of the Clergy*' (1911)
—— *The Puritans in Power* (1913)
Tayler, J. J., *A Retrospect of the Religious Life of England* (1876)
Toulmin, J., *Historical View of the State of Protestant Dissenters in England* (1814)
Townsend, H., *The Claims of the Free Churches* (1949)
Townsend, W. J., Workman, H. B., and Eayrs, G., *A New History of Methodism* (1909)
Transactions of the Baptist Historical Society
Transactions of the Congregational Historical Society
Transactions of the Presbyterian Historical Society
Transactions of the Unitarian Historical Society
Underwood, A. C., *A History of the English Baptists* (1947)
Vaughan, R., *English Nonconformity* (1862)
Vickers, J., *History of Independent Methodism* (1920)
Watton, A. C., *History of the British Churches of Christ* (1947)
Wearmouth, R. F., *Methodism and the Working-Class Movements of England: 1800-1850* (1932)
—— *Methodism and the Struggle of the Working Classes: 1850-1900* (1954)
—— *Methodism and the Trade Unions* (1959)
Whitley, W. T., *A History of British Baptists* (1923)
Whiting, C. E., *Studies in English Puritanism, 1660-1688* (1931)
Wilbur, E., *A History of Unitarianism*, 2 vols (1952)
Wilson, W., *History and Antiquities of the Dissenting Churches of London*, 2 vols (1808)
Wodrow, *History of the Church of Scotland* (1721)
Workman, H. B., *Methodism* (1912)

INDEX

INDEX